William Faulkner

Annotations to the Novels

Edited by
James B. Meriwether
University of South Carolina

Advisory Editor
Dianne Luce

A GARLAND SERIES

The Garland Faulkner Annotation Series

Series Editor: James B. Meriwether
Advisory Editor: Dianne Luce

MOSQUITOES

Annotated by
Edwin T. Arnold

Garland Publishing, Inc.
New York & London
1989

Library of Congress Cataloging-in-Publication Data

Arnold, Edwin T.
Mosquitoes/ Annotated with an introduction by Edwin T. Arnold.
p. cm.—(William Faulkner: annotations to the novels)
ISBN 0-8240-4234-4 (alk. paper)
1. Faulkner, William, 1897–1962. Mosquitoes. I. Title.
II. Series.
PS3511.A86M634 1989   89-1283
813'.52—dc19

The volumes in this series have been printed on
acid-free, 250-year-life paper.

Manufactured in the United States of America

Preface by Series Editor

The annotations in the volumes of this series are intended to assist the reader of Faulkner's novels to understand obscure or difficult words and passages, including literary allusions, dialect, and historical events that Faulkner uses or alludes to in the twenty works included. The scope of these annotations varies, necessarily, from volume to volume. But throughout the series the goal has been to provide useful, brief explanations or definitions for what may be puzzling in Faulkner's text.

Obviously what is puzzling to one reader may be clear to another, and these annotations are provided for a varied and changing audience. For many readers today, especially those from the American South, explanations of dialect words and spellings may be unnecessary. The same may be true of many of the historical and geographical annotations. But with the passage of time, a steadily increasing percentage of Faulkner's readers will need help with such points, and what may be foreign today only to Faulkner's readers from other countries, will be increasingly foreign to American readers in the years to come.

Though the annotations have usually been kept brief, each volume is intended to be inclusive, and useful independently of the others. As a rule words that can be found in standard unabridged dictionaries are not annotated, but this rule has not been followed consistently. Usefulness and clarity rather than consistency have been the criteria for this series.

The pioneering work in this field was Calvin Brown's *A Glossary of Faulkner's South* (Yale University Press, 1976). Though our volumes obviously can go into very much greater detail than could Professor Brown's book, almost every volume in this series is indebted to his more substantially than the acknowledgments for individual annotations can show. Even when we have expanded, corrected, or disagreed with him, we have always been conscious of how much this series owes to his knowledge and his labors.

All those involved in this project are fully aware that no such endeavor can ever be complete or difinitive. Further close reading of Faulkner's texts and further study of his sources and influences will reveal new allusions. Further linguistic research will provide additional information about his use of dialect. Such progress in the study of Faulkner will be never-ending, with obvious consequences for such reference works as these. Accordingly, in order to correct and update the information provided in these volumes, there will be a regular department in the *Mississippi Quarterly* devoted to notes and queries, addenda and corrigenda, concerning these annotations.

J.B.M.

Introduction

Written in 1925–26 and published in 1927, *Mosquitoes* was William Faulkner's second novel. It is today probably his least read and is usually considered the most "un-Faulknerian" of his full-length works. The book is set in New Orleans (a locale Faulkner had employed extensively in early sketches published in the *New Orleans Times-Picayune* and would later use in such non-Yoknapatawpha County works as *Pylon* and *The Wild Palms*) and on board a luxury yacht stranded off the shore of Lake Pontchartrain. It is, in one sense, an attempt at sophisticated comedy, a social satire owing much to such writers as Aldous Huxley and Sinclair Lewis. The yacht *Nausikka* is pictured as a ship of fools, and the novel uses this confined, artificial setting to reveal the passengers' comic delusions and shortcomings, expressed through their endless talk and often pointless activities. However, more seriously, the novel is also a study of the artist, of his role and responsibility in society. This was a subject that greatly concerned the young Faulkner, one which he often examined in both his prose and poetry. In this sense, the book fits into the general category of the *Kunstlerroman*, exemplified at the time by James Joyce's *A Portrait of the Artist as a Young Man*, a book that is, not surprisingly, often echoed in Faulkner's novel. In addition, *Mosquitoes* reflects aspects of Faulkner's emotional and private life, most specifically his relationships with Helen Baird, with whom he was in love, and the writer Sherwood Anderson, who had served as his literary mentor and friend. Altogether, *Mosquitoes* stands as a summation of Faulkner's artistic, intellectual, and emotional growth at this important point in his life and career, the end of his period of literary apprenticeship.

The year 1925 had been an extremely important and productive one for Faulkner. He spent the first six months living in New Orleans, writing short, experimental sketches inspired by the local scene and working on his first novel, *Soldiers' Pay*. In New Orleans he grew close to Sherwood Anderson, whom he had met briefly in 1924 in New York. Anderson was then among the leading writers in America, and he and Faulkner talked at great length and, to a lesser extent, shared their writings. In New Orleans, Faulkner also became associated with the local literary scene, especially that centered around the *Double Dealer*, the most significant "little magazine" to come out of the South in the 1920s. *Mosquitoes* would be written in part as a comment on this artistic community. Faulkner would satirize the posturing and self-importance he found there among the local literati. However, he would also pay qualified homage to his friend Anderson, represented by the character Dawson Fairchild, whom he would draw with a mixture of amusement and affection.

During the second half of 1925 (from July to December), Faulkner made his first trip to Europe. He sailed with his friend and roommate, the artist William Spratling, to Genoa, Italy. On the way he threw overboard manuscripts that had failed to meet his satisfaction, a kind of preparatory cleaning house. After landing, Faulkner and Spratling parted company, and Faulkner went on alone through Italy and Switzerland to Paris and finally to England (much as does the character David West in *Mosquitoes*. Faulkner's letters are often echoed in the book). In Europe Faulkner soaked up the atmosphere, observed the people, and attempted new writings. One work he mentioned to his mother in a letter from Paris (23 August 1925) was a book called *Mosquitoe*, which he had put aside because "I dont think I am quite old enough to write it as it should be written—dont know quite enough about people." The recently-revealed 46-page manuscript of *Mosquitoes*-related material, acquired by the Alderman Library of the University of Virginia, suggests that *Mosquitoe* was an early attempt at the *Mosquitoes* story. The manuscript is made up of discontinuous sections that appear largely in the first half of the published novel: Talliaferro's first meeting with the Mrs. Maurier character and her niece Pat; Talliaferro's meeting with Fairchild and his guests at Broussard's; the beginning of the voyage; Pat and Jenny's sexual experimentation. However, it also contains a version of Pat and David's journey through the swamp found in the second half, and it shows Faulkner experimenting with the New Orleans nighttime sequence that appears in Section 9 of the Epilogue in the published book. At this time, Faulkner apparently intended to include it in Section 9 of the Prologue, before the ill-fated voyage of the *Nausikka* rather than after. If this manuscript does date to Faulkner's stay in Paris, if it is the *Mosquitoe* work he mentioned to his mother, then we can see that Faulkner was very quickly trying to put his New Orleans experience into perspective and was, at this point, failing.

After putting aside the *Mosquitoe* story, Faulkner then began work on another comic novel, *Elmer*. It, too, was to be a satire of the artistic world, centered on the aspiring painter Elmer Hodge. There are numerous similarities between *Elmer* and *Mosquitoes*, for both grew from the same concerns. The two works share character types, thematic ideas, and even important scenes. But *Elmer* also came to a dead end. At the end of his six months, Faulkner returned to America with no finished work in hand but with a richness of possibilities in mind.

It is likely that Faulkner wrote most of *Mosquitoes* during the spring of 1926, during which time he was also working on his poems to Helen Baird. He typed the book during the summer, which he spent in Pascagoula, Mississippi, at the family summer home of his friend Phil Stone. The sole surviving typescript (there may have been more than one typed version) is dated 1 September 1926, but it was then heavily revised by Faulkner and edited by others (to Faulkner's consternation) before it was published by Boni and Liveright in April, 1927. Although the book was favorably reviewed by such knowledgeable critics as Conrad Aiken and Lillian Hellman, both of whom recognized Faulkner's considerable talent, it sold poorly and did little to advance Faulkner's reputation.

Faulkner next began work on *Father Abraham,* his initial entry into what would become the world of Yoknapatawpha, and *Mosquitoes* was largely forgotten. Faulkner would later say of it, "That one, if I could write that over, I probably wouldn't write it at all. . . . I was still learning my craft." However, he added, "I'm not ashamed of it, because that was the chips, the badly sawn planks that the carpenter produces while he's learning to be a first-rate carpenter. . . ." And indeed it is from this perspective that the book is most interesting: while few today would read it for its story, its satire, or its ideas, *Mosquitoes* is important for what it tells us about Faulkner's development as an artist. It shows us, for example, how Faulkner used previously written material—unpublished stories such as "Don Giovanni" and "Adolescence"; unfinished work such as *Elmer,* much of the early poetry. It also anticipated characters and stories that were yet to come—Quentin Compson in *The Sound and the Fury,* Popeye and Horace Benbow in *Sanctuary,* Eula Varner in *The Hamlet,* Thomas Sutpen's marriage in *Absalom, Absalom!,* Harry and Charlotte's affair and flight in *The Wild Palms,* and more. Although *Mosquitoes* is clearly an apprentice novel, it proves once again that the groundwork for Faulkner's masterpieces was laid in his early attempts, his lesser achievements. I have attempted to point out some of these connections between early and later work, although the Faulkner reader will easily note others as well.

In addition, because *Mosquitoes* belongs to that period when Faulkner had not completely found his own narrative voice (or voices), it more clearly reveals the influences that helped shape him as a young writer, influences that had not yet been so thoroughly absorbed into his own manner of thought or expression. These influences are diverse and wide-ranging, and they show us (if there is still any doubt) that Faulkner was well-read and very much aware of the prevailing literary, intellectual, and cultural movements of the time. Among the sources suggested or directly referred to in *Mosquitoes* are, for example, the myths of Ovid, the fables of Aesop, and the fairy tales of Perrault; the poetry of Keats, Baudelaire, Swinburne, Housman, Eliot, and Pound; the fiction of Flaubert, Gautier, Wilde, and Conrad, the contemporary writings of Mann, Joyce, Huxley, Michael Arlen, Sinclair Lewis, Sherwood Anderson, Joseph Hergesheimer, and F. Scott Fitzgerald; the philosophical, psychological, and critical works of Emerson, Freud, Havelock Ellis, Walter Pater, and Clive Bell. *Mosquitoes* is filled with such references.

This is not to say that in every case Faulkner was deliberately echoing or directly alluding to the works or sources suggested in the following notes.

Many of the ideas were simply in the air, easily absorbed by an eager, attentive mind. One of the purposes of these annotations is to illustrate the extent to which these ideas permeated the culture out of which Faulkner wrote. Nevertheless, it is also true that Faulkner *was* often deliberately enriching his writings through references to other writers, trying his hand at their devices, measuring his art against theirs. In this sense, *Mosquitoes* appears a remarkably self-assured and even boldly experimental work.

One of the main topics of discussion in the book is the nature and proof of the true artist. In *Mosquitoes* Faulkner was on the threshold of discovering his own artistic genius. This work today offers us an intriguing glimpse of what was yet to come.

Edwin T. Arnold

Annotations to Mosquitoes

Dedication: To/HELEN: Mosquitoes was the third
work Faulkner dedicated to Helen Baird (1904-72),
the girl who served as a model for Patricia Robyn.
He first presented her the hand-lettered and
hand-bound allegorical novelette Mayday, dated 17
January 1926, which bore the inscription "to thee/O
wise and lovely/this:/a fumbling in darkness"
(Mayday, ed. Carvel Collins [South Bend, Indiana:
University of Notre Dame Press, 1976]). In the
summer of 1926 Faulkner gave her a book of fifteen
sonnets, also hand-lettered and hand-bound, entitled To Helen: A Courtship. (See Helen: A
Courtship and Mississippi Poems. Introductory
essays by Carvel Collins and Joseph Blotner.
Published jointly by Tulane University and Yokna-
patawpha Press, 1981. For further discussion of
these poems, see Joseph Blotner, Faulkner: A
Biography [New York: Random House, 1974], I, 439,
510-11; Cleanth Brooks, William Faulkner: Toward
Yoknapatawpha and Beyond [New Haven and London:
Yale University Press, 1978], pp. 52-60; and Carvel
Collins, "Biographical Background for Faulkner's
Helen," his introductory essay in Helen: A
Courtship and Mississippi Poems.) On 11 January
1927 Faulkner wrote to Horace Liveright concerning
the publication of Mosquitoes: "Enclosing a
dedication for `Mosquitoes.' Will you please put
it in for me? I made the promise some time ago,
and you can lie to women, you know, but you cant
break promises you make 'em. That infringes on
their own province. And besides, you dont dare"
(Selected Letters of William Faulkner, ed. Joseph
Blotner [New York: Random House, 1977], p. 34).
The typescript dedication to the novel reads: "To
Helen, Beautiful and Wise." The phrase "Beautiful
and Wise," which was omitted from the published
dedication, is taken from Conrad Aiken's poem
"Discordants" (Turns and Movies [New York:
Houghton Mifflin Company, 1916]):

For it was in my heart you moved among them,
And blessed them with your hands and with your
                                          eyes;
And in my heart they will remember always,--
They knew you once, O beautiful and wise [p. 24].

Faulkner had earlier quoted this stanza in his
review of Aiken's book and had written of the poem,

"This is one of the most beautifully, impersonally
sincere poems of all time." (Quoted in <u>William</u>
<u>Faulkner</u>: <u>Early</u> <u>Prose</u> <u>and</u> <u>Poetry</u>, ed. Carvel
Collins [London: Jonathan Cape, 1963], p. 76. For
further discussion of Aiken's influence on
Faulkner, see Judith L. Sensibar, <u>The</u> <u>Origins</u> <u>of</u>
<u>Faulkner's</u> <u>Art</u> [Austin: University of Texas Press,
1984], pp. 105-25.) (See Notes 145.7-8, 228.6-13.)

(8).1-2 "<u>In</u> <u>spring</u> . . . <u>idiotic</u> <u>birds</u>": Cf.
"sparrows delirious in a mimosa" ("Out of
Nazareth," <u>William</u> <u>Faulkner</u>: <u>New</u> <u>Orleans</u> <u>Sketches</u>,
ed. Carvel Collins [New York: Random House, 1968],
p. 102). Cf. "The song of birds came up on the
dawn, and the young spring waking freshly, golden
and white and troubling: flowers were birdcries
about meadows unseen and birdcries were flowers
necklaced about the trees" (<u>Mayday</u>, p. 3). Cf.
"Mockingbirds in the ancient oak/In golden madness
swing and shake" (Poem IX in <u>A</u> <u>Green</u> <u>Bough</u> [New
York: Harrison Smith and Robert Haas, 1933]; <u>The</u>
<u>Marble</u> <u>Faun</u> <u>and</u> <u>A</u> <u>Green</u> <u>Bough</u> [New York: Random
House, 1965], p. 29). Cf. "Sparrows were delirious
in ivy . . . " (<u>Soldiers'</u> <u>Pay</u> [New York: Boni &
Liveright, 1926], p. 57).

(8).4-14 "<u>they</u> <u>were</u> <u>little</u> . . . <u>sheer</u> <u>repe-</u>
<u>tition</u>.": In this epigraph Faulkner establishes
his practice of refusing to identify the ambiguous
"they" as mosquitoes; the word does not appear
throughout the book. Phyllis Franklin has suggested that this technique was taken from Joseph
Hergesheimer's <u>The</u> <u>Bright</u> <u>Shawl</u> (New York: Alfred
A. Knopf, 1922), of which Faulkner had written in
his 1922 review, "The induction to The Bright Shawl
is good--he talks of the shawl for a page or so
before one is aware of the presence of the shawl as
a material object, before the word itself is said;
it is like being in a room full of people, one of
whom one has not yet directly looked at, though
conscious all the time of his presence" (<u>EP&P</u>,
p. 102). (See Phyllis Franklin, "The Influence of
Joseph Hergesheimer Upon <u>Mosquitoes</u>," <u>Mississippi</u>
<u>Quarterly</u>, 22 (Summer 1969), 207-13.) A possible
source for the mosquitoe image is a one-act play by
Paul Eldridge entitled "The Carnival" which
appeared in the New Orleans "little magazine" <u>The</u>
<u>Double</u> <u>Dealer</u> (V [January 1923], 4-29). The play

is set in a decayed garden, in the center of which
is a well "filled with dirty water, about which
swarms of giant mosquitoes make great circles"
(4). As the play continues, the mosquitoes "become
supreme masters of the situation" (5) until, in the
last scene, the "Hand of the Jester of the Gods
splashes in the well" and chases them and the world
of illusion they represent away (28). (See Note
169.1-2.)

(8).7 "moon of decay and death": Cf. "How strange
the moon seems! She is like a woman rising from a
tomb. She is like a dead woman. You would fancy
she was looking for dead things" (Oscar Wilde,
Salome, trans. by Lord Alfred Douglas, illus. by
Aubrey Beardsley [New York: Three Sirens Press,
1906], p. 25). This is the first of a number of
moon images in _Mosquitoes_, for which Faulkner was
indebted to the French Symbolists and to Wilde.
Cf. "Moon of death, moon of bright despair"
(Fragment of undated poem, ts. carbon at University
of Texas, listed by Keen Butterworth, "A Census of
Manuscripts and Typescripts of William Faulkner's
Poetry," _Mississippi_ _Quarterly_, 26 [Summer 1973],
357). Cf. "the moon of decay and death" (_Elmer_,
ed. Dianne L. Cox [Northport, Alabama: Seajay
Press, 1983], p.92). (For other examples of the
Symbolists' influence on Faulkner's early work, see
Collins, "Biographical Background for Faulkner's
Helen," Noel Polk's introduction to _The_ _Marionettes_
[Charlottesville, Va.: University of Virginia
Press, 1977], p. xi, and Judith Sensibar, _The_
Origins _of_ _Faulkner's_ _Art_, pp. 77-101.)

(8).11-12 "a biblical plague": A probable
reference to the swarms of flies and locusts
brought by Moses to Egypt. Cf. Exodus 8:20-21, 24;
and Exodus 10:12-19.

9.4 "The sex instinct": Sigmund Freud's theories
concerning the importance of sexual instincts in
man's development--physically, mentally, and
artistically--were quite popular and often
discussed in the New Orleans circle of which
Faulkner was a part. (See Blotner, I, 396.) In
interviews later in life, Faulkner denied having
read Freud. In 1956 he told Jean Stein, "Everybody
talked about Freud when I lived in New Orleans, but

I have never read him" (<u>Lion</u> <u>in</u> <u>the</u> <u>Garden</u>:
<u>Interviews</u> <u>with</u> <u>William</u> <u>Faulkner</u>, <u>1926</u>-<u>1962</u>, ed.
James B. Meriwether and Michael Millgate [New
York: Random House, 1968], p. 251). The next year
he told an audience at the University of Virginia
that "the writer don't have to know Freud to have
written things which anyone who does know Freud can
divine and reduce into symbols" (<u>Faulkner</u> <u>in</u> <u>the</u>
<u>University</u>, ed. Frederick L. Gwynn and Joseph L.
Blotner [New York: Vintage Books, 1965], p. 147).
It seems probable from <u>Mosquitoes</u> and other works
that Faulkner had at least passing knowledge of
Freud's basic concepts. (See Carvel Collins'
arguments on Faulkner and Freud in "The Interior
Monologues of <u>The</u> <u>Sound</u> <u>and</u> <u>the</u> <u>Fury</u>" in <u>The</u>
<u>Merrill</u> <u>Studies</u> <u>in</u> <u>The</u> <u>Sound</u> <u>and</u> <u>the</u> <u>Fury</u>, compiled
by James B. Meriwether [Columbus, Ohio: Charles E.
Merrill Publishing Company, 1970], pp. 59-79, and,
more recently, in his Afterward to <u>Mayday</u>. See
also Brooks' discussion of Faulkner and Freud in
<u>WF</u>: <u>TYB</u>, pp. 376-77, and Sensibar, <u>Origins</u> <u>of</u>
<u>Faulkner's</u> <u>Art</u>, pp. 117, 165-66.) (See Note
248.20-21; 250.3-6; 251.29-30.)

9.4 "Mr. Talliaferro": For the character of
Ernest Talliaferro (pronounced Tolliver), Faulkner
drew on some of his earlier work as well as other
established literary sources. In 1925, while in
New Orleans before leaving for Europe, Faulkner
created an early version of Talliaferro in his
then-unpublished short story "Don Giovanni."
Herbie, the protagonist of this story, suffers the
same uncertainties and humiliations as does
Talliaferro, episodes which Faulkner incorporated
into <u>Mosquitoes</u>. (See "Don Giovanni" in
<u>Uncollected</u> <u>Stories</u> <u>of</u> <u>William</u> <u>Faulkner</u>, ed. Joseph
Blotner [New York: Random House, 1979], pp. 480-
88. For specific borrowings from the story, see
Notes 31.28-30; 32.21-33.25; 305.5-312.31; 340.24-
349.5.) In developing Talliaferro's past, Faulkner
partly relied on an earlier unpublished story
"Adolescence," written probably in 1922. (See
"Adolescence" in <u>Uncollected</u> <u>Stories</u>, pp. 459-73.
Also see Note 32.7-12.) As Frederick L. Gwynn has
noted, Talliaferro owes a good many of his charac-
teristics to T. S. Eliot's J. Alfred Prufrock.
(See "Faulkner's Prufrock--And Other Observations,"
<u>JEGP</u>, 52 [January 1953], 63-70, and following

Notes.) In addition, there are a number of
similarities between Talliaferro and Denis Stone in
Aldous Huxley's <u>Crome Yellow</u> (New York: Harper &
Brothers, 1922). (See Edwin T. Arnold, III,
"Faulkner and Huxley: A Note on <u>Mosquitoes</u> and
<u>Crome Yellow</u>," <u>Mississippi Quarterly</u>, 30 [Summer
1977], 433-36.)

9.4-5 "careful cockney": "Cockney" is the dialect
spoken in the East End of London. For Talliaferro,
this accent indicates an affectation of speech, an
attempt to pass himself off as a sophisticate.
However, since the cockney dialect is associated
with lower class English speech, Talliaferro's
posing seems all the more foolish. It is also
possible that this character may represent a kind
of self-parody on Faulkner's part, for he himself
was guilty of a similar affectation. According to
Blotner, Faulkner, on occasion, used a "clipped,
upper-class English" accent, apparently picked up
during his RAF days (Blotner, I, 410, 421). There
are, in fact, a number of similarities between
Talliaferro and the young Faulkner. (See Blotner,
I, 233, 268-69; see also Michael Millgate, <u>The
Achievement of William Faulkner</u> [New York: Random
House, 1966], pp. 5, 8.)

9.7-8 "Frankness . . . no friendship":
Talliaferro's association of the "sex instinct" and
friendship is quite similar to the theory expressed
by Elsie Clews Parsons in her essay on "Sex" in
<u>Civilization in the United States: An Inquiry by
Thirty Americans</u>, ed. Harold E. Stearns (New York:
Harcourt, Brace and Company, 1922), pp. 309-18:

My own conclusion or guess in regard to perversion
in this country is that part of the commonly
observed spirit of isolation or antagonism between
the sexes, and part of the spirit of competition
between individuals, are associated with homosexual
or masturbatory tendencies which get expressed in
varying degrees according to varying circumstances. Most particularly the lack of warmth in
personal intercourse which makes alike for American
bad manners and in the more intellectual circles,
for cheerlessness and aridity is due, I think, to
failure of one kind or another in sex relations
. . . [p. 311].

<u>Civilization</u> <u>in</u> <u>the</u> <u>United</u> <u>States</u> was one of the
most famous attacks on "American Culture" of the
1920's.

9.8-9 "two people . . . `get' each other": i.e.,
understand, communicate with each other.

9.16 "Bluebeard's closet . . . severed clots":
Bluebeard was the murderous husband in Charles
Perrault's fairy tale "Barbe-bleue," included in
<u>Histories</u> <u>ou</u> <u>contes</u> <u>du</u> <u>temps</u> <u>passe</u> (1697). In the
story, Bluebeard gives each of his new brides a set
of keys but warns her not to open the door to a
certain room, behind which are hung the butchered
bodies of his previous wives. Most translations of
this tale, such as A. E. Johnson's in his <u>Old-Time</u>
<u>Stories</u> <u>told</u> <u>by</u> <u>Master</u> <u>Charles</u> <u>Perrault</u> (New York:
Dodd, Mead & Company, 1921), describe the floor of
this chamber as "entirely covered with clotted
blood," which perhaps explains Faulkner's grotesque
phrase. Faulkner may have also known the story of
Bluebeard through Joris Karl Huysmans' novel <u>La-Bas</u>
(1891), trans. by Keene Wallis (New York: Albert &
Charles Boni, 1924), and reviewed by Sam Gilmore in
<u>The</u> <u>Double</u> <u>Dealer</u>, VII (November-December 1924),
77-79. (See Note 54.25-29.) In this work Huysmans
recounts the history of Gilles de Rais (1404-1440),
a Marshal of France who fought alongside Joan of
Arc but later turned to satanism and was thought to
be the model for Perrault's villain. (See also
Iona and Peter Opie, <u>The</u> <u>Classic</u> <u>Fairy</u> <u>Tales</u>
[London: Oxford University Press, 1974], pp. 103-
09, for a discussion and translation of the
Bluebeard legend.) Cf. Temple Drake's "clotted
curls" in <u>Sanctuary</u> (New York: Cape and Smith,
1931, p. 65).

10.1-4 "Mr. Talliaferro . . . habit of
masturbation in his youth": See Note 9.7-8.

10.10-18 "His entire sleeve . . . he always
returned": Talliaferro's fastidiousness is one of
a number of similarities he shares with Eliot's
Prufrock (see Note 9.4). Cf. "My morning coat, my
collar mounting firmly to the chin,/My necktie rich
and modest, but asserted by a simple pin" ("The
Love Song of J. Alfred Prufrock," first published

in <u>Poetry</u> magazine [1915], included in <u>Prufrock</u> <u>and</u>
<u>Other</u> <u>Observations</u> [1917]. See <u>Poems</u>: <u>1909-1925</u>
[London: Faber and Gwyer, 1925], p. 11).
Frederick L. Gwynn has pointed out a number of
possible borrowings from Eliot's early poetry in
this section of <u>Mosquitoes</u>. See following Notes.

10.22-23 "while light came across roofs and
chimney pots . . . becoming weary": Cf.

> Six o'clock.
> The burnt-out ends of smoky days.
> . . . .
> The showers beat
> On broken blinds and chimney-pots.

(T. S. Eliot, "Preludes" [1915), included in
<u>Prufrock</u> <u>and</u> <u>Other</u> <u>Observations</u> [1917]. See <u>Poems</u>,
p. 21.)

Cf. "With the smoke coming down above the house-
tops" (Eliot, "Portrait of a Lady" [1915], included
in <u>Prufrock</u> <u>and</u> <u>Other</u> <u>Observations</u> [1917]. See
<u>Poems</u>, p. 20). Both sources noted by Gwynn.

10.27 "vieux carre": The French Quarter of New
Orleans, located below Canal Street to the south-
west and bounded by Esplanade Avenue to the north-
east, North Rampart Street to the north-west, and
the Mississippi River to the south-east. The Vieux
Carre, or "Old Square," occupies what was once the
location of the walled city of Nouvelle Orleans.
In the 1920's it was the center of New Orleans'
artistic community.

10.28-29 "faintly tarnished languor . . .
smokefilled room": Cf. Charles Baudelaire's
"Epilogue" to <u>Les</u> <u>Fleurs</u> <u>du</u> <u>Mal</u> (1857), in which he
compares Paris to a prostitute:

> But, like an old and faithful lecher, fain
>   To drink delight of that enormous trull
> Whose hellish beauty makes me young again.
> . . . .
> I love thee, infamous city!

Cf. "The Tourist--New Orleans": "A courtesan, not
old and yet no longer young, who shuns the sunlight

that the illusion of her former glory be preserved"
(<u>William</u> <u>Faulkner</u>:   <u>New</u> <u>Orleans</u> <u>Sketches</u>, ed.
Carvel Collins [New York: Random House, 1968],
p. 49). Cf. <u>Elmer</u>, in which Faulkner refers to New
Orleans' "quiet vitiating twilight soft and oppressive as smoke in the streets . . . like the sigh of
a dark and passionate woman no longer young"
(p. 43).

10.29-30 "avid yet weary too of ardent ways": Cf.
the villanelle written by Stephen Dedalus in James
Joyce's <u>A</u> <u>Portrait</u> <u>of</u> <u>the</u> <u>Artist</u> <u>as</u> <u>a</u> <u>Young</u> <u>Man</u>
(New York: B. W. Huebsch, 1916), which begins:
"<u>Are</u> <u>you</u> <u>not</u> <u>weary</u> <u>of</u> <u>ardent</u> <u>ways</u>,/<u>Lure</u> <u>of</u> <u>the</u>
<u>fallen</u> <u>seraphim?</u>/<u>Tell</u> <u>no</u> <u>more</u> <u>of</u> <u>enchanted</u> <u>days</u>"
(pp. 255, 262). (See Note 272.17-22.)

10.30-31 "the bowled weary passion of the sky":
Cf. "And that inverted Bowl we call The Sky/ Where-
under crawling coopt we live and die" (Stanza LII
of Edward FitzGerald, <u>Rubaiyat</u> <u>of</u> <u>Omar</u> <u>Khayyam</u> <u>of</u>
<u>Naishapur</u>, 1st ed. [1859]; in <u>Letters</u> <u>and</u> <u>Literary</u>
<u>Remains</u> <u>of</u> <u>Edward</u> <u>FitzGerald</u> [London: Macmillan
and Co., Ltd., 1903], VII, p. 27). Cleanth Brooks
also suggests the "Telemachus" chapter from James
Joyce's <u>Ulysses</u> as a possible source. (See <u>WF</u>:
<u>TYB</u>, p. 132.) The "Telemachus" chapter had
appeared in <u>The</u> <u>Little</u> <u>Review</u> in March, 1918. (See
Richard Ellmann, <u>James</u> <u>Joyce</u> [New York: Oxford
University Press, 1959], p. 456, for a listing of
publication dates of <u>Ulysses</u> chapters in <u>The</u> <u>Little</u>
<u>Review</u>.) Cf. "Look, the black bowl of the sky
inverted above you/Is chipped at the east, and
slowly fills with light;" ("The World and Pierrot.
A Nocturne.", one of the poem series in <u>Visions</u> <u>in</u>
<u>Spring</u>, the booklet Faulkner gave to Estelle
Franklin in 1921. (See <u>Visions</u> <u>in</u> <u>Spring</u>, Introduction by Judith L. Sensibar [Austin: University
of Texas Press, 1984], p. 27.) Cf. "Outside the
sky was clear, an inverted bowl of dark water
floating with stars . . ." ("Adolescence,"
<u>Uncollected</u> <u>Stories</u>, p. 469). Cf. "the weary bowl
of the sky" (<u>Elmer</u>, p. 70). Cf. "The bowled pale
sky" (<u>SP</u>, p. 225). (See Note 163.20-31.)

10.31-33 "Spring and the cruellest months . . .
comfort of Time": Cf. "April is the cruellest
month/. . . stirring/Dull roots with spring rain"

(T. S. Eliot, <u>The</u> <u>Waste</u> <u>Land</u> [Richmond, Surrey:
Hogarth Press, 1923], p. 1). By extension,
Faulkner might also be alluding to Chaucer's
General Prologue to <u>The</u> <u>Canterbury</u> <u>Tales</u>, which
Eliot deliberately echoes.

10.33-11.1 "August was on the wing": Cf. "The
Bird of Time has but a little way/To fly--and Lo!
the Bird is on the Wing" (Stanza VII of <u>Rubaiyat</u> <u>of</u>
<u>Omar</u> <u>Khayyam</u>, Vol. VII of <u>Letters</u> <u>and</u> <u>Literary</u>
<u>Remains</u> <u>of</u> <u>Edward</u> <u>FitzGerald</u>, p. 18).

11.1-2 "a month . . . regretful as woodsmoke":
Cf. "Spring will come! rejoice! But still is
there/An old sorrow sharp as woodsmoke on the air"
(<u>GB</u>, XXXV, p. 58. Butterworth identifies this poem
under the ts. title "Indian Summer" and dates it
"10 September 1924." See "Census . . . of William
Faulkner's Poetry," 342). Cf. ". . . with Indian
summer upon the land and an ancient sadness sharp
as woodsmoke on the still air" (<u>Flags</u> <u>in</u> <u>the</u> <u>Dust</u>
[New York: Random House, 1973], p. 267).

11.2-6 "But Mr. Talliaferro's youth . . . is not
deathless": Talliaferro's concern with youth and
youthful desires is echoed in other early Faulkner
works. Cf. especially "The Priest," written in
1925 as part of Faulkner's series "Mirrors of
Chartes Street," some of which were published in
the <u>New</u> <u>Orleans</u> <u>Times-Picayune</u>: "He passionately
desired a surcease and an easing of the appetites
and hunger of his blood and flesh . . . he expected
something like sleep, a condition to which he would
attain in which those voices in his blood would be
stilled. Or rather, chastened. Not to trouble him
more, at least . . . ." "Is it youth I want? Is
it youth in me crying out to youth in others which
troubles me?" ("The Priest," <u>Uncollected</u> <u>Stories</u>,
pp. 348, 351. The work was first published in the
<u>Mississippi</u> <u>Quarterly</u>, 29 [Summer 1976], 445-50.)

11.19-30 "As you entered . . . integrity of your
being": Panthea Reid Broughton, in her study
<u>William</u> <u>Faulkner</u>: <u>The</u> <u>Abstract</u> <u>and</u> <u>the</u> <u>Actual</u>
(Baton Rouge and London: LSU Press, 1974),
identifies <u>Mosquitoes</u> as the one work in which
Faulkner "explicitly considers aesthetic issues"
(p. 25). Gordon's statue stands as a complex

symbol of the conflicting nature of Art. In 1956,
Faulkner said, "The aim of every artist is to
arrest motion, which is life, by artificial means
and hold it fixed so that 100 years later when a
stranger looks at it, it moves again since it is
life. Since man is mortal, the only immortality
possible for him is to leave something behind him
that is immortal since it will always move. This
is the artist's way of scribbling `Kilroy was here'
on the wall of the final and irrevocable oblivion
through which he must someday pass" (<u>Lion</u>,
p. 253). However, Faulkner also distinguished
between the stasis of Art and the motion of Life:
"people exist only in life. . . .   Life is motion
. . ." (p. 253). Cf. his early criticism of the
works of Joseph Hergesheimer: "He has never
written a novel--someone has yet to coin the word
for each unit of his work. . . .   It is more like a
lovely Byzantine frieze: a few unforgettable
figures in silent arrested motion, forever beyond
the reach of time and troubling the heart like
music. His people are never actuated from within
. . . they are like puppets assuming graceful but
meaningless postures in answer to the author's
compulsions, and holding these attitudes until he
arranges their limbs again in other gestures as
graceful and meaningless" (<u>EP&P</u>, pp. 101-02).
There are any number of possible sources or
influences from which Faulkner may have derived his
artistic concepts. Cf. Clive Bell's discussion of
Art in "The Aesthetic Hypothesis":

Art transports us from the world of man's activity
to a world of aesthetic exaltation. For a moment
we are shut off from human interests; our antici-
pations and memories are arrested; we are lifted
above the stream of life. . . .   And let no one
imagine, because he has made merry in the warm
tilth and quaint nooks of romance, that he can even
guess at the austere and thrilling raptures of
those who have climbed the cold, white peaks of
Art.

(Clive Bell, <u>Art</u> [1913; New York: Capricorn Books,
1958], pp. 27, 31. One of the books Elmer Hodge
takes with him to Europe is by Bell. Also
mentioned is Elie Faure's <u>The Outline of Art</u>
[1909-14]. See <u>Elmer</u>, p. 4.) Another likely

source is Joyce's <u>A</u> <u>Portrait</u> <u>of</u> <u>the</u> <u>Artist</u> <u>as</u> <u>a</u>
<u>Young</u> <u>Man</u>, in which Stephen Dedalus discusses his
concept of Art and Beauty:

Beauty expressed by the artist cannot awaken in us
an emotion which is kinetic or a sensation which is
purely physical. It awakens, or ought to awaken,
or induces, or ought to induce, an esthetic stasis,
an ideal pity or an ideal terror, a stasis called
forth, prolonged and at last dissolved by what I
call the rhythm of beauty. . . . To speak of these
things and to try to understand their nature and,
having understood it, to try slowly and humbly and
constantly to express, to press out again, from the
gross earth or what it brings forth, from sound and
shape and colour which are all the prison gates of
our soul, an image of the beauty we have come to
understand--that is art [pp. 241-42].

Cf. Willa Cather, <u>The</u> <u>Song</u> <u>of</u> <u>the</u> <u>Lark</u> (Boston and
New York: Houghton Mifflin and Company, 1915):

. . . what was art but an effort to make a sheath,
a mould in which to imprison for a moment the
shining, elusive element which is life itself,
--life hurrying past us and running away, too
strong to stop, too sweet to lose. The Indian
women held it in their jars. In the sculpture she
had seen in the Art Institute, it had been caught
in a flash of arrested motion. In singing, one
made a vessel of one's throat and nostrils and held
it on one's breath, caught the stream in a scale of
natural intervals [p. 304].

Faulkner sometimes listed Cather as among the best
of American writers and admired her work.

11.25-29 "the virginal breastless torso of a girl
. . . darkness of the world": Cf. Theophile
Gautier's <u>Mademoiselle</u> <u>De</u> <u>Maupin</u> ([1835]; New
York: Boni & Liveright, 1918), a novel Faulkner
owned (see <u>William</u> <u>Faulkner's</u> <u>Library</u>: <u>A</u>
<u>Catalogue</u>, compiled by Joseph Blotner [Charlottes-
ville, Va.: University Press of Virginia, 1964],
p. 94) and often echoed in <u>Mosquitoes</u>. In the
novel, d'Albert confesses:

I begin to believe that I am in the wrong, and that

I am asking more from nature and society than they
can give. What I seek has no existence, and I
ought not to complain for having failed to find
it. Yet if the woman of our dreams is impossible
to the conditions of human nature, what is it that
causes us to love her only and none other, since we
are men, and our instinct should be an infallible
guide? Who has given us the idea of this imaginary
woman? From what clay have we formed this invisible statue? [p. 21].

D'Albert constantly thinks of this ideal beauty in
terms of statuary:

I decidedly believe that I must become a sculptor,
for to see such beauty and to be unable to express
it in one way or another is sufficient to make a
man furious and mad. . . . Sculpture has all the
reality that anything completely false can possess;
it has a multiple aspect, casts a shadow and may be
touched [p. 193].

Cf. Stephen Dedalus: "He wanted to meet in the
real world the unsubstantial image which his soul
so constantly beheld. He did not know where to
seek it or how but a premonition which led him on
told him that this image would, without any overt
act of his, encounter him . . ." (<u>Portrait</u> <u>of</u> <u>the</u>
<u>Artist</u>, p. 71). Cf. Joseph Hergesheimer's <u>Linda</u>
<u>Condon</u> (New York: Alfred A. Knopf, 1919), a book
which Faulkner had earlier reviewed (see Note
11.19-30). In it, the young girl Linda is told of
the cult of the "worship of beauty . . . developed
mostly at Florence in the Platonic Academy of
Cosmos and Pico della Mirandola. Love was the
supreme force, and its greatest expression a desire
beyond the body" (p. 32). The description of this
desire is appropriate to Gordon's statue:

The old gesture toward the stars, the bridge of
perfection, the escape from the fatality of flesh.
Yet it was a service of the body made incredibly
lovely in actuality and still never to be grasped.
Never to be won. It ought to be clear to you that
realized it would diminish into quite a different
thing----
      'La <u>figlia</u> <u>della</u> <u>sua</u> <u>mente</u>, l'<u>amorosa</u> <u>idea</u>'"
[p. 34].

Later in the book, Linda looks at a statue which
she has inspired the sculptor Dodge Pleydon to
create and thinks: "Dodge had, in his love,
absorbed her, and that resulted in the statues the
world applauded. . . . But at last she could see
that he had preserved her spirit, her secret self,
from destruction. He had cheated death of her
fineness. The delicate perfection of her youth
would never perish, never be dulled by old age or
corrupted in death. It had inspired and entered
into Pleydon's being, and he had lifted it on the
pedestal . . ." (pp. 302-03). Cf. Michael Arlen's
<u>The Green Hat</u> (New York: George H. Doran Company,
1924), one of the most popular novels of its day:
"They call it . . . `the desire-for-I-know-not-
what.' They will find it one day when we are dead
and all things that live now are dead. They will
find it when everything is dead but the dreams we
have no words for. . . . There is one taste in us
that is unsatisfied. I don't know what that taste
is, but I know it is there" (p. 37). Underlying
all of these possible sources--and the one Faulkner
most clearly and often referred to--is John Keats'
"Ode on a Grecian Urn." Cf.

Heard melodies are sweet, but those unheard
   Are sweeter; therefore, ye soft pipes, play on;
Not to the sensual ear, but, more endear'd
   Pipe to the spirit ditties of no tone: [ll. 11-
14]

In Faulkner's own early work, cf. Elmer Hodge's
ideal beauty: "a dianalike girl with an
impregnable integrity, a slimness virginal and
impervious to time or circumstance" (<u>Elmer</u>,
p. 38). Elmer draws pictures of "people armless
and sweeping upward in two simple lines from a
pedestal-like base: lines that entranced him with
clean juxtaposition, pure and meaningless as
marble" (p. 38) Cf. Horace Benbow's description of
glass figurines in <u>Flags</u>: "Sheerly and tragically
beautiful. Like preserved flowers, you know.
Macabre and inviolate; purged and purified as
bronze, yet fragile as soap bubbles. Sounds of
pipes crystallized" (p. 153).

12.2-3 "the room . . . drain has been opened":
Cf. "Before this green cathedral of trees he stood

for a while, empty as a sheep, feeling the dying
day draining from the world as a bath-tub drains,
or a cracked bowl . . . ." ("Nympholepsy," written
by Faulkner apparently in late 1924 or early 1925.
See <u>Uncollected</u> <u>Stories</u>, pp. 332-33. The sketch
was first published in the <u>Mississippi</u> <u>Quarterly</u>,
26 [Summer 1973], 149-55.)

12.4-5 "a face . . . heavy hawk": This is the
first of a number of hawk images used to describe
Gordon. Joyce W. Warren, in "Faulkner's `Portrait
of the Artist'," (<u>Mississippi</u> <u>Quarterly</u>, 19 [Summer
1966], 121-31), has pointed out Gordon's numerous
similarities to Stephen Dedalus in Joyce's <u>A</u>
<u>Portrait</u> <u>of</u> <u>the</u> <u>Artist</u> <u>as</u> <u>a</u> <u>Young</u> <u>Man</u>, chief among
them being the hawk symbolism. Cf. Stephen's
identification with "the hawklike man whose name he
bore soaring out of his captivity on osier wings
. . ." (p. 264). That this figure is an emblem of
the aspiring artist in Stephen's mind is also made
clear in the novel: ". . . a hawklike man flying
sunward above the sea, a prophecy of the end he had
been born to serve and had been following through
the mists of childhood and boyhood, a symbol of the
artist forging anew in his workshop out of the
sluggish matter of the earth a new soaring
impalpable imperishable being" (p. 196). Cf.
Gerald March in <u>The</u> <u>Green</u> <u>Hat</u>, who has "a face as
dark as night and the nose of a hawk and the eyes
of one who has seen Christ crucified in vain"
(p. 62). Cf. Col. John Sartoris, "with his
bearded, hawklike face and the bold glamor of his
dreams" (<u>Flags</u>, p. 5); and the "hawklike planes of
[Bayard Sartoris's] face" (<u>Flags</u>, p. 38).

12.25-26 "the slim yellow gleam of his straight
malacca stick": The malacca cane is another
example of Talliaferro's dandyism, and, again, its
origins can be traced to Faulkner himself. Carvel
Collins has noted that in 1920 Faulkner imported to
the Mississippi campus "not only the works of
French Symbolists but a walking stick . . ."
(Introduction to <u>EP&P</u>, p. 13). While in New
Orleans, Sherwood Anderson also carried a walking
stick with him; see, for example, William
Spratling's illustration of Anderson in <u>Sherwood</u>
<u>Anderson</u> <u>&</u> <u>Other</u> <u>Famous</u> <u>Creoles</u> ([New Orleans:
Pelican Bookshop Press, 1926]; Austin and London:

University of Texas Press, 1966). A possible
literary source for the stick is Stephen Dedalus's
"ashplant," which he carries throughout <u>Ulysses</u>
([1922], New York: The Modern Library, 1934):
"Damn your yellow stick," Lynch tells him in the
"Circe" section (p. 426), which did not appear in
<u>The</u> <u>Little</u> <u>Review</u>. Cf. Elmer's "yellow stick"
which he uses after his wartime accident: he
"nursed his yellow varnished stick between his
knees . . ." (<u>Elmer</u>, p. 23).

13.7 "characteristic plunging movements": Cf. the
"characteristic plunging movements" of old Bayard
Sartoris in <u>Flags</u> (p. 86).

13.15 "Descending a final stair": Cf. "Time to
turn back and descend the stair" ("Prufrock,"
<u>Poems</u>, p. 11. Noted by Gwynn.)

13.25-30 "His match flared . . . darkness more
intense": Cf. <u>The</u> <u>Green</u> <u>Hat</u>: "I went before her
up the dark narrow stairs, sideways, lighting and
dropping matches, after the custom of six years"
(pp. 17-18). Cf. the opening scene of <u>The</u> <u>Wild</u>
<u>Palms</u>: "The knocking sounded again, at once
discreet and preemptory, while the doctor was
descending the stairs, the flashlight's beam
lancing on before him down the brown-stained
stairwell and into the brown-stained tongue-
and-groove box of the lower hall" ([New York:
Random House, 1939], p. 3).

13.32-14.8 "an undimensional feathered square
. . . street": Jackson Square, originally a parade
ground known as the Place d'Armes but in 1856 made
into a formal garden by the Baroness de Pontalba,
is perhaps the most famous square in New Orleans.
In the center is the ten-ton statue of Andrew
Jackson, noted for "the manner in which the
sculptor succeeded in effecting a perfect balance
in the posture of the horse without props" (<u>New</u>
<u>Orleans</u> <u>City</u> <u>Guide</u>, written and complied by the
Federal Writers' Project, 1938; revised by Robert
Tallant [Boston: Houghton Mifflin and Company,
1952], p. 247). Cf. "Out of Nazareth": "Sparrows
were upon Andrew Jackson's head as, childishly
conceived, he bestrode his curly horse in terrific
arrested motion" (<u>NOS</u>, p. 101). The Square is

bound by St. Ann, St. Peter, Decatur, and Chartres
streets. The Pontalba Buildings flank the Square
north-east and south-west, on St. Ann and St. Peter
streets. They were also built by the Baroness in
1849, originally as apartment houses. Sherwood
Anderson lived in the lower Pontalba on St. Peter
while Faulkner was in New Orleans in 1925 (Blotner,
I, 388). Each of the buildings is four stories
high but runs the length of the Square, thus giving
an appearance of "long unemphasis." St. Louis
Cathedral, built in 1794, is located on Chartres
Street and faces the Square from the north-west.
The three spires of the Cathedral were added in
1851 when it was remodeled. On the two sides of
the Cathedral are St. Anthony's Alley and Orleans
Alley, later renamed Pirate's Alley for the tourist
trade (Collins, <u>NOS</u>, p. 21). Both run into Royal
Street, located behind the Cathedral. From
Faulkner's description, Talliaferro would appear to
be in a building on Orleans Alley. Faulkner
himself lived with William Spratling in such a
building at 624 Orleans Alley, where Spratling had
a studio similar to Gordon's. (See Blotner, I,
401-02.)

14.28-29 "Pontalba and cathedral . . . pasted flat
on a green sky": Cf. Stephen Crane's famous simile
in <u>The</u> <u>Red</u> <u>Badge</u> <u>of</u> <u>Courage</u>: "The red sun was
pasted in the sky like a wafer" ([New York:
D. Appleton and Company, 1896], p. 99).

14.30 "palms . . . soundless explosions": Cf.
"Here each/Slow exploding oak and beech/Blaze up
. . ." (<u>The</u> <u>Marble</u> <u>Faun</u> [Boston: The Four Seas
Company, 1924]; <u>The</u> <u>Marble</u> <u>Faun</u> <u>and</u> <u>A</u> <u>Green</u> <u>Bough</u>,
p. 41). Cf. "the crest of a cabbage palm exploded
raggedly . . ." (<u>The</u> <u>Wild</u> <u>Palms</u>, p. 36).

14.31 "Royal street": The <u>Rue</u> <u>Royale</u> was once the
main street of the old French city. It runs from
north to south behind the St. Louis Cathedral and
is noted for its curio and antique shops.

15.1-2 "inflated rubber": Electric street cars
such as were used in New Orleans at this time ran
on rubber tires.

15.5-12 "He walked . . . passive and motionless":

Cf. Stephen Crane, <u>Maggie</u>: <u>A Girl of the Streets</u>
(New York: D. Appleton and Company, 1896):

     Eventually they entered into a dark region
where, from a careening building, a dozen gruesome
doorways gave up loads of babies to the streets and
the gutter. A wind of early autumn raised yellow
dust from cobbles and swirled it against an hundred
windows. Long streamers of garments fluttered from
fire-escapes. In all unhandy places there were
buckets, brooms, rags and bottles. In the street
infants played or fought with other infants or sat
stupidly in the way of vehicles. Formidable women,
with uncombed hair and disordered dress, gossiped
while leaning on railings, or screamed in frantic
quarrels. Withered persons, in curious postures of
submission to something, sat smoking pipes in
obscure corners. A thousand odors of cooking food
came forth to the street. The building quivered
and creaked from the weight of humanity stamping
about in its bowels [pp. 12-13].

15.9-10 "soft south European syllables": i.e.,
Italian. Prominent settlements of Italians were
found in the neighborhood of Jackson Square near
the French Market. (See <u>New Orleans City Guide</u>,
pp. 44, 246.) Cf. "The Cobbler" (<u>NOS</u>, pp. 131-34)
for an early example of Faulkner's representation
of this dialect.

15.21 "broad West End accent": It is unclear what
accent Faulkner is referring to here. Mr. Talliaferro's cockney would have been prominent in the
East Side of London (see Note 9.4-5). The West End
of New Orleans refers to that section located in
the northwest at Pontchartrain Boulevard and Lake
Pontchartrain, but the grocer's own accent would
seem out of place in this neighborhood, which was
not primarily Italian.

15.24 "thick reluctant thighs": Cf. the "thick
reluctant hips" of Ike Snopes in <u>The Hamlet</u> (New
York: Random House, 1940), p. 192.

16.4 "tacked": To sail a ship diagonally against
the wind, a nautical term suitable to Mrs. Maurier.

16.6-8 "Her hand bloomed . . . hothouse face":

This image is presumably an extension of "hothouse
flower" and is perhaps explained by a letter
Faulkner wrote to his mother while in Paris (6
September 1925) in which he refers to "good healthy
hardy flowers, not hothouse ones" (_Letters_, p. 18).
That Mrs. Maurier is being described as unhealthy
or artificial is supported by lines from Edmond
Rostand's _Cyrano de Bergerac_, a play which is
echoed several times in _Mosquitoes_:

> Have you not seen great gaudy hothouse flowers,
> Barren, without fragrance?--Souls are like that:
> Forced to show all, they soon become all show--
> The means to Nature's end ends meaningless!

(_Cyrano de Bergerac_, trans. by Brian Hooker [New
York: Modern Library, 1923], Act III, p. 168).
Cf. _Flags_, in which Belle "flowered like a hothouse
bloom, brilliant and petulant and perverse"
(p. 167).

16.12 "Mrs. Maurier": Blotner has suggested that
the model for Mrs. Maurier was Elizabeth Werlein
(1887-), "who was thought to have a penchant for
artists and intellectuals and appeared very
soignee" (I, 515). However, according to _Who's Who
in America_ 1928-29 (ed. Albert Nelson Marquis
[Chicago: The A. N. Marquis Company, 1928], XV,
2186-87), Mrs. Werlein was a newspaper woman, a
former public relations head, an author, a museum
restoration worker, and an airplane pilot, all of
which accomplishments would make her an unlikely
Mrs. Maurier. See also Spratling's drawing of her
in _SA&OFC_, which does not at all fit Faulkner's
description of Mrs. Maurier. There is likewise no
reason to believe that Helen Baird's aunt, Mrs.
E. B. Martin, whom Faulkner knew and who lived in
Pascagoula, Mississippi, where _Mosquitoes_ was
written, influenced the creation of Pat Robyn's
aunt in the novel (Blotner, I, 510). As Cleanth
Brooks has put it, "Mrs. Maurier is a rather broad
caricature, and I daresay that she is an entirely
composite figure who owes more to Faulkner's
imagination and his reading that to any woman he
ever met" (_WF_: _TYB_, p. 378). However, Brooks goes
on to suggest that Mrs. Maurier might be partially
based on Sherwood Anderson's third wife, Elizabeth
Prall (p. 378). Martin Kreiswirth draws

interesting parallels between Mrs. Maurier and Mrs.
Aldwinkle in Aldous Huxley's <u>Those</u> <u>Barren</u> <u>Leaves</u>
(1925), a book which he argues also served as a
model for Faulkner in writing <u>Mosquitoes</u>. (See
Kreiswirth, <u>William</u> <u>Faulkner</u>: <u>The</u> <u>Making</u> <u>of</u> <u>a</u>
<u>Novelist</u> [Athens: University of Georgia Press,
1983], pp. 82-83.) Faulkner used the Maurier
character in works other than <u>Mosquitoes</u>. In the
ts. of "Carcassonne" (in the Alderman Library,
University of Virginia), a Mrs. Maurier is
mentioned: "She'd make a poet of you too, if you
didn't work anywhere. She believed that, if a
reason for existing were not acceptable to her, it
was not a reason. With her, if you didn't have a
steady job, you were either a poet or a tramp.
Maybe you were. Women are so wise. They have
learned how to live unconfused by reality" (p. 4).
In the published, slightly revised version, her
name is changed to Widdrington, but her character
remains the same. (See <u>Collected</u> <u>Stories</u> <u>of</u>
<u>William</u> <u>Faulkner</u> [New York: Random House, 1950],
pp. 897-98.) Faulkner had also used the name
Maurier in <u>SP</u>: "Harrison Maurier from Atlanta" is
considered as a possible suitor for Cecily Saunders
(p. 99). And there are similarities between Mrs.
Maurier and Mrs. Monson in <u>Elmer</u>: her relationship
with her daughter Myrtle resembles that of Mrs.
Maurier and her niece Pat Robyn (see Book II of
<u>Elmer</u>, pp. 46-72.) (See also Note 16.21-17.1.)

16.12-14 "Mrs. Maurier . . . amazed at chance . . .
instigated it": Cf. Anse Bundren in <u>As</u> <u>I</u> <u>Lay</u> <u>Dying</u>
([1930]; New York: Random House, 1964): "He looks
around, blinking, in that surprised way, like he
had wore hisself down being surprised and was even
surprised at that" (p. 31).

16.20-21 "examining . . . cool uninterest": Cf.
"The eyes that fix you in a formulated phrase"
("Prufrock," <u>Poems</u>, p. 11). Noted by Gwynn.

16.21-17.1 "The older woman . . . pity on us,
also?'": One of Faulkner's probable models for
Mrs. Maurier is the unnamed patroness of Eliot's
"Portrait of A Lady." Cf.:

You do not know how much they mean to me, my
    friends,

And how, how rare and strange it is, to find
In a life composed so much, so much of odds and
     ends
[For indeed I do not love it . . . you know? you
     are not blind!

How keen you are!]
To find a friend who has these qualities,
Who has, and gives
Those qualities upon which friendship lives.
How much it means that I say this to you--
Without these friendships--life, what <u>cauchemar</u>!
                                   [<u>Poems</u>, p. 16].

16.22-23 "the Quarter": i.e., The French Quarter
(see Note 10.27).

16.28 "Miss Robyn": It has been well established
that Helen Baird served as chief inspiration for
the character of Patricia Robyn. (See Note to
Dedication. In addition to Collins' "Biographical
Background for Faulkner's <u>Helen</u>," see Brooks, <u>WF</u>:
<u>TYB</u>, pp. 51-60. Thomas McHaney has discussed the
possible reflection of the Faulkner-Baird relationship in <u>The Wild Palms</u> in <u>William Faulkner's The
Wild Palms</u>: <u>A Study</u> [Jackson: University Press of
Mississippi, 1975], pp. 21-24. Also see Blotner,
I, 438; II, 982.) There are also a number of
fictional models Faulkner may have used in the
creation of Pat Robyn, among them the boyish
Magdalen de Maupin in Gautier's <u>Mademoiselle De
Maupin</u>, and Madeleine Robin, the Roxane of <u>Cyrano
de Bergerac</u>, from whom Pat's name is presumably
taken. In addition, Faulkner was surely drawing on
the "flapper" figure made famous by F. Scott
Fitzgerald; compare Pat, for example, with the
character of Ardita Farnam in "The Off-Shore
Pirate," a story to which <u>Mosquitoes</u> bears several
similarities. ("The Off-Shore Pirate" was first
published in the <u>Saturday Evening Post</u> [29 May
1920]; collected in <u>Flappers and Philosophers</u> [New
York: Charles Scribner's Sons, 1920]). Cf. also
T. S. Eliot's "Cousin Nancy," which appeared in
<u>Prufrock And Other Observations</u> (1917) and appro-
priately describes Pat's relationship with her
aunt, Mrs. Maurier:

     Miss Nancy Ellicott smoked

And danced all the modern dances;
And her aunts were not quite sure how they felt
     about it,
But they knew that it was modern.

[<u>Poems</u>, p. 30]

17.5 "Chicago": According to Blotner, the Baird
family owned a mansion in Nashville, Tennessee, but
spent their summers at their summer home in
Pascagoula, Mississippi. However, Helen Baird
attended a finishing school for girls on Lakeshore
Drive in Chicago, which could explain Pat Robyn's
acquaintance with the city (see Blotner, I, 509;
see also New Orleans <u>Times-Picayune</u> [1 May 1927],
Sec. 3, p. 4, for reference to this connection).

18.19 "Maecenas": Gaius Maecenas (?-8 B. C.), a
Roman knight who acted as counselor and diplomatic
agent to Octavian, but whose fame rests in his
patronage of Virgil and Horace and in his general
support of the arts. His own writings were
considered affected and pompous. Cf. <u>Cyrano de
Bergerac</u>, in which the character Ragueneau, the
would-be poet, is facetiously referred to as
"Patron of the Arts--Maecenas!" (Act I, p. 14).
Cf. Eliot's "Prufrock":

No! I am not Prince Hamlet, nor was meant to be;
Am an attendant lord, one that will do
To swell a progress, start a scene or two,
Advise the prince; no doubt, an easy tool,
Deferential, glad to be of use,
Politic, cautious, and meticulous;
Full of high sentence, but a bit obtuse
[<u>Poems</u>, p. 14].

18.21-25 "I had hoped . . . delicacy of soul":
Cf. Walter Pater: "What is important, then, is not
that the critic should possess a correct abstract
definition of beauty for the intellect, but a
certain kind of temperament, the power of being
deeply moved by the presence of beautiful objects"
(<u>The Renaissance: Studies in Art and Poetry</u>
[London: Macmillan and Co., Ltd., 1910], p. x).

18.27-28 "Ah, to be a man . . . to create": Cf.
Magdalen de Maupin's feelings concerning the
relative states of men and woman:

     As for us, our life is clear and may be pierced
at a glance. It is easy to follow us from our home
to the boarding-school, and from the boarding-school
to our home. . . . Our life is not a life, it is a
species of vegetation like that of mosses and
flowers. . . . The period of our education is spent
not in teaching us something, but in preventing us
from learning something.
     We are really prisoners in body and mind . . . .
                                        [pp. 152-53]

18.30-19.3 "I looked in on him . . . long lonely
road": Cf. Clive Bell's proclamation on the life of
the Artist:

Let the artist have just enough to eat, and the
tools of his trade: ask nothing of him. Materially
make the life of the artist sufficiently miserable
to be unattractive, and no one will take to art save
those in whom the divine daemon is absolute. . . .
The artist and the saint do what they have to do,
not to make a living, but in obedience to some
mysterious necessity. They do not produce to live--
they live to produce. There is no place for them in
a social system based on the theory that what men
desire is prolonged and pleasant existence. You
cannot fit them into the machine, you must make them
extraneous to it. You must make pariahs of them,
since they are not a part of society but the salt of
the earth [Art, p. 172].

For a more satiric view of the artist, cf. John
Telfer in Sherwood Anderson's Windy McPherson's Son:

In books and stories the great men starve in
garrets. In real life they are more likely to ride
in carriages on Fifth Avenue and have country places
on the Hudson. . . . Visit the starving genius in
his garret. It is a hundred to one that you will
find him not only incapable in money getting but
also incapable in the very art for which he starves.

([New York: John Lane Company, 1916], p. 79).

19.18-19 "the sweet young curve . . . legs of a
bird": Cf. "A girl stood before him in midstream.
. . . Her long slender bare legs were delicate as a
crane's . . ." (Portrait of the Artist, p. 199).

19.20-21 "Her hat was a small brilliant bell about
her face": Pat Robyn is wearing a cloche, a helmet-
or bell-like narrow-brimmed hat popular during the
1920's. Cf. Crome Yellow, in which Mary Brace-
gridle's hair hangs "in a bell of elastic gold about
her cheeks" (p. 26).

20.4-5 "Artistic temperament . . . so spiritual":
Cf. Clive Bell: "Whatever the world of aesthetic
contemplation may be, it is not the world of human
business and passion; in it the chatter and tumult
of material existence is unheard, or heard only as
the echo of some more ultimate harmony" (Art,
p. 55).

20.8-9 "undimensional angular flatness . . .
carving": Early Egyptian carvings were normally
done in a form of relief sculpture, lacking perspective and thus giving the figures a flattened,
sharply angled appearance. Cf. "Even those who
carved those strange flat-handed creatures on the
Temple of Rameses must have dreamed New Orleans by
moonlight" ("Mirrors of Chartres Street," NOS,
p. 54).

21.4 "flowers cut and delicately vased": It was
customary for luxury cars such as Mrs. Maurier's
limousine to have flower vases in the back
compartment where the passangers sat.

21.10-11 "clean young odor . . . young trees": Cf.
The Sound and the Fury ([New York: Cape and Smith,
1929]; New York: The Modern Library, 1966): "Caddy
smelled like trees and like when she says we were
asleep" (p. 5). (See Note 27.31-33.)

21.21 "dives": Normally, a disreputable
establishment or public place, but used also to
describe any place of bad repute.

22.16 "like a round platter stood on edge": Cf.
Sinclair Lewis's description of George Babbitt:
"But he was in earnest, and when he had finished the
formal paper he talked to them, his hands in his
pockets, his spectacled face a flashing disk, like a
plate set up on edge in the lamplight" (Babbitt [New
York: Harcourt, Brace and Company, 1922], p. 166).
(See Note 33.19-22 for mention of Babbitt; see also

Notes 34.12; 35.33-36.2; and 37.31.) Cf. Faulkner's
story "Peter," which Blotner dates from Summer 1925:
"Peter's face is round as a cup of milk with a dash
of coffee in it." "Peter with his face round and
yellow as a new penny . . ." (<u>Uncollected</u> <u>Stories</u>,
pp. 489, 490). Cf. Clarence Snopes in <u>Sanctuary</u>
(New York: Cape and Smith, 1931): "Snopes lit a
cigar, his face coming out of the match like a pie
set on edge" (p. 245).

22.19-20 "to brave the lion in his den":   "And
darest thou then/To beard the lion in his den,/The
Douglas in his hall?" (Sir Walter Scott, <u>Marmion</u>: <u>A</u>
<u>Tale</u> <u>of</u> <u>Flodden</u> <u>Field</u>, Canto VI, xiv, ll. 431-33, in
<u>The</u> <u>Complete</u> <u>Poetical</u> <u>Works</u> <u>of</u> <u>Sir</u> <u>Walter</u> <u>Scott</u>,
Cambridge Edition [Boston and New York: Houghton,
Mifflin and Company, 1900], p. 144). (See Note
325.33-326.1.)

22.25 "Ah, Mr. Gordon, how I envy you this
freedom": Cf. Clive Bell:

The one good thing Society can do for the artist is
to leave him alone. Give him liberty. The more
completely the artist is freed from the pressure of
public taste and opinion, from the hope of rewards
and the menace of morals, from the fear of absolute
starvation or punishment, and from the prospect of
wealth or popular consideration, the better for him
and the better for art, and therefore the better for
everyone. Liberate the artist: here is something
that those powerful and important people who are
always assuring us that they would do anything for
art can do [<u>Art</u>, pp. 167-68].

22.28 "two tired looking stars of the fourth
magnitude": Stars are classed according to their
magnitude, their degree of brilliancy. Stars of the
first magnitude are the brightest and most easily
seen; those of the sixth magnitude are barely
visible to the eye.

23.15-17 "You both know how sensitive to beauty
 . . . denied the creative impulse myself": Martin
Kreiswirth notes that in Aldous Huxley's <u>Those</u>
<u>Barren</u> <u>Leaves</u>, Mrs. Aldwinkle says, "I'm one of
those unfortunate people . . . who have an artistic
temperament without any artistic powers" ([London:

Chatto and Windus, 1925], p. 58.   See Kreiswirth,
The Making of a Novelist, p. 83).

23.32-24.1   "Her jaw in profile was heavy . . .
masculine about it":   Cf. Faulkner's description of
Helen Baird in an undated letter: "I remember a
sullen-jawed yellow-eyed belligerent gal in a linen
dress and sunburned legs sitting on Spratling's
balcony and not thinking even a hell of a little bit
of me that afternoon, maybe already [having] decided
not to" (see Brooks, WF: TYB, p. 52).   Cf.
Charlotte Rittenmeyer in The Wild Palms: ". . . the
dark-haired woman with queer hard yellow eyes in a
face whose skin was drawn thin over prominent
cheekbones and a heavy jaw . . ." (p. 5).

24.6-7   "It's like me":   Cf. Linda Condon's emotions
on seeing Dodge Pleydon's statue (see Note 11.21-
25).

24.27-30   "Gordon examined . . . like a calf or
colt":   Cf. "The Kid Learns":   "Down the street she
came, swinging her flat young body with all the awk-
ward grace of youth, swinging her thin young arms;
beneath her hat he saw hair neither brown nor gold,
and gray eyes.   Clean as a colt she swung past him
. . ." (NOS, p. 163).   In 1943 Faulkner described
the young Lauren Bacall: "[Humphrey Bogart]'s got a
new girl friend . . . . She's like a young colt"
(Blotner, II, 1156).

25.4-5   "Of course you can't have it . . . see that,
don't you?":   Cf. Joseph Hergesheimer, Cytherea (New
York: Alfred A. Knopf, 1922), in which Mina Raff
sees the doll Cytherea which Lee Randon keeps on his
mantle.   Randon worships this doll as "the reward of
all our fineness and visions and pleasures, the idol
of our supreme accomplishments" (p. 366), much as
Gordon regards his statue.   When Mina first notices
the doll, she says to Lee, "What a wonderful doll.
. . . Where did you get her?   But that doesn't
matter: do you suppose, would it be possible for
me, could I buy her?" (p. 51).   Randon answers, "I'm
sorry . . . we can't do without her" (pp. 51-52).

25.17   "Why are you so black?":   Cf. Sanctuary, in
which Temple Drake describes Popeye as a "black man"
(p. 48).   (See Note 144.32-145.8.)

26.2-4 "The spirit of youth . . . dust": Cf. "When
my arms wrap you round I press/My heart upon the
loveliness/That has long faded from the world . . ."
(William Butler Yeats, "He Remembers Forgotten
Beauty," The Wind Among the Reeds [1889]). Cf. "I
desire to press in my arms the loveliness which has
not yet come into the world" (Joyce, Portrait of the
Artist, p. 297). Cf. Mina Raff in Cytherea: "Mina
realized to the last possible indefinite grace the
ideal, always a silver abstraction, of youth; the
old worn simile of an April moon, distinguished in
her case by the qualification wistful, was the most
complete description of her he possessed. Young men
. . . were worshippers of the moon, the unattainable; and when they happily attained a reality they
hid it in iridescent fancy" (p. 177). Cf. Linda
Condon, in which Pleydon's statue, the "Winged
Victory," represents "the goddess of the other
world, of the spirit" (p. 119). Cf. Ardita Farnam
in "The Off-Shore Pirate": "Oh, [men] talk about me
. . . . They tell me I'm the spirit of youth and
beauty" (Flappers and Philosophers, p. 31). Cf. "I
want to gain a part of that beauty which shall not
pass from the earth, of companionship, of love,
perhaps-- who knows?" ("Home," NOS, p. 76). Cf.
Myrtle Monson in Elmer: "Myrtle was like a star,
clean and young and unattainable for all of
her----Henry James would have called it vulgarity
----humanness"(p. 19). Cf. "The Priest": "But ah,
God, ah, God: youth is so much in the world! it is
everywhere in the young bodies of girls dulled with
work over typewriters or behind counters in stores,
uncaged and free at last and crying for the heritage
of youth, taking their soft agile bodies aboard
street cars, each with her own dreams, of who knows
what?" (Uncollected Stories, p. 351). Cf. Mr.
Compson in TS&TF, who tells Quentin, "You are not
thinking of finitude you are contemplating an
apotheosis in which a temporary state of mind will
become symmetrical above the flesh and aware both of
itself and of the flesh" (p. 220). (See also Note
11.19-30.)

26.4-6 "Desire . . . any particular object at all":
Cf. Freud's Libido theory concerning sexual desire.
Under normal circumstances, sexual "energy" is
directed toward a specific, socially acceptable
object. When this transference does not occur,

various "perversions" of this energy may occur, such
as "narcissism," in which the desire is directed
toward the Ego, which replaces the object (see
<u>Beyond</u> <u>the</u> <u>Pleasure</u> <u>Principle</u> ([London: Hogarth
Press, Ltd., 1922], pp. 63-66). Talliaferro offers
one example of the theme of narcissism which runs
throughout the novel.

26.7-19 "What--what does it signify . . . pure form
untrammeled by any relation to a familiar or utili-
tarian object": Cf. Clive Bell's theory of "Significant Form":

. . . lines and colours combined in a particular
way, certain forms and relations of forms, stir our
aesthetic emotions. These relations and combinations of lines and colours, these aesthetically
moving forms, I call `Significant Form'; and
`Significant Form' is the one quality common to all
works of visual art. . . . Any system of aesthetics
which pretends to be based on some objective truth
is so palpably ridiculous as not to be worth
discussing. We have no other means of recognizing a
work of art than our feelings for it [<u>Art</u>, pp. 17-
18].

Bell's ideas were strongly influenced by the "Art
for Art's Sake" movement of the late 19th Century.
Cf. <u>Mademoiselle</u> <u>De</u> <u>Maupin</u>: "There is nothing truly
beautiful but that which can never be of any use
whatsoever; everything useful is ugly, for it is the
expression of some need, and man's needs are ignoble
and disgusting like his own poor and infirm nature.
The most useful place in a house is the water-
closet" (p. xxi). Cf. Oscar Wilde: "As long as a
thing is useful or necessary to us, or affects us in
any way, either for pain or for pleasure, or appeals
strongly to our sympathies, or is a vital part of
the environment in which we live, it is outside the
proper sphere of art. To art's subject-matter we
should be more or less indifferent" ("The Decay of
Lying" in <u>Intentions</u>, vol. V of <u>The</u> <u>Complete</u> <u>Works</u>
<u>of</u> <u>Oscar</u> <u>Wilde</u> [Garden City, N.Y.: Doubleday, Page
& Company, 1923], p. 24). Cf. Walter Pater: "Great
passions may give us this quickened sense of life,
ecstasy and sorrow of love, the various forms of
enthusiastic activity, disinterested or otherwise,
which come naturally to many of us. . . . Of such

wisdom, the poetic passion, the desire of beauty,
the love of art for its own sake, has most. For
art comes to you proposing frankly to give nothing
but the highest quality to your moments as they
pass, and simply for those moments' sake" (<u>The
Renaissance</u>, pp. 238-39). For a more contemporary
view, see Joseph T. Shipley, "The Esthetic
Emotion," <u>The</u> <u>Double</u> <u>Dealer</u>, VII (October 1924),
61-64. Cf. also Joel Elias Spingarn, "The Seven
Arts and the Seven Confusions" in <u>A</u> <u>Modern</u> <u>Book</u> <u>of</u>
<u>Criticism</u>, ed. Ludwig Lewisohn (New York: Boni &
Liveright, 1919): "[Beauty] aims neither at morals
nor at truth. Her imaginary creations, by
definition, make no pretense to reality, and cannot
be judged by reality's tests. Art is expression,
and poets succeed or fail by their success or
failure in completely and perfectly expressing
themselves" (p. 164). According to Blotner,
Faulkner took this book with him to Europe on the
<u>West</u> <u>Ives</u> in 1925 (I, 444, 467). Cf. <u>Linda</u> <u>Condon</u>,
in which Linda says, on seeing one of Dodge
Pleydon's creations: "It is beautiful, isn't it?
I think it's the first thing I ever noticed like
that. You know what I mean--the first thing that
hadn't a real use." Pleydon answers, "But it has.
. . . Do you think it is nothing to be swept into
heaven? I suppose by 'real' you mean oatmeal and
scented soap. Women usually do. But no one, it
appears, has any conception of the practical side
of great art. You might try to remember that it is
simply permanence given to beauty. . . . That is
all, and it is enough" (pp. 115-16).

26.24-26 "This is my feminine ideal . . . talk to
me": Faulkner is drawing in part on the story of
Pygmalion recorded by Ovid in the <u>Metamorphoses</u>.
His description of the sculptor and his statue is
applicable to Gordon and his creation:

     Pygmalion had seen these women spending their
lives in shame, and, disgusted with the faults
which in such full measure nature had given the
female mind, he lived unmarried and long was
without a partner of his couch. Meanwhile, with
wondrous art he successfully carves a figure out of
snowy ivory, giving it a beauty more perfect than
that of any woman ever born. And with his own work
he falls in love. The face is that of a real

maiden, whom you would think living and desirous of
being moved, if modesty did not prevent. So does
his art conceal his art. Pygmalion looks in
admiration and is inflamed with love for this
semblance of a form.

(Ovid, <u>Metamorphoses</u>, trans. Frank Justus Miller
[New York: G. P Putnam's Sons, 1918], vol. II,
Book x, pp. 81-83.)

   Cf. D'Albert's proclamation in <u>Mademoiselle</u> <u>De</u>
<u>Maupin</u>:

In women I have sought nothing but the exterior,
and as those that I have seen up to the present are
far from answering to the idea that I have formed
of beauty, I have fallen back on pictures and
statues;--a resource which is after all pitiful
enough when one has senses so inflamed as mine.
However, there is something grand and beautiful in
loving a statue, in that the love is perfectly
disinterested, that you have not to dread the
satiety or disgust of victory, and that you cannot
reasonably hope for a second wonder similar to the
story of Pygmalion. The impossible has always
pleased me [p. 90].

A woman possesses this unquestionable advantage
over a statue, that she turns of herself in the
direction that you wish, whereas you are obliged to
walk round the statue and place yourself at the
point of sight;--which is fatiguing [p. 142].

Your sculptured differs from your veritable
mistress only in this--that she is a little harder
and does not speak--two very trifling defects!
[p. 193].

26.30-27.3 "`Not,' she added quickly . . . `Or is
it the Bible of which I am thinking?'": Cf. Clive
Bell:

Patronage of the Arts is to the cultivated classes
what religious practice is to the lower-middle, the
homage that matter pays to spirit, or, amongst the
better sort, that intellect pays to emotion.
Neither the cultivated nor the pious are genuinely
sensitive to the tremendous emotions of art and

religion; but both know what they are expected to
feel, and when they ought to feel it [<u>Art</u>, p. 176].

27.30-31 "Gordon's hawk face . . . remote and
insufferable with arrogance": Cf. Stephen Dedalus
in <u>Portrait</u> <u>of</u> <u>the</u> <u>Artist</u>: "I will try to express
myself in some mode of life or art as freely as I
can and as wholly as I can, using for my defence
the only arms I allow myself to use, silence, exile
and cunning" (p. 291). Noted by Warren. (See
Notes 12.4-5; 153.27-28.)

27.31-33 "The niece . . . straight as a poplar":
Sherwood Anderson often used this dryad image, as
did Faulkner himself. Cf. "Her legs and arms were
like the slender top branches of trees swaying in a
gentle wind" ("Out of Nowhere Into Nothing," <u>The</u>
<u>Triumph</u> <u>of</u> <u>the</u> <u>Egg</u> [New York: B. W. Huebsch, Inc.,
1921], p. 178). Cf. Faulkner's early poem "A
Poplar": "You are a young girl/Trembling in the
throes of ecstatic modesty,/A white objective
girl/Whose clothing has been forcibly taken away
from her" (<u>EP&P</u>, p. 60). Cf. <u>Marionettes</u>, in which
Marietta is described as "a slender birch tree
stripped by a storm, she is a birch tree shivering
at dawn upon the dim border of a wood; no she is a
young poplar, between a river and a road" (p. 42).
Cf. Cecily Saunders in <u>SP</u>: "She was like a flower
stalk or a young tree relaxed against the table:
there was something so fragile, so impermanent
since robustness and strength were unnecessary, yet
strong withal as a poplar is strong through very
absence of strength . . ." (p. 80). (See Note
21.10-11.)

27.33-28.1 "Mrs Maurier implored him . . . eyes
doglike, temporarily silent": Cf. "Carcassonne":
"but the woman with the woman with the dog's eyes
to knock my bones together and together" (<u>Collected</u>
<u>Stories</u>, p. 898). In "Carcassonne" the reference
seems to be to Clytemnestra (see Brooks, <u>WF</u>: <u>TYB</u>,
pp. 62-63). For Mrs. Maurier the emphasis is
placed on the pleading nature of her expression.
(See Note 171.32-172.11.)

28.8-9 "Don't you fail me . . . people fail me":
Cf. "I am always sure that you understand/My
feelings, always sure that you feel,/Sure that

across the gulf you reach your hand" (Eliot,
"Portrait of a Lady," <u>Poems</u>, p. 17).

30.6 "shimmy": <u>Chemise</u>: a woman's undergarment.

30.13-14 "Oh, haul in your sheet. . . . You're
jibbing": The "sheet" is the rope which controls
the boom of the main sail of a ship. The "jib" is
a triangular sail which stretches from the mast to
the jib-boom in most sailing ships. To "jibe" is
to allow the sail and boom to be blown across the
deck of the ship and thus to change directions.
One would "haul in the sheet" to avoid "jibing."
Faulkner's spelling--or Pat's pronunciation--is
incorrect.

30.20-22 "She seemed not only unable to get new
men . . . hold to the old ones, even": Cf.:

I have been wondering frequently of late
          . . . .
Why we have not developed into friends.
          . . . .
For everyone said so, all our friends,
They all were sure our feelings would relate
So closely! I myself can hardly understand.
We must leave it now to fate

(Eliot, "Portrait of a Lady," <u>Poems</u>, p. 19).

30.25-26 "O beautiful . . . salutation and
farewell": "O beautiful and wise" from Aiken's
"Discordants." (See Note to Dedication.)

31.8 "Don Juan": In legend, a young nobleman of
Seville who gained a reputation as a seducer of
women. His story inspired numerous works of art,
including Mozart's opera <u>Don Giovanni</u> (1787), in
which a statue plays an important part. The
character who anticipates Talliaferro in <u>Mosquitoes</u>
is first seen as Herbie in Faulkner's story "Don
Giovanni" (<u>Uncollected Stories</u>, pp. 480-88). (See
Notes 9.4 "Mr. Talliaferro"; 31.28-30; 32.21-33.25;
305.5-312.31; 340.24-349.5.)

31.28-30 "Mr. Talliaferro had been married . . .
these eight years": Cf. "Don Giovanni": "He had
been married while quite young by a rather

plain-faced girl whom he was trying to seduce,and
now, at thirty-two, he was a widower" (<u>Uncollected
Stories</u>, p. 480).

31.31 "the final result of some rather casual
biological research":   Cf. <u>Mayday</u>, in which,
according to the running head on p. 29, Galwyn
"Carries On His Biological Research" with the
Princess Aelia.   In a 1927 letter to Horace
Liveright Faulkner indicated that he was "going on
an expedition with a lady friend for purposes of
biological research" (Blotner, I, 557).   James B.
Meriwether informs me that in his reply, Liveright
suggested that Faulkner surely meant "gynocological
research."

32.2-4 "The family originated . . . impulse in the
race":   Cf. <u>Elmer</u>:   "His family, like the sun, had
a westward tendency, as though the eastward
direction of the earth's motion prevented them ever
rooting anywhere" (p. 7).

32.5-6 "Horace Greeley . . . observed it himself":
Horace Greeley (1811-72) was a founder and editor
of the <u>New</u> <u>York</u> <u>Tribune</u>.   The slogan "Go West,
Young Man" has been popularly attributed to him,
although he denied having originated it.   (See
<u>Dictionary</u> <u>of</u> <u>Quotations</u>, collected and arranged
with comments by Bergen Evans [New York: Delacorte
Press, 1968], p. 745.)

32.7-12 "His brothers were various . . .
California":   Cf. "Adolescence":

Paternity rested but lightly upon him [the
father]:   like the male of his kind, he regarded
the inevitable arrival of children as one of the
unavoidable inconveniences of marriage, like the
risk of wetting the feet while fishing.
     In regular succession thereafter appeared
Cyril, one day to be sent to the State Legislature,
Jeff Davis, who was finally hung in Texas for
stealing a horse; then another boy whom, her spirit
broken, she [the mother] was too apathetic to name
at all and who, as a matter of convenience,
answered to Bud, and became a professor of Latin
with a penchant for Catullus at a small mid-western
university [<u>Uncollected</u> <u>Stories</u>, pp. 459-60].

Cf. <u>The</u> <u>Hamlet</u>:

He [an unnamed farmer] was a man past middle age,
who with nothing to start with but sound health and
a certain grim and puritanical affinity for
abstinence and endurance, had made a fair farm out
of the barren scrap of hill land which he had
bought at less than a dollar an acre and married
and raised a family on it and fed and clothed them
all and even educated them after a fashion, taught
them at least hard work, so that as soon as they
became big enough to resist him, boys and girls
too, they left home (one was a professional nurse,
one a ward-heeler to a minor county politician, one
a city barber, one a prostitute; the oldest had
simply vanished completely) . . . [pp. 218-19].

32.12-13 "They never did know . . . Mr.
Talliaferro's sister": Cf. <u>Elmer</u>, in which Elmer's
sister Jo-Addie leaves home when Elmer is a child,
sends him paint and brushes, and then disappears
from his life, although Elmer thinks he sees her
fleetingly in New Orleans. Cf. Candace Compson in
<u>TS&TF</u> and in "Appendix: The Compsons 1699-1945,"
which first appeared in <u>The</u> <u>Portable</u> <u>Faulkner</u>, ed.
Malcolm Cowley ([New York: The Viking Press,
1946).

32.21-33.25 "His marriage . . . oppress him": Cf.
"Don Giovanni" (<u>Uncollected</u> <u>Stories</u>, pp. 480-81),
in which Herbie has also been victim to an unhappy
marriage.

32.28-32 "women's clothing section . . . wholesale
buyer": In addition to Herbie in "Don Giovanni,"
there is in <u>SP</u> a minor character named Schluss who
is also a buyer: "I got a swell line of ladies'
underthings," he tells the soldiers on the train
(p. 16).

33.5-6 "he remained faithful . . . an invalid": A
similar situation is portrayed at some length in a
later Faulkner story "The Brooch," begun in late
1930 or early 1931 although not published until
1936. (See "The Brooch," <u>Scribner's</u>, 99 [January
1936], pp. 7-12; also <u>Collected</u> <u>Stories</u>, pp. 647-
65, in which Howard Boyd takes care of his invalid
mother at the expense of his own marriage. The

mother lies in bed "propped bolt upright, in the
darkness, watching the invisible door" [<u>Collected
Stories</u>, p. 649].)

33.10-12 "he became accustomed . . . freedom was
an unexplored field to him": Cf. "The Brooch":
"He [Howard] had begun to drink after his mother's
stroke, in the beginning of what he had believed to
be his freedom . . ." (<u>Collected</u> <u>Stories</u>, p. 664).

33.13-14 "his solitary routine of days": Cf.:

For I have known them all already, known them
      all:--
Have known the evenings, mornings, afternoons,
I have measured out my life with coffee spoons
            [Eliot, "Prufrock," <u>Poems</u>, p. 11].

33.14-17 "of walking home . . . to say him nay":
Cf. "The Priest":

     Walking the streets, his problem became no
clearer. The streets were filled with women:
girls going home from work, their lithe young
bodies became symbols of grace and beauty, of
impulses antedating Christianity. "How many of
them have lovers?" he wondered [<u>Uncollected
Stories</u>, p. 350].

33.19-22 "Mr. Talliaferro did Europe . . .
Complete": Cf. "We were foul with dust, numbed
with cold, aching with tiredness, and this was
because we had `done' the six hundred odd miles
from Cannes in two days and a few hours" (Arlen,
<u>The</u> <u>Green</u> <u>Hat</u>, p. 134). Writing to his mother (13
September 1925) of Vance Carter Witt and her
daughter, relatives Faulkner met while in Europe,
he noted: "They are very nice, of the purest
Babbitt ray serene. They carry their guidebooks
like you would a handkerchief. . . . Europe has
made no impression on them whatever other than to
give them a smug feeling of satisfaction for having
`done it'" (<u>Letters</u>, p. 22). Cf. <u>Elmer</u>: "Elmer had
a remote Jove-like perspective on things now.
Perhaps because he was a war veteran, perhaps
because he had `done' the war . . ." (p. 22).

33.22 "His only alarm . . . thinning hair": Cf.

"They will say: `How his hair is growing thin!'"
(Eliot, "Prufrock," Poems, p. 11). Noted by Gwynn.

33.25 "celibacy . . . oppress him": Cf. "The
Priest":

And he wondered how many priests leading chaste
lives relieving human suffering, were virgin, and
whether or not the fact of virginity made any
difference. . . . It was as though a man were
given certain impulses and desires without being
consulted by the donor, and it remained with him to
satisfy them or not. He himself could not do this,
though; he could not believe that sexual impulses
could disrupt a man's whole philosophy, and yet
might be allayed in such a way [Uncollected
Stories, p. 350].

33.26 "Broussard's": Located at 819 Conti Street,
Broussard's is one of the finest New Orleans
restaurants, known for its oysters a la Broussard.
(See Note 38.4.)

33.27 "Dawson Fairchild, the novelist": Fairchild
is patterned on Faulkner's friend and mentor
Sherwood Anderson (1876-1941). Faulkner had first
met Anderson in 1924 through Anderson's wife,
Elizabeth Prall, for whom Faulkner had worked in
New York in 1921 in the Doubleday bookshop at Lord
& Taylor's. Anderson later used Faulkner as a
rather odd, yet not unadmirable character in his
story "A Meeting South," published in The Dial in
1925. In one sense, Faulkner was repaying
Anderson, presenting him in Mosquitoes as a likable
yet limited artist. However, Faulkner's portrayal
of Anderson is by no means cruel or unfair, and,
when compared with Anderson's representation of
Faulkner in "A Meeting South," illustrates
Faulkner's more acute perception. (For a detailed
discussion of Faulkner and Anderson in New Orleans,
see Carvel Collins' Introduction to NOS, pp. 17-
20. See also James B. Meriwether, "Faulkner's
Essays on Anderson," in Faulkner: Fifty Years
After The Marble Faun, ed. George H. Wolfe
[University, Alabama: The University of Alabama
Press, 1976], pp. 159-81. For a different
perspective, see Max Putzel, "The Break With
Anderson," in Genius of Place: William Faulkner's

Triumphant _Beginnings_ [Baton Rouge and London: LSU
Press, 1985], pp. 73-85.)

34.12 "Mr. Hooper": Hooper represents a type of
character made famous by Sinclair Lewis--the
middle-class, upward-bound, morally-blind
businessman. There are a number of similarities
between Hooper and George Babbitt, Lewis's
best-known character. _Babbitt_ was published in
1922 and Faulkner was familiar with the book. (See
Notes 22.16; 33.19-22; 35.33-36.2.) Other probable
sources for the character of Hooper are Almus
Pickerbaugh in _Arrowsmith_ (1925) and Mr. Barbecue-
Smith in Huxley's _Crome_ _Yellow_. (See Note 9.4 and
following Notes.)

34.14-16 "a man . . . thwarted Sunday school
superintendent": Cf. the Chief Engineer in _Elmer_:
"His smooth-shaven face was cast like a conscien-
tious Sunday school superintendent's, in a sort of
flouted frenzy of conviction . . ." (p. 4). Cf.
the judge in _The_ _Wild_ _Palms_ who passes sentence on
Harry Wilbourne: "his face which was not a
lawyer's face at all but that of a Methodist Sunday
School superintendent who on week days was a banker
and probably a good banker, a shrewd banker . . ."
(p. 317).

34.18-19 "a tall, ghostly young man . . . mouth":
According to Blotner (I, 517), Mark Frost is drawn
from the character of Samuel Louis Gilmore, Jr.
(1896-1972), a New Orleans poet and regular contributor to _The_ _Double_ _Dealer_. Martin Kreiswirth
draws a parallel between Frost and the poet Francis
Chelifer in _Those_ _Barren_ _Leaves_ (see _The_ _Making_ _of_
_a_ _Novelist_, p. 83). (See also Notes 65.3-4; 334.9-
19.)

34.19 "a pale prehensile mouth": Cf. the figure
of Hunger in _Mayday_: "a small green design with a
hundred prehensile mouths" (p. 4). Cf. the
"obscuring prehensileness" of Cecily Saunders'
mouth in _SP_ (p. 212).

34.19-20 "a bald Semitic man . . . sad quizzical
eyes": Julius Kauffman is based on Julius Weis
Friend (1896-1962), one of the founders and editors
of _The_ _Double_ _Dealer_ (see Blotner, I, 517; also see

Brooks, <u>WF</u>: <u>TYB</u>, pp. 378-80). However, Faulkner
also uses characteristics of the "Wealthy Jew" from
his New Orleans sketches in his development of
Julius (see <u>NOS</u>, pp. 37-38, and following Notes).
Kreiswirth notes similarities between Julius and
"Mr. Cardon" in <u>Those Barren Leaves</u> (see <u>The Making
of a Novelist</u>, p. 83). (See Note 16.12.)

35.4-6 "Except for this southern laziness . . .
possibilities": Cf. Sherwood Anderson's <u>Poor White</u>
(New York: B. W. Huebsch, Inc., 1920):

> Practically all of the people of Hugh's
> [McVey] home town were of Southern origin. Living
> originally in a land where all physical labor was
> performed by slaves, they had come to have a deep
> aversion to physical labor. In the South their
> fathers, having no money to buy slaves of their own
> and being unwilling to compete with slave labor,
> had tried to live without labor. . . . Their food
> was meager and of an enervating sameness and their
> bodies degenerate. . . . The more energetic among
> them, sensing dimly the unfairness of their
> position in life, became vicious and dangerous.
> . . . In Southern Indiana and Illinois they were
> merged into the life about them and with the
> infusion of new blood they a little awoke
> [pp. 18-19].

Cf. "Damon and Pythias, Unlimited": "These people
in the South ain't got the pep we have at all"
(<u>NOS</u>, p. 61). Cf. <u>Elmer</u>: "New Orleans soothed
him, someway. Its voluptuous inertia mocking all
briskness with a mild polite derision; its
atmosphere that made even those who had the virus
of Progress in their blood go through their ritual
of efficiency with tongue in cheek . . ." (p. 43).

35.15-27 "I am glad . . . to himself": Cf. Almus
Pickerbaugh, the public health director in Sinclair
Lewis's <u>Arrowsmith</u> (New York: Harcourt, Brace &
Company, 1925), who considers himself the "Billy
Sunday of the [public health] movement" (p. 195).
Pickerbaugh writes verses of "instruction and a
little pep" (p. 196) and boasts: "Still, you'll
readily see how one of these efforts of mine, just
by having a good laugh and a punch and some melody
in it, does gild the pill and make careless folks

stop spitting on the sidewalks, and get out into
God's great outdoors and get their lungs packed
full of ozone and lead a real hairy-chested
he-life" (p. 197). Cf. <u>Crome</u> <u>Yellow</u>, in which Mr.
Barbecue-Smith writes books of "comfort and
spiritual teaching" for the multitude (p. 52).

35.33-36.2 "What did you think of my idea . . .
miss something good by staying away?": Cf. George
Babbitt: "The more manly and practical a fellow
is, the more he ought to lead the enterprising
Christian life" (p. 212). Babbitt proposes raising
attendance at Sunday School by "going right at it
as if it were a merchandizing problem . . ."
(p. 215). (See <u>Babbitt</u>, pp. 204-17.) Cf. Almus
Pickerbaugh, who leads a "Go-to-Church"
Demonstration in <u>Arrowsmith</u>: "That was a dandy
meeting! We increased church attendance here
seventeen per cent!" (p. 196). Cf. Faulkner's
account of the Al Jackson family in a letter to
Sherwood Anderson written in 1925. At the age of
nine, Jackson's mother "increased attendance at her
church three hundred percent with some sort of a
secret recipe for communion wine, including among
other things, grain alcohol" ("Al Jackson,"
<u>Uncollected</u> <u>Stories</u>, p. 474). (See Notes 66.22;
277.4-281.15.)

36.20 "a member of Rotary": The Rotary is a
world-wide organization composed largely of
representatives from businesses, trades, and other
professions in a community. The Club was
established in Chicago in 1905; by the 1920's it
had become synonymous with conservative, middle-
class thinking and was therefore the subject of
ridicule to the more liberal thinkers in the
country. Sinclair Lewis, especially, scorned the
Rotary in works such as <u>Babbitt</u> and <u>Arrowsmith</u>, in
which Pickerbaugh is the "founder of the first
Rotary Club in Iowa" (p. 198). In Elizabeth Prall
Anderson's memoirs <u>Miss</u> <u>Elizabeth</u> (New York:
Little, Brown & Company, 1969), she recounts an
exchange between Gertrude Stein and Ernest
Hemingway:

    Gertrude once told Hemingway, "After all, you
are ninety per cent Rotarian."
    "Can't you make it eighty per cent?" he asked,

trying to make it a joke.
        "No," she said, with sincere regret, "I can't"
[p. 170].

Cf. <u>Elmer</u>: When arrested in Venice, "Elmer felt
quite like a rotarian as he wondered what he had
done . . ." (p. 84).

36.29-37.2 "He is just the man . . . meaning of
service, hey, Talliaferro?": An apparent reference
to Bruce Barton's best-selling and controversial
book <u>The</u> <u>Man</u> <u>Nobody</u> <u>Knows</u>: <u>A</u> <u>Discovery</u> <u>of</u> <u>the</u> <u>Real</u>
<u>Jesus</u> (Indianapolis, Indiana: Bobbs-Merrill Co.,
1925). Barton argued that Jesus was "The Founder
of Modern Business":

Manufacturers of building equipment, of clothes, of
food; presidents of railroads and steamship
companies; the heads of banks and investment
houses--<u>all</u> of them tell the same story. "Service
is what we are here for," they exclaim. They call
it the "spirit of modern business"; they suppose,
most of them, that it is something very new. But
Jesus preached it more than nineteen hundred years
ago [pp. 165-66].

According to Barton, the first "main" point of
Jesus's "business philosophy" is "Whoever will be
great must render great service" (p. 177).

37.10-17 "I run my day to schedule . . . what do
you do with them?": Cf. George Santayana, "The
Genteel Tradition in American Philosophy": "Good-
will became the great American virtue; and a
passion arose for counting heads, and square miles,
and cubic feet, and minutes saved--as if there had
been anything to save them for" (<u>Winds</u> <u>of</u>
<u>Doctrine</u>: <u>Studies</u> <u>in</u> <u>Contemporary</u> <u>Opinion</u> [New
York: Charles Scribner's Sons, 1913], p. 91).

37.23-25 "Our forefathers . . . existence to
fetiches": Benjamin Franklin, in his <u>Poor</u>
<u>Richard's</u> <u>Almanack</u> (1732-57), made popular many
aphorisms and household proverbs which have
remained in use to this day. The best known of
these proverbs were found in <u>The</u> <u>Way</u> <u>to</u> <u>Wealth</u>
(1757), the preface to his last <u>Almanack</u>. Most of
these maxims were concerned with money, and they

have contributed to Franklin's reputation as a
materialist, although, in truth, they make up only
a small portion of his sayings. The idea of a
fetiche, as used by Sigmund Freud, referred to any
object irrationally worshipped or adored. Freud
linked this extreme attraction to a fear of
castration. (See "Fetishism" in _The Standard
Edition_ _of_ _the_ _Complete_ _Works_ _of_ _Sigmund_ _Freud_, ed.
James Strachey [The Hogarth Press and the Institute
of Psychoanalysis, 1916], XXI, 149-58.)

37.31 "pep": An abbreviation of "pepper," "pep"
became synonymous with energy and initiative c.
1914. In _Babbitt_, George Babbitt's Booster Club
button "displayed two words: `Booster--Pep!'"
(p. 10). Cf. _Elmer_: The Second Officer on the
transatlantic voyage tells Elmer, "You'd think
. . . that a man would have lots of time to read
and improve his mind in this profession. But he
just lazes around . . . . Nothing to pep him up to
reading books" (p. 19). (See Note 35.4-6.)

38.2 "George": An irreverent form of address to a
stranger. Cf. Clarence Snopes to a train porter in
Sanctuary: "Here, George . . . have a cigar"
(p. 213).

38.4 "Mr. Broussard": Joseph Broussard,
proprietor of Broussard's restaurant. (See Note
33.27.)

38.21 "Monteleone hotel, three blocks away": The
Monteleone hotel, located at 214 Royal Street.

38.30-39.1 "When you are young . . . high
ideals": The stated purpose of the Rotary was to
"serve humanity." (See Note 36.20.)

39.7-9 "And when you've made a form of behavior
. . . public nuisance": This idea is quite similar
to Sherwood Anderson's theory of the "Grotesques"
in "The Book of the Grotesque" which begins
Winesburg, _Ohio_ (New York: B. W. Huebsch, 1919):

   That in the beginning when the world was young
there were a great many thoughts but no such thing
as a truth. Man made the truths himself and each
truth was a composite of a great many vague

thoughts. All about in the world were the truths
and they were all beautiful. . . .   And then the
people came along. Each as he appeared snatched up
one of the truths and some who were quite strong
snatched up a dozen of them.
      It was the truth that made the people
grotesque . . . the moment one of the people took
one of the truths to himself, called it his truth,
and tried to live his life by it, he became a
grotesque and the truth he embraced became a
falsehood [pp. 4-5].

Cf. <u>Elmer</u>: "How magnificent convictions are, being
so short-lived, so quickly replaced. . . .   But
then, people busy getting born and getting children
and getting dead have no time for lasting convictions. And if it lasted very long it wouldn't be a
conviction: someone would adopt it and shout it
from the untroubled eaves of houses, and in time it
would become divine, or (worse still) a custom"
(p. 5).

40.24 "an Elk or a Boy Scout": The Benevolent and
Protective Order of Elks is a fraternal and
charitable organization founded in 1868. The Boy
Scouts, founded by Lt. Gen. R.S.S. Baden-Powell in
Great Britain in 1907, is a youth organization for
boys, built on a semi-militaristic system. These
groups and the Rotary would be representative of
middle-class American values. (See Note 36.20.)
However, Faulkner served as master of the local boy
scout troop in 1924 until he was dismissed,
probably for his drinking.

41.24-42.2 "So you believe the sole accomplishment
of education . . . just as bad, and perhaps
worse": Cf. Robert Morss Lovett's article on
"Education" in <u>Civilization</u> <u>in</u> <u>the</u> <u>United</u> <u>States</u>,
in which he refers to Barrett Wendell's description
of education as "the Great American Superstition"
(p. 77) and adds: "Education is the propaganda
department of the State, and the existing social
system. Its resolute insistence upon the essential
rightness of things as they are, coupled with its
modest promise to reform them if necessary, is the
basis of the touching confidence with which it is
received" (p. 89). Cf. Sherwood Anderson's <u>A</u> <u>Story</u>
<u>Teller's</u> <u>Story</u> (New York: B. W. Huebsch, 1924):

Books I have always had access to and I am sure
there is no other country in the world where people
in general are so sentimentally romantic on the
subject of books and education. Not that we read
the books or really care about education. Not we.
What we do is to own books and go to colleges and I
have known more than one young man without money
work his way patiently through college without
paying much attention to what the colleges are
presumed to teach [p. 156].

42.4-13 "But to go back to religion . . . weak to
resist": Cf. Bruce Barton's defense of Jesus in
the introduction to <u>The</u> <u>Man</u> <u>Nobody</u> <u>Knows</u>: "A
physical weakling! Where did they get that idea?
Jesus pushed a plane and swung an adze; he was a
successful carpenter. He slept outdoors and spent
his days walking around his favorite lake. His
muscles were so strong that when he drove the
money-changers out, nobody dared to oppose him!"
(p. [4]).

43.3-20 "`Oh, he'll come, I guess' . . . he
agreed": Cf. Clive Bell:

     The cultured . . . who expect in every picture
at least some reference to a familiar masterpiece,
create, unconsciously enough, a thoroughly
unwholesome atmosphere. For they are rich and
patronising and liberal. They are the very
innocent but natural enemies of originality, for an
original work is the touchstone that exposes
educated taste masquerading as sensibility.
Besides, it is reasonable that those who have been
at such pains to sympathise with artists should
expect artists to think and feel as they do.
Originality, however, thinks and feels for itself;
commonly the original artist does not live the
refined, intellectual life that would benefit the
fancy-man of the cultured classes. He is not
picturesque; perhaps he is positively inartistic;
he is neither a gentleman nor a blackguard; culture
is angry and incredulous. Here is one who spends
his working hours creating something that seems
strange and disquieting and ugly, and devotes his
leisure to simple animalities; surely one so
utterly unlike ourselves cannot be an artist? So
culture attacks and sometimes ruins him. If he

survives, culture has to adopt him. He becomes
part of the tradition, a standard, a stick with
which to beat the next original genius who dares to
shove an unsponsored nose above water [Art, pp.
177-78].

Cf. Faulkner's story "Artist at Home": "Why do you
feel compelled to lodge and feed these people?
Can't you see they consider you an easy mark? that
they eat your food and wear your clothes and
consider us hopelessly bourgeois for having enough
food for other people to eat, and a little soft-
brained for giving it away?" (Collected Stories,
p. 631).

43.23-25 "The fact that . . . assured position in
the creative world . . .": In the 1920's, Sherwood
Anderson was often ranked as one of the leading
writers in the United States. (See Notes 209.15-
16; 209.17; 241.26-28.)

46.1-3 "`How's it coming, Josh?' . . . three
inches long": Helen Baird's twin brother Peter was
known as Josh, according to Blotner (I, 509).
Josh's consuming interest in his pipe, to the
exclusion of human companionship, is similar to
that of Henry Wimbush in Crome Yellow, who is "more
at home" with his oaken drainpipes and finds that
people "don't very much interest me. They aren't
in my line" (p. 286). Cf. Elmer's infatuation with
his tubes of paint: he "hovered over them with a
brooding maternity, taking up one at a time those
fat portentous tubes in which was yet wombed his
heart's desire, the world itself--thick-bodied and
female and at the same time phallic: hermaphrodite" (p. 5). (See Notes 46.24-26; 46.27-29;
252.17.)

46.9-10 "A thin pencil of smoke": Cf. "pencils of
sun slanted in the trees" (TS&TF, p. 167). Cf. "a
narrow rosy pencil of sunlight" (Sanc., p. 334).

46.23 "Gus": Here used as a common nickname
between the twins. Cf. "Country Mice" (NOS, pp.
193-207), in which the bootlegger speaks of his
brother Gus who runs whiskey to New Haven for a
football game. Josh Robyn plans to attend Yale in
Mosquitoes (see pp. 256-58).

46.24-26 "They were twins . . . feminine about
his": Twinships and intense relationships between
brothers and sisters are quite common in Faulkner's
early works, most notably Elmer and Jo-Addie Hodge
in <u>Elmer</u>; John and Bayard Sartoris in <u>Flags</u>; Horace
and Narcissa Benbow in <u>Flags</u> and <u>Sanctuary</u>; Quentin
and Candace Compson in <u>TS&TF</u>; Darl and Dewey Dell
Bundren in <u>AILD</u>. Patricia and Josh Robyn very much
fit into this mold. (For a thorough discussion of
this theme in Faulkner, see John T. Irwin, <u>Doubling
and Incest/Repetition and Revenge</u>: <u>A Speculative
Reading of Faulkner</u> [Baltimore and London: The
Johns Hopkins Press, 1975].) The image of the
hermaphrodite, central to the theme of <u>Mosquitoes</u>
and reflected in Gordon's statue, is summoned up in
this passage. Josh--or Theodore, his actual name--
and Pat share masculine and feminine characteristics, and neither exhibits a normal interest in
sex. In developing these two characters, Faulkner
may have had in mind Michael Arlen's <u>The Green Hat</u>,
in which Iris Storm and her twin brother Gerald
March have a special relationship: "But you can't,
you see, get rid of the funny love between twins
like Gerald and me just by the word ˜hate.' . . .
There was something peculiarly <u>us</u> about Gerald and
me, something of blood and bone peculiarly us which
nothing but death could destroy" (p. 142). Another
possible influence is Gautier's <u>Mademoiselle De
Maupin</u>, in which Magdalen de Maupin impersonates
and finally becomes the effeminate Theodore de
Serannes. Cf. also George Moore, <u>Louis Seymour and
Some Women</u>, in which Seymour compares himself to
the statue of Hermaphroditos: "Well, there are
traces of the woman in me" (Carra Edition of <u>The
Collected Works of George Moore</u> [New York: Boni &
Liveright, 1922], I, 96). Faulkner owned a copy of
this novel (see <u>William Faulkner's Library</u>, p.
77). (See Notes 46.27-29; 252.17-19.)

46.27-29 "For God's sake . . . waving your legs
around?": Pat's attraction to her brother, her
tendency even to attack him, however playfully (see
Note 315.4-25), echoes the myth of Hermaphroditos
as told by Ovid: the fountain nymph Salmakis falls
in love with the handsome, unresponsive
Hermaphroditos. When he rejects her, she leaps upon
him and wraps herself around him while he is
bathing. Finally, as a result of her prayers, she

is united with him, fused into one person with both
masculine and feminine characteristics. (See
<u>Metamorphoses</u>, vol. I, Book IV, 199-205.) Cf.
Charlotte Rittenmeyer in <u>WP</u>: "I liked my oldest
brother the best but you cant sleep with your
brother and he and Rat roomed together in school so
I married Rat and now I've got two girls, and when
I was seven years old I fell in the fireplace, my
brother and I were fighting, and that's the scar.
It's on my shoulder and side and hip too and I got
in the habit of telling people about it before they
would have time not to ask and I still do it even
when it doesn't matter anymore" (p. 40).

46.30 "yellow negro": A Negro with light skin,
taken as a sign of Caucasian ancestry and once
resulting in higher caste.

47.4 "fool fool you have work to do": Cf.
Faulkner's poem "Study": "While I can think of
nothing else at all/Except the sunset in her eyes'
still pool./(Work, work, you fool--)" (<u>EP&P</u>,
p. 62).

47.4-5 "o cursed of god cursed and forgotten":
Cf. Thomas Mann's story "Tonio Kroger" (1903):
"Don't talk about `calling.' . . . Literature is
not a calling, it is a curse, believe me! When
does one begin to feel the curse? Early, horribly
early. At a time when one ought by rights still to
be living in peace and harmony with God and the
world" (<u>Stories</u> <u>of</u> <u>Three</u> <u>Decades</u> [New York: Alfred
A. Knopf, 1938], p. 104). Cf. also in the same
story Kroger's desire to "live free from the curse
of knowledge and the torment of creation, live and
praise God in blessed mediocrity!" (p. 128).
Faulkner often expressed his admiration for Mann.

47.5 "form shapes cunningly sweated cunning to
simplicity": See Note 27.30-31.

47.6 "shapes out of chaos": A reference to the
artist as creator, as god. In mythology, Chaos was
the first state of the universe and was sometimes
personified as the most ancient of gods. Ovid, in
the <u>Metamorphoses</u> (Book I) described how order was
brought to Chaos resulting in the individualization
of the separate elements: Earth, Sea, and Sky. In

<u>Paradise</u> <u>Lost</u>, John Milton presents Chaos as both
place and "Anarch" of that place (Book II,
1. 988). "Nature," or the created world, causes
Chaos "to retire/As from her outmost works a broken
foe,/With tumult less and with less hostile din"
(11. 1038-40). (See <u>The</u> <u>Complete</u> <u>Poetical</u> <u>Works</u> <u>of</u>
<u>John</u> <u>Milton</u>, ed. by Douglas Bush [Boston: Houghton
Mifflin Company, 1965], pp. 254, 255.) Cf. "Tonio
Kroger": "I am looking into a world unknown and
formless, that needs to be ordered and shaped; I
see into a whirl of shadows of human figures who
beckon to me to weave spells to redeem them . . ."
(<u>Stories</u> <u>of</u> <u>Three</u> <u>Decades</u>, p. 132).

47.7 "a madmans dream": The artist as inspired
madman is perfectly illustrated in Samuel Taylor
Coleridge's "Kubla Khan" (1797), a poem which
Faulkner knew well. (See Blotner, I, 246-47.)

47.7-8 "le garcon vierge of the soul": The virgin
boy of the soul.

47.8-9 "horned by utility o cuckold of derision":
Horns upon the forehead are symbols of the
cuckold. Here the artist is cuckold by necessity;
the demands of the actual cheat and defile his
artistic vision.

47.10-11 "formal rectangle without perspective":
A cubist image relating to the modern art school of
cubism which often employed abstract geometrical
forms rather than realistic depictions of nature.
The two-dimensionality of the image is in implied
contrast to the three-dimensionality of the plastic
arts which Gordon employs (see Note 11.25-29).
However, Faulkner often used the appearance of
two-dimensionality to indicate incompleteness, as
in his description of Popeye in <u>Sanctuary</u>: "he had
that vicious depthless quality of stamped tin"
(p. 4).

47.15-20 "Beneath it, within the somber gloom . . .
passing on": Cf. <u>Elmer</u>: "the docks where he
walked smelling the rich smells of earth in a quick
hastened fecundity, an overripeness: sugar and
fruit, resin and dusk and warmth, like the sigh of
a dark and passionate woman no longer young"
(p. 43). Cf. <u>WP</u>: "a wall of soft muted brick above

which the crest of a cabbage palm exploded raggedly
and from beyond which came a heavy smell of sugar
and bananas and hemp from the docks, like inert
wisps of fog or even paint" (p. 36).

47.23 "the unseen river": i.e. the Mississippi
River which runs through New Orleans to the Gulf of
Mexico.

47.28 "the Point": Probably the Nine-Mile Point,
located where the Huey P. Long bridge now spans the
Mississippi River.

47.29-48.21 "Gordon paused . . . died away":
Faulkner here refers to the myth of Narcissus, one
to which he attached great importance in his early
fiction. Andre Bleikasten, in <u>The Most Splendid
Failure</u> (Bloomington/London: Indiana University
Press, 1976), has discussed at length the theme of
narcissism in Faulkner's work, although he deals
only superficially with <u>Mosquitoes</u>. One should
also see Noel Polk's introduction to <u>The
Marionettes</u>, which points out Faulkner's use of the
Narcissus myth in that early play. According to
myth, Narcissus, a most handsome boy, spurned the
affections of the nymph Echo, who then wasted away
to a voice alone. Seeing his reflection in a pool,
Narcissus became so entranced with his own beauty
that he stayed by the spring until he died of
longing, or, in some versions, fell into the water
and drowned. In Ovid's retelling of the story,
Narcissus's reflection is "like a statue carved
from Parian marble. . . . O fondly foolish boy,
why vainly seek to clasp a fleeing image? What you
seek is nowhere; but turn yourself away, and the
object of your love will be no more. That which
you behold is but the shadow of a reflected form
and has no substance of its own" (<u>Metamorphoses</u>, I,
155). Cf. Pan "Stays and broods upon the scene/
Beside a hushed pool where lean/His own face . . ."
(<u>MF</u>, p. 16). Cf. also <u>The Marionettes</u>, in which
Marietta constantly stares into the pool and
Pierrot into the mirror; <u>Mayday</u>, which begins and
ends with Sir Galwyn of Arthgyl seeing his and
other faces in a stream (pp. 39-40); Quentin
Compson in <u>TS&TF</u>, who ponders his own suicide while
staring at his shadow in the water (pp. 110-11);
Horace Benbow, who sees his and Popeye's reflection

in the water at the beginning of <u>Sanctuary</u> (p.1).
Cf. d'Albert in <u>Mademoiselle De Maupin</u>: "Perhaps,
too, finding nothing in the world worthy of my
love, I shall end by adoring myself, like the late
Narcissus of egotistical memory. To secure myself
against so great misfortune, I look into all the
mirrors and all the brooks that I come across. In
truth, with my reveries and aberrations, I am
tremendously afraid of falling into the monstrous
or unnatural. It is a serious matter, and I must
take care" (p. 38). Cf. <u>Portrait of the Artist</u>:
After writing his first poem, the young Stephen
Dedalus "went into his mother's bedroom and gazed
at his face for a long time in the mirror of her
dressing table" (p. 78). Cf. Faulkner's letter (10
September 1925) from Paris to his aunt, Mrs. Murry
Faulkner: "I have just finished the most beautiful
short story in the world. So beautiful that when I
finished it I went to look at myself in a mirror.
And I thought, Did that ugly ratty-looking face,
that mixture of childishness and unreliability and
sublime vanity, imagine that? But I did. And the
hand doesn't hold blood to improve on it" (<u>Letters</u>,
p. 20). (See Note 26.4-6.)

47.31-48.4 "stars in my hair . . . autogethsemane":
A reference to Christ, specifically the garden
outside Jerusalem where Jesus awaited his arrest
and crucifixion. Gordon sees himself, the artist,
as a Christ or savior, agonizing and sacrificing
himself in the act of creation. However, Gordon's
similarities with Quentin Compson are also quite
striking: Quentin is, like Gordon, caught up in
egotistical musings and is haunted by the realities
of nature, especially sexual nature: "Delicate
equilibrium of periodical filth between two moons
balanced. Moons he said full and yellow as harvest
moons her hips thighs. . . . With all that inside
of them shapes an outward suavity waiting for a
touch to. Liquid putrefaction like drowned things
floating like pale rubber flabbily filled getting
the odour of honey-suckle all mixed up" (<u>TS&TF</u>,
p. 159).

48.8-9 "israfel . . . relation": In Arabic
folklore, Israfel is the "burning one," the angel
of resurrection and song who will blow his trumpet
on Judgment Day. According to legend, he, too,

will be destroyed in the conflagration following
his third blast, but will be revived by Allah.
Still, he grieves for those who will be damned
(Shorter Encyclopedia of Islam, ed. H. A. R. Gibb
and J. H. Kramers [Leiden: E. J. Brill, 1953], p.
184). Faulkner may also have had in mind Edgar
Allan Poe's poem "Israfel," in which the angel is
seen primarily as the angel of song, removed from
the realities and constraints of the earth:

        The ecstasies above
        With thy burning measures suit;
    Thy grief, thy joy, thy hate, thy love,
        With the fervor of thy lute:
        Well may the stars be mute!

(The Works of Edgar Allan Poe, collected and edited
by Edmund Clarence Stedman and George Edward
Woodberry [New York: Charles Scribner's Sons,
1914], X, 31.) Hervey Allen's biography of Poe,
entitled Israfel: The Life and Times of Edgar
Allan Poe, 2 vols. (New York: George H. Doran
Company, 1926) presented a heavily romantic picture
of Poe the artist which may be compared with
Faulkner's portrayal of Gordon. Cf.:

        One can imagine him [Poe], after taps, waiting
    for his roommates to drift off into the dreamless
    sleep which was so often denied him by their
    mutterings, and by the beating at the bars of the
    restless wings of his own spirit. . . . How could
    they know, these heavy sleepers, these solemn
    memorizers of the banalities of textbooks--that in
    their midst, brooding over them in the long hours
    of the night, sat a spirit whose song was sweeter
    and clearer than that of the archangels of God!
    . . . Out of this gigantic and almost insane pride
    of heart welled up the lines of the poem . . . [I,
    287-88].

In the typescript, Faulkner consistently refers to
Araphael, a minor angel of the Seventh Heaven
mentioned in the apocryphal book of Enoch (3:18)
rather than to Israfel.

48.10 "small white belly": Cf. Poem XI in GB:

        And a small white belly yielded up

That they might try to make
Of youth and dark and spring a cup
That cannot fail nor slake [p. 31].

48.12 "bitter and new as a sunburned flame":   Cf.
The Marionettes:

Then we will be one in the silence,
    Love!
The pool and the flame,
'Till I am dead or you become a flame [p. 18].

Cf. Poem IV in GB: "o bitter and new as fire"
(p. 21). Butterworth identifies this poem under
the ts. title "Guidebook" and gives the date of
composition as "Paris/27 Aug 1925" (see "Census of
. . . William Faulkner's Poetry," 340). Brooks
discusses the poem as part of the sonnet sequence
To Helen: A Courtship (see WF: TYB, p. 55). A
possible source for this image is Walter Pater's
famous dictum concerning the love of art: "To burn
always with this hard, gemlike flame, to maintain
this ecstasy, is success in life" (The Renaissance,
p. 236). (See Note 249.25.)

48.13-14 "two little silken snails . . . horned
pinkly": Cf. Poem IV of GB:

let lean march teasing the breasts of spring
horned like reluctant snails within
pink intervals [p. 20].

48.14-15 "wax your wings . . . odorless moisture
of her thigh": Israfel had four wings (see Note
48.8-9). In her article "Faulkner's Women," Ilse
Dusoir Lind discusses this passage in terms of
Faulkner's description of "the biological facts of
female life": "In Mosquitoes, which both announces
and launches his program of naturalistic physical
representation, he describes Gordon at one point as
engaging in an erotic fantasy involving Pat Robyn
in which the sculptor imagines himself an Israfel
whose wings are `waxed by the thin odorless
moisture of her thighs,' a biologically precise
reference to the functioning of the glands of
Bartholen" (in The Maker and the Myth: Faulkner
and Yoknapatawpha 1977, ed. Evans Harrington and
Ann J. Abadie [Jackson: University Press of

Mississippi, 1978], p. 94). Lind suggests that
Faulkner's information came from Dr. Louis Berman's
book <u>The</u> <u>Glands</u> <u>Regulating</u> <u>Personality</u> (New York:
Macmillan, 1921), owned by Phil Stone. Cf. Poem
XLIII of <u>GB</u>:

    between two brief balloons
    of skirts I saw grave chalices of knees
    and momently the cloyed and cloudy bees
    where hive her honeyed thighs those little moons
                                              [p. 66].

Faulkner dates this poem "off Minorca/1 Aug 1925"
("Census of . . . William Faulkner's Poetry,"
342). Cf. <u>Elmer</u>: "Virginity has no odor at all"
(p. 77).

48.15-16 "strangle your heart with hair": Cf.
Poe's "Israfel":

    In Heaven a spirit doth dwell
    Whose heart-strings are a lute;
    None sing so wildly well
    As the angel Israfel
            [<u>Works</u> <u>of</u> <u>Edgar</u> <u>Allan</u> <u>Poe</u>, X, 30].

Cf. Robert Browning, "Porphyria's Lover" (1836):

That moment she was mine, mine, fair,
    Perfectly pure and good: I found
A thing to do, and all her hair
    In one long yellow string I wound
    Three times her little throat around,
And strangled her.

(See Note 48.8-9.)

48.17-21 "He flung back his head . . . died
away": The myth of Narcissus and Echo. (See Note
47.29- 48.21.)

48.21-30 "He went on treading the dark resin-
scented wharf . . . dark leaf": Faulkner is
probably describing the Toulouse Street Wharf on
the Mississippi River which is within walking
distance of Jackson Square. According to the <u>New</u>
<u>Orleans</u> <u>City</u> <u>Guide</u>, freight sheds on this wharf
were torn down in 1930, allowing one to see Jackson

Square from the dock. At the foot of Esplanade
Avenue were located the freight yards of the
Southern Pacific Railroad, cars of which were
carried across the river by the Third District
Ferry to Algiers, from which the trains would
continue their westward run. The <u>Guide</u> notes that
chief imports at these docks were coffee and
bananas (see pp. 272, 273).

48.31-32 "There was a moon . . . old coin": Cf.
"the moon is a flat Roman coin suspended upon her
breast" (<u>Marionettes</u>, p. 5). Cf. "the pale broken
coin of the moon" (<u>SP</u>, p. 291).

49.1 "tall pickets": i.e., the fence surrounding
Jackson Square.

49.5 "like coral in a tideless sea": Cf.

  We have lingered in the chambers of the sea
  By sea-girls wreathed with seaweed red and brown
  Till human voices wake us and we drown

(Eliot, "Prufrock," <u>Poems</u>, p. 11). Cf. "rigid as
coral in a mellow tideless sea" (<u>SP</u>, p. 290).

49.20-26 "I don't mind the heat . . . he's good as
any of 'em": Cf. Sherwood Anderson, <u>Tar</u>: "Old
horses like Passenger Boy are like some old men Tar
knew long afterwards, when he was a man. You've
got to warm the old ones up a lot--prod 'em--but
when they get going the right kind--boy, look out.
What you've got to do is heat them up" (p. 177).
Cf. Anderson's letter to his brother Karl: "It is
hot, but like an old horse I feel better, in the
heat" (<u>Letters</u> <u>of</u> <u>Sherwood</u> <u>Anderson</u>, ed. Howard
Mumford Jones with Walter B. Rideout [Boston:
Little, Brown & Company, 1953], p. 128; noted by
Blotner, I, 76 [Notes]).

50.15-16 "But he won't last very long . . . than
you did": See Note 43.3-20.

50.17-20 "But he ought to keep a line on her . . .
swap it for something, you know": The image here
is quite close to the "dream" Faulkner described
Anderson's having told him, in which Anderson "was
riding around the country on a horse--had ridden

for days. At last I met a man, and I swapped him
the horse for a night's sleep. . . . But the
fellow never showed up--left me standing there all
night, holding the horse." (See "Sherwood
Anderson" which first appeared in the Dallas
<u>Morning</u> <u>News</u> [26 April 1925]; rptd. in <u>NOS</u>, pp.
132-39. A longer, slightly different version of
this dream appears in "A Note on Sherwood
Anderson," found in <u>Essays</u>, <u>Speeches</u> & <u>Public</u>
<u>Letters</u>, ed. James B. Meriwether [New York: Random
House, 1966], pp. 3-10.)

51.23-28 "But then, you are not an artist . . .
wood or stone": This judgment on Fairchild, and
through him on Anderson, although voiced by Julius
Kauffman, would seem to be more Faulkner's than
Julius Friend's. In his remarks on Anderson in the
<u>Morning</u> <u>News</u> (see Note 50.17-20), Faulkner wrote
that "Mr. Anderson is interested in his reactions
to other people, and very little in himself. That
is, he has not enough active ego to write
successfully of himself" (<u>NOS</u>, p. 138). Julius
Friend, on the other hand, wrote very highly of
Anderson's talents: "Sherwood Anderson is the
healthiest writer I know. He is too robust for
that delicate sensualist, the esthete. He is,
indeed, the touchstone of sanity." (See Friend's
review of <u>A</u> <u>Story</u> <u>Teller's</u> <u>Story</u> in <u>The</u> <u>Double</u>
<u>Dealer</u>, VII [October 1924], 72; also see Friend's
later article "The Philosophy of Sherwood
Anderson," <u>Story</u>, 19 [September-October 1941],
37-41. See also Brooks' comments on the subject in
<u>WF</u>: <u>TYB</u>, pp. 379-80.) (See Notes 33.27; 241.26-
28.)

52.1 "esthetic foster sisters of both sexes":
Cf. "All over the room elderly women were dancing
with young men of both sexes" (<u>The</u> <u>Green</u> <u>Hat</u>, p.
162). (See Note 209.20-21.)

52.7 "Corn belt . . . Indiana talking": Anderson
was born in Clyde, Ohio, as Faulkner knew. (See
"Sherwood Anderson," <u>NOS</u>, pp. 132-33, in which in
an extended metaphor Faulkner compares Anderson to
"a lusty corn field.")

52.8 "booster complex": To "boost" means to
advance, often through exaggerated praise. In the

1920's, Booster Clubs which extolled the virtues of
the United States were not uncommon. George
Babbitt, for example, is a member of such a club
(_Babbitt_, p. 4). "Complex" is a term established
by C. G. Jung in 1907 which became synonymous with
the idea of a mental obsession.

52.10 "Oh, well, we Nordics are at a
disadvantage": Cf. "Al Jackson": "But Al is the
one I wish to meet. He is considered by every one
who knows him to be the finest time of American
manhood, a pure Nordic" (_Uncollected_ _Stories_, p.
477). (See Notes 181.19; 328.6-7.)

52.12-15 "We've got to fix our idea on a
terrestrial place . . . old home town, you know":
Cf. Sherwood Anderson, _A_ _Story_ _Teller's_ _Story_:

     As for the men of Jewish blood, so many of
whom I found quick and eager to meet me half way,
my heart went out to them in gratitude. They were
wanting love and understanding, had in their
natures many impulses that were destructive. Was
there a sense of being outlaws? They did not want
their own secret sense of separateness from the
life about them commented upon but it existed.
They themselves kept it alive and I thought they
were not unwise in doing so. I watched them
eagerly. Did they have, in their very race
feeling, the bit of ground under their feet it was
so hard for an Ohio man to get in Cleveland,
Cincinnati or Chicago or New York? . . . One had
always to remember that we Americans were in the
process of trying to make a race. The Jews had
been a part of the life of almost every race that
had come to us and were for perhaps that very
reason in a better position than the rest of us to
help make our own race [pp. 395-96, 397].

Cf. "Wealthy Jew": "No soil is foreign to my
people, for have we not conquered all lands with
the story of your Nativity?" (_NOS_, p. 38).

52.21-24 "Now, you lay off our New Orleans . . .
charming futility about it": Anderson had warm
feelings toward New Orleans, which he expressed in
"New Orleans, The Double Dealer and the Modern
Movement in America" (_The_ _Double_ _Dealer_, III [March

1922], 119-26). In New Orleans Anderson found
"culture," which he defined as "the enjoyment of
life, leisure and a sense of leisure. It means
time for a play of the imagination over the facts
of life, it means time and vitality to be serious
about really serious things and a background of joy
in life in which to refresh the tired spirits"
(p. 126).

52.25-26 "croquet": Croquet was often played in
Oxford, Mississippi, while Faulkner was growing
up. According to Calvin Brown, "In my childhood
lots of people in Oxford played croquet on their
lawns, and it was a notorious source of quarrels
and fights among children." While in Paris in 1925
Faulkner wrote his mother that "the old men who at
home would sit in the court-house yard and sleep,
play croquet. Always a big gallery at the croquet
games, which run all day" (<u>Letters</u>, p. 14). He
later admitted, "I have got to be a croquet fiend:
I waste half the day watching youths and taxi
drivers and senators play croquet in the
Luxembourg" (p. 21).

52.30 "go-getter": An active, enterprising
person. The term dates from the 1920's.

53.3-4 "Two ferry boats . . . barren cycle of
courtship": A probable reference to the Third
District Ferries which ran from the docks at the
foot of Esplanade Avenue to Algiers on the west
bank of the Mississippi. (See Faulkner's "Sunset"
[<u>NOS</u>, pp. 147-57] for a use of this setting.) Cf.
"Frankie and Johnny": "When I seen you coming down
the street back yonder it was like them two ferry
boats hadn't seen each other until then, and they
would stop when they met instead of crossing each
other, and they would turn and go off side by side
together where they wasn't nobody except them"
(<u>NOS</u>, p. 40).

54.3 "The <u>Nausikka</u>": There are two probable
sources for the yacht's name. In the <u>Odyssey</u>,
Odysseus is shipwrecked by Poseidon and his men are
drowned, but he is saved through divine
intervention and, exhausted, reaches land. There
he is found by Nausikka, daughter of Alkinoos, King
of the Phaiakes, when she comes to wash her clothes

at the shore. Odysseus is received by the King,
given gifts, allowed to tell his tale, and finally
presented with a magic ship, which is later turned
into stone by the still angry Poseidon. A second
source surely known to Faulkner was the "Nausicaa"
episode in James Joyce's <u>Ulysses</u>. This section had
appeared in <u>The Little Review</u> in April, May and
June of 1920, and it is likely that Faulkner had
read the book by 1926. (See Robert M. Slabey,
"Faulkner's <u>Mosquitoes</u> and Joyce's <u>Ulysses</u>," <u>Revue
des Langues Vivantes</u>, 28 [1962], 435-37, for a
fuller discussion of Faulkner's apparent borrowings
from <u>Ulysses</u>.) The actual voyage described in
<u>Mosquitoes</u> appears to be loosely based on an outing
on Lake Pontchartrain undertaken by Faulkner,
Sherwood and Elizabeth Prall Anderson, Sam Gilmore,
Lillian Marcus, Virginia Parker Nagle, Colonel
Charles Glenn Collins, and others, on board the
<u>Josephine</u> (see Blotner, I, 417-18). Slightly
different versions of this trip have been described
by Elizabeth Anderson in <u>Miss Elizabeth</u> (pp.117-21)
and William Spratling in <u>File on Spratling</u>
([Boston: Little, Brown & Company, 1967], p. 29).
(See Note 169.1-2.)

54.3 "the basin": The New Basin Canal.

54.5 "yacht club flag": The Southern Yacht Club,
the second oldest in the United States, is located
in the West End of New Orleans, on Lake Pontchartrain. The Club was housed in a two-story building
on the left bank of the New Basin Canal (<u>New
Orleans City Guide</u>, pp. 283-84).

54.10 "inferior macadam road": A road made by
compressing layers of broken stone into a solid
mass, originated by John Loudon McAdam (1756-1836),
for whom the process was named. Macadam roads were
largely obsolete by 1926.

54.12 "less-than-one-percent": i.e., beverages
containing less that one per cent alcohol. Calvin
Brown points out that Faulkner probably meant less
than <u>one-half</u> per cent, which was "the limit (by
volume) of alcohol content of legal beverages fixed
by the Volstead Act." (See <u>A Glossary of
Faulkner's South</u> [New Haven and London: Yale
University Press, 1976], p. 118.)

54.25-29 "Mark Frost . . . incompletely
performed": Samuel Louis Gilmore, Jr. (see Note
34.18-19), the probable model for Mark Frost,
produced one book of poetry, privately printed,
<u>Vine</u> <u>Leaves</u> <u>and</u> <u>Flowers</u> <u>of</u> <u>Evil</u>. The first half
consisted of his poems and the second half was a
translation of Baudelaire. As a contributor to <u>The</u>
<u>Double</u> <u>Dealer</u>, he published a number of poems which
have been described as "always clever, always
mocking, uniformly brittle" (Frances Jean Bowen,
"The New Orleans <u>Double</u> <u>Dealer</u>: 1921-May 1926, A
Critical History," Dissertation, Vanderbilt
University, 1954, p. 235). Gilmore's poems are
also consistently short, as suggested by Faulkner's
description. Cf. "Artist at Home": "[Poetry] has
to be fed to me by hand. . . . In words of one
syllable. . . . I'm glad his racket is poetry,
something you can perpetrate in two lines"
(<u>Collected</u> <u>Stories</u>, p. 634).

54.29-55.2 "He wore ironed serge . . . as was his
way": Gilmore had a reputation for borrowing
cigarettes and stretching out on any level
surface. In fact, a fresco of him reclined hung
over the fireplace in the <u>Double</u> <u>Dealer</u> office.
(See Blotner, I, 417. See also Spratling's drawing
of Gilmore in <u>SA&OFC</u>.) Cf. Gilmore's poem "Deity"
(in <u>Poetry</u>: <u>A</u> <u>Magazine</u> <u>of</u> <u>Verse</u>, II [June 1918],
132-33):

        In incense before gods He rises
        In the blue smoke of cigarettes He curls,
        He dwells in the eyelids of the Buddha;
        He is in the lotus.

55.10-11 "a soft blonde girl in a slightly soiled
green dress": Cf. <u>Elmer</u>, whose first sexual
experience is with a woman remembered as "a full
red mouth never quite completely closed, a young
body seemingly on the point of bursting out of its
soiled expensive dress in soft rich curves" (p.
38). The identification of soiled clothes and
female sexuality is most clearly made in <u>TS&TF</u>,
with its central image of Caddy's soiled
underwear. However, also see the little Italian
girl Quentin meets on the last day of his life: "a
little dirty child with eyes like a toy bear's and
two patent-leather pig-tails" (p. 155). (See Notes

87.13-14; 294.11- 12.)

55.21-22 "ˇPete' . . . slanted stiff straw hat":
Carvel Collins has suggested that Pete was modeled
on a local New Orleans bootlegger named Slim (NOS,
pp. 23-24). Faulkner had earlier used a similar
character in several of his New Orleans sketches:
cf. "Home," in which one of the gangsters is named
Pete (NOS, p. 74); "Country Mice," in which the
unnamed bootlegger resembles Pete at the end of
Mosquitoes. Cf. especially "ˇOnce Aboard the
Lugger--'" (Contempo, I [February 1, 1932], 1, 4;
reprinted as "Once Aboard the Lugger (I)" along
with "Once Aboard the Lugger (II)" [previously
unpub- lished] in Uncollected Stories, pp. 352-
67): "Pete was about nineteen, in a silk shirt of
gold and lavender stripes, and a stiff straw hat,
and all day long he squatted in the bows, holding
his hat and saying Jesus Christ to himself"
(Uncollected Stories, p. 352). In some ways, Pete
anticipates Faulkner's most famous gangster Popeye
in Sanctuary. Like Pete, Popeye is always smoking,
wears a "slanted straw hat" (p. 2), and expresses
his exasperation through his oath "Jesus Christ."

56.14 "Genevieve Steinbauer": Cf. "Don Giovanni,"
in which Herbie attempts to seduce an Miss
Steinbauer (Uncollected Stories, p. 486). Jenny's
name is quite similar to that of Gertrude
Stegbauer, who worked as a stenographer for
Faulkner's friend Phil Stone in his Charleston,
Mississippi, law office. "Bill fancied he was in
love with her," Phil Stone remembered (Susan Snell,
Phil Stone of Yoknapatawpha [Ann Arbor: University
Microfilms, 1978], pp. 308-09). "Jenny" might
possibly have been suggested by Dante Gabriel
Rossetti's poem "Jenny," which deals with a
prostitute (see Note 127.5-6). There are also at
least surface similarities between Jenny and
Lorelei Lee (whom Faulkner called "that elegant
moron of a cornflower" [Letters, p. 32]) in Anita
Loos' Gentlemen Prefer Blondes (New York: Boni &
Liveright, 1925), a book Faulkner read and enjoyed
before writing Mosquitoes. This type of lush
femininity repre- sented by Jenny anticipates
Faulkner's paragon of female allurement, Eula
Varner, who appeared in Father Abraham begun
immediately after Mosquitoes (see Blotner, I,

526-31; also see James B. Meriwether's Introduction
to <u>Father</u> <u>Abraham</u> [original limited edition
published by Red Ozier Press, 1983; subsequently
published New York: Random House, 1983].)

56.27 "I ain't a sailor": Cf. Pete in "Once
Aboard the Lugger (I)," who is constantly seasick
and argues with the Captain. Pete is murdered by
rival bootleggers in "Once Aboard the Lugger (II)."

57.32-33 "Shake it up, Josh": A nautical
colloquialism meaning "to hurry." However, the
term (and other variations on it) also mean "to
masturbate," a definition worth noting given the
sexual tension that exists between Pat and Josh.

58.24 "Jenny's bovine white placidity": Cf. Eula
Varner in <u>The</u> <u>Hamlet</u>, pp. 107-15.

58.28-29 "turn out to be so wet": i.e., dull,
stupid.

59.4 "Holmes": D. H. Holmes Company, Ltd.,
located at 1819 Canal Street, one of the oldest
department stores in New Orleans, having been
established in 1842.

59.8 "He's her heavy, I gather": A steady or
important date; in sexual terms, a passionate
relationship. The word may also refer to a
hoodlum. In Pete's case, all meanings apply.

59.17 "She's a complete washout": A failure or
disappointment; socially inept.

59.19 "Gabriel's pants": I have found no specific
source for this oath. "Gabriel" was sometimes used
as slang for a trumpet player, in reference to the
biblical angel Gabriel. Since his Arabic
counterpart is Israfel (see Note 48.8-9), who is
associated with Gordon, there may be some intended
connection, but it is more likely an example of
current slang or Pat's own coinage.

60.7 "Mrs. Wiseman": Apparently modeled on Julius
Weis Friend's sister Lillian Friend Marcus, who
acted as business manager of <u>The</u> <u>Double</u> <u>Dealer</u>
during its last years. She was known for her

caustic wit, but was not a poet as is Eva Wiseman
(see Blotner, I, 518-19). Martin Kreiswirth draws
a parallel between her and Mary Thirplow, a
novelist in Huxley's <u>Those</u> <u>Barren</u> <u>Leaves</u> (see
<u>Making</u> <u>of</u> <u>a</u> <u>Novelist</u>, p. 83).

60.8 "Miss Jameson": Dorothy Jameson appears to
have been created by Faulkner for the novel.
Although he recounts her background in detail, no
real-life counterpart has been identified.

60.23 "birds": A slang term for any person
considered somewhat odd.

61.29 "Major Ayers": Faulkner apparently modeled
Major Ayers on Colonel Charles Glenn Collins, a
Scot who had, according to Carvel Collins,
adventured in India, spent time in the New Orleans
jail, and been mixed up in several shady dealings
(see <u>NOS</u>, pp. 22- 23). Max Putzel less
convincingly suggests that Charles J. Finger, "an
adventurous English business- man who gave up
railroading to become a writer" was also a model
for the Major. Finger was editor of <u>Reedy's</u> <u>Mirror</u>
and later of his own magazine <u>All's</u> <u>Well</u> (see
<u>Genius</u> <u>of</u> <u>Place</u>, p. 17, n. 3). However, Faulkner
had also observed "swell-looking Lords and dukes"
during his visit to England in 1925 (see <u>Letters</u>,
pp. 26-27), and had included some English
characters in his <u>Elmer</u> material before giving it
up (see Thomas L. McHaney, "The <u>Elmer</u> Papers,"
<u>Mississippi</u> <u>Quarterly</u>, 26 [Summer 1973], 281-311.)
Faulkner was also probably influenced by the
English characters of Aldous Huxley in his creation
of Major Ayers. Cf. Freddie Ayers in "Yo Ho and
Two Bottles of Rum" (<u>NOS</u>, pp. 209-23): ". . . Mr.
Ayers was the soul of joviality and wit as he sat
in the saloon clasping his tumbler, sucking his
straight short pipe, so palpably and blatantly
British with mackerel eye and his moth-eaten
Guardsman's moustache" (p. 214). (See Note
282.13-23.)

61.32-33 "No teeth, no tiffin": In England,
"tiffin" refers to a light meal; i.e. "tea."
Without his teeth, Major Ayers would not be able to
eat.

62.25 "Blackbeard": Popular name given to Edward
Teach (?-1718), a British pirate who terrorized the
Carolina and Virginia coasts between 1716 and 1718
in his ship the <u>Queen Anne's Revenge</u>. He was
killed in a battle with the HMS <u>Pearl</u> on 21
November 1718, and his head was taken to Virginia
on a stake. However, Pat is alluding, at least in
part, to Gordon's beard (although it is red) and to
his threatening disposition. (See Note 25.17.)

63.24-65.11 "Fairchild, watching him . . . `all
Americans are constipated,' Fairchild suggested":
This discussion of constipation is similar to Sir
Ferdinando Lapith's "spiritual" preoccupation with
privies and sanitation in Huxley's <u>Crome Yellow</u>
(p. 102). See also the description of Mark Frost's
poetry on p. 54 of <u>Mosquitoes</u>.

64.9 "tweaky": To tweak is to pull with a
twisting motion, a meaning inappropriate as Major
Ayers uses it. In slang usage, "twee" may mean
"small" or "dainty," which may be what the Major
means. However, this usage dates from the 1930's
(see Eric Partridge, <u>A Dictionary of Slang and
Unconventional English</u>, 7th ed. [New York: The
Macmillan Company, 1970], p. 1485).

65.3-4 "I have a better idea . . . golden rule on
the other": The Golden Rule is "Do Unto Others As
You Would Have Them Do Unto You." This is perhaps
an oblique reference to Louis Gilmore's (and Mark
Frost's) homosexuality, which was recognized by his
New Orleans companions. (See Note 334.9-19.)

66.12-15 "A hundred odd years ago . . . lick hell
out of him": The Battle of New Orleans took place
on 8 January 1815. The British forces, under the
command of Major General Sir Edward Pakenham,
numbered some 7500 men, most of whom were
veterans. General Andrew Jackson (1767-1845) led a
motley force composed of a few regular troops,
Jackson's own Tennessee and Kentucky veterans, and
a group of volunteer militia: in all this force
numbered 3100 men. There were also 2000 untrained
and poorly equipped militia held in reserve. The
Battle was fought in the Chalmette Swamps. (See
<u>The Encyclopedia of Military History</u>, ed. R. Ernest
Dupuy and Trevor N. Dupuy; rev. ed. [New York:

Harper & Row, 1970], p. 802.)

66.22 "Al Jackson": A fictitious character,
invented by Faulkner and Anderson, who acted as the
central figure in a number of "tall tales" the two
writers swapped during this period in New Orleans.
H. Edward Richardson, in "Faulkner, Anderson, and
Their Tall Tale" (American Literature, 34 [May
1962], 287-91), argued that these tales were
largely Anderson's invention, but Walter B. Rideout
and James B. Meriwether, in "On the Collaboration
of Faulkner and Anderson" (American Literature, 35
[March 1963], 85-87), showed that Faulkner owed
little to Anderson in these tales and that the
example given in Mosquitoes (see pp. 277-81) was
Faulkner's, not Anderson's, work. For an example
of an Anderson tale, see Letters of Sherwood
Anderson, pp. 162-64; for another example of
Faulkner's work in this genre, see "Al Jackson"
(Uncollected Stories, pp. 474-79). See also
Faulkner's own comments on this collaboration in "A
Note on Sherwood Anderson," (ES&PL, pp. 3-10).

66.32 "Old Hickory that licked you folks in
1812": "Old Hickory" was the popular name given to
Andrew Jackson, one which he used extensively in
his campaign for the U. S. Presidency. As
previously noted, the battle occurred in 1815, not
1812 (see Note 66.12-15).

67.2-3 "congress boots": High boots with elastic
sides.

67.10 "round china-blue eyes": Cf. Mary
Bracegirdle in Crome Yellow: "She had large blue
china eyes, whose expression was one of ingenuous
and often puzzled earnestness" (p. 26).

67.20-23 "Well, the old general bought a place in
Florida . . . herd of horses": The tall tale
element is at work here. Andrew Jackson's home in
Tennessee was known as the "Hermitage." Although
he did much trading in land, there is no record of
a "stock farm" in Florida. In 1814, Jackson had
led his Tennessee forces against the Creek Indians
at Horseshoe Bend in Florida, a victory which
resulted in his being named commander in defense of
New Orleans. (See Note 66.12-15.)

68.1 "hotels at Palm Beach": Located in
southeasten Florida on the Atlantic Coast, Palm
Beach is famed as a luxurious winter resort. In
the 1920's, especially, it was a favorite vacation
spot for the wealthy and famous.

68.18-21 "We're a simple people . . . national
temperament, Major": Cf. Harold E. Stearns'
preface to <u>Civilization</u> <u>in</u> <u>the</u> <u>United</u> <u>States</u>: "For
American civilization is still in the embryonic
stage, with rich and with disastrous possibilities
for growth. But the first step in growing up is
self-conscious and deliberately critical
examination of ourselves, without sentimentality
and without fear" (p. vii). Cf. a section of
Anderson's <u>A</u> <u>Story</u> <u>Teller's</u> <u>Story</u>, not included in
the 1924 edition but the sentiments of which he
might easily have expressed to Faulkner: "I had
read Mr. Van Wyck Brooks on <u>America's</u> <u>Coming</u> <u>of</u> <u>Age</u>
and had been deeply stirred by what he had to say.
. . . He had been writing about such men as myself
(it is to be kept in mind that I think of myself--
no matter what anyone else may think--as a
thorough-going American) and had proved pretty
conclusively that we were immature--children in
fact." (See <u>A</u> <u>Story</u> <u>Teller's</u> <u>Story</u>: <u>A</u> <u>Critical</u>
<u>Text</u>, ed. Ray Lewis White [Cleveland: The Press of
Case Western University, 1968], p. 279.) Cf.
Faulkner's early statements concerning Americans in
"American Drama: Inhibitions" (<u>EP&P</u>, pp. 93-97).

68.25-26 "It's the custom that makes the man, you
know": Cf. "Custom is all" (James Branch Cabell,
<u>Jurgen</u>: <u>A</u> <u>Comedy</u> <u>of</u> <u>Justice</u> [New York: Grosset &
Dunlap, 1919], p. 198).

69.2 "Eton": A public school for boys in England.

71.19 "rutting": The sex act in an animalistic
sense.

71.24-25 "Gordon . . . tall and shabby and
arrogant": Cf. Dodge Pleydon in <u>Linda</u> <u>Condon</u>, who
is large and carelessly dressed: "His features,
Linda saw, were rugged and pronounced; he was very
strong" (p. 113). (See Note 82.5-10.)

72.26 "Squire Western's hollo": A character in

Henry Fielding's <u>Tom Jones</u> (1749), Western is
portrayed as a foxhunting squire of violent temper
and rough good humor. He is the father of Sophia
Western, with whom Tom falls in love. In a 1931
interview with Marshall J. Smith, Faulkner said, "I
haven't written a real novel yet. . . . I'm too
young in experience. It hasn't crystallized enough
for me to build a book upon one of the few funda-
mental truths which mankind has learned. Perhaps
in five years I can put it over. Perhaps write a
<u>Tom Jones</u> or a <u>Clarissa Harlowe</u>" (<u>Lion</u>, p. 11).

72.31-32 "Freedom . . . is in wartime": Cf. John
Dos Passos, <u>Three Soldiers</u> (1921): "It's great to
be a soldier. . . . Ye kin do anything ye goddam
please" ([New York: The Modern Library, 1932],
p. 37). Cf. <u>Elmer</u>: "But Angelo had not been
sickened by war, not by a hell of a lot. He had
been able to do things in wartime which in
peacetime the police, government, all people who
were able to override him through the circumstance
of birth, would have made impossible. Of course
war was bad, but so is traffic . . ." (p. 91). Cf.
Caspey in <u>Flags</u>: "we wuz in de army, whar a man
kin do whut he wants as long as dey'll let him
. . ." (p. 56).

73.2-4 "England full of your beastly expeditionary
forces . . . not so damned many of you": Great
Britain declared war on Germany on 4 August 1914.
Canada sent its first troops--approximately 33,000
--to complete training in England in October,
1914. The first Canadian soldiers landed in France
on 11 February 1915, and by 1916 there were four
divisions of the Canadian Expeditionary Force in
the fighting. America did not enter the war until
6 April 1917, and troops did not begin arriving in
France until 26 June 1917. Many Americans joined
the Canadian forces in order to begin battle before
America had officially declared war. Faulkner
himself joined the RAF in June 1918 and left for
Canada in July of the same year for training.

73.11-16 "Can't have another war right off . . .
overdid it": Cf. Exodus in <u>The Wishing Tree</u>
(written in 1927): "I never seed a soldier yet
that ever won anything in a war. But then,
whitefolks' wars is always run funny. Next time

the whitefolks has a war, I think I ain't goin'.   I
think I'll jes' stay in the army instead" ([New
York: Random House, 1964], p. 48).

73.20 "bunk": i.e., nonsense; an abbreviation of
"bunkum," derived from Buncombe County, N. C.,
noted for its political shenanigans.

74.14 "riding the blinds": In hobo slang, the
"blind" referred to that section of a railroad car
used to pass from one car to another; it was
protected from view and allowed tramps to hide from
conductors. "Beating" or "riding" the "blinds"
thus meant to steal a ride on a train.

76.7-10 "He stood . . . staring at the engine with
rapture:" Cf. ". . . to Adams the dynamo became a
symbol of infinity. As he grew accustomed to the
great gallery of machines, he began to feel the
forty-foot dynamos as a moral force, much as the
early Christians felt the cross" (Henry Adams, "The
Dynamo and the Virgin" in The Education of Henry
Adams [Boston: Massachusetts Historical Society,
1918], p. 380). Cf. Henry Wimbush in Crome Yellow,
who believes in "the perfectibility of machinery"
and wants "to live in a dignified seclusion,
surrounded by the delicate attentions of silent and
graceful machines, and entirely secure from any
human intrusion" (p. 288).

76.10-19 "It was as beautiful as a racehorse . . .
wings of energy and flame. . . .": Faulkner often
used the Pegasus image to indicate moments of
transcendence--artistic, emotional, or otherwise.
Cf. "Carcassonne": "Still galloping, the horse
soars outward; still galloping, it thunders up the
long blue hill of heaven, its tossing mane in
golden swirls like fire" (Collected Stories, p.
899). Cf. Flags: "The beast burst like unfolding
bronze wings . . . as the gate splintered to
matchwood beneath its soaring volcanic thunder" (p.
119).

78.24 "Mandeville ferry": Mandeville, a popular
summer resort on Lake Pontchartrain, could be
reached by a ferry which ran from New Orleans
across the lake. This service was ended in 1936.

80.29-81.4 "Above this one-sided merriment . . .
passive astonishment": Pat's diving ability is
simlilar to that of Ardita Farnam in Fitzgerald's
"The Off-Shore Pirate." In that story, Ardita
makes three dives from a cliff, each dive higher
than the previous one, to prove her courage and her
"enormous faith in myself." As she explains:
". . . courage to me meant ploughing through that
dull gray mist that comes down on life--not only
overriding people and circumstances but overriding
the bleakness of living. A sort of insistence on
the value of life and the worth of transient
things" (_Flappers_ _and_ _Philosophers_, p. 37).

82.5-10 "She clasped his hard wrists . . . hard
high chest": Cf. _Linda_ _Condon_: "She turned, to
thank Dodge Pleydon for all his goodness to her,
when he lifted her--was it toward heaven?--and
kissed her mouth" (p. 126). Cf. Caddy and Dalton
Ames in _TS&TF_: "their shadow one shadow her head
rose it was above his on the sky higher their two
heads" (p. 192). Quentin thinks of Caddy and
Dalton in terms of a centaur and his captive.

82.11-18 "`Swing you again?' . . . a glory he
could not see": Cf. "The Off-Shore Pirate":

     And then dawn slanted dynamically across the
deck and flung the shadows reeling into gray
corners. The dew rose and turned to golden mist,
thin as a dream, enveloping them until they seemed
gossamer relics of the late night, infinitely
transient and already fading. For a moment sea and
sky were breathless, and dawn held a pink hand over
the young mouth of life--then from out of the lake
came the complaint of a rowboat and the swish of
oars.
     Suddenly against the golden furnace low in the
east their two graceful figures melted into one,
and he was kissing her spoiled young mouth.
     "It's a sort of glory," he murmured after a
second.
     She smiled up at him."
     "Happy, are you?"
     Her sigh was a benediction--an ecstatic surety
that she was youth and beauty now as much as she
would ever know. For another instant life was
radiant and time a phantom and their strength

eternal . . ." [<u>Flappers</u> <u>and</u> <u>Philosophers</u>, p. 44].

Cf. <u>Cyrano</u> <u>de</u> <u>Bergerac</u>:

> You know how, after looking at the sun,
> One sees red suns everywhere--so, for hours
> After the flood of sunlight that you are,
> My eyes are blinded by your burning hair
>   [III, p. 169].

82.18-19 "her taut simple body . . . fleeting hips
of a boy": Cf. "Her boy's breast and the plain
flanks of a boy" in "To Helen: Swimming," the
first sonnet in <u>To</u> <u>Helen</u>: <u>A</u> <u>Courtship</u>.

82.18-19 "an ecstasy in golden marble": Cf. the
statue of Pygmallion (see Note 26.24-26). Cf.
<u>Marionettes</u>: "How beautiful she is! She is like
an ivory tower builded by black slaves and
surrounded by flames, she is like a little statue
of ivory and silver for which blood has been spilt"
(p. 41).

82.28-83.9 "while the last of day . . . without
ceiling or floor": Cf. Joseph Conrad's <u>Heart</u> <u>of</u>
<u>Darkness</u> (1902): "Going up that river was like
travelling back to the earliest beginnings of the
world, when vegetation rioted on the earth and the
big trees were kings. An empty stream, a great
silence, an impenetrable forest. The air was warm,
thick, heavy, sluggish" (<u>The</u> <u>Works</u> <u>of</u> <u>Joseph</u> <u>Conrad</u>
[London: William Heinemann, 1921], V, 112). (See
Notes 83.17; 121.16-23; 135.5-6; 164.5-6; 169.19-
30; and 262.21-22 for further references to this
work which Faulkner greatly admired.)

83.11 "morose hatted duenna": A chaperon; usually
refers to an elderly woman who oversees a younger,
although here it describes Pete.

83.17 "Mr. Talliaferro's dry interminable voice":
Cf. Eliot's "The Hollow Men" (1925):

> Our dried voices, when
> We whisper together
> Are quiet and meaningless
> As wind in dry grass [<u>Poems</u>, p. 95].

The reference is an appropriate one here because of
the poem's connection with <u>Heart of Darkness</u>
through Eliot's epigraphic quote, "Mistah Kurtz--he
dead" (<u>Works of Joseph Conrad</u>, V, 183).

84.14 "dogwatch": The short or half watch on a
ship which runs from 4 to 6 o'clock p.m. or from 6
to 8 o'clock p.m. The term may also apply to any
night shift.

86.28 "fisherd": "Fisherd" is a word apparently
coined by Faulkner. Cf. "Al Jackson": Al's boy
Herman, who works for a time as a "fish grader at
the fish market," dies after reading the complete
works of Sir Walter Scott in twelve and a half
days: "The Benevolent Order of Carp, assisted by
his college fraternity, R.O.E., buried him with
honors; and his funeral is said to have been one of
the largest ever held in the fish-herding circles"
(<u>Uncollected Stories</u>, pp. 478-79).

86.29-32 "Did you see the sunset . . . takes years
and years": Joseph Mallord William Turner
(1755-1851) was the leading English romantic
landscape painter of the 19th Century, famed in
part for his representations of the sea. An
endless experimenter in the effects of light and
color in his paintings, he moved away from physical
representation and anticipated the Impressionists
in his evocation of atmosphere. In the 1920's, in
the wake of the post-Impressionist movement,
Turner's reputation suffered, as is reflected in
this passage, but he is now recognized as one of
the great innovators in painting. Cf. Oscar Wilde:

Nobody of any real culture . . . ever talks
nowadays about the beauty of a sunset. Sunsets are
quite old-fashioned. They belong to the time when
Turner was the last note in art. To admire them is
a distinct sign of provincialism of temperament.
Upon the other hand they go on. Yesterday evening
Mrs. Arundel insisted on my going to the window,
and looking at the glorious sky, as she called it.
. . . And what was it? It was simply a very
second-rate Turner, a Turner of a bad period, with
all the painter's worst faults exaggerated and
over- emphasized ["The Decay of Lying,"
<u>Intentions</u>, vol. V of <u>The Complete Works of Oscar</u>

<u>Wilde</u>, p. 49].

87.13-14 "Jenny . . . a piece of bread in her
hand": Cf. the Italian girl in <u>TS&TF</u>: "The little
girl watched me, holding the bread against her
dirty dress" (p. 158). (See Note 294.11-12.)

87.18 "Esplanade": Esplanade Avenue in New
Orleans, once called the "Promenade Publique"
because of the prominent people who lived on it.
By the 1920's, the avenue had lost many of its
wealthier residents and much of its former allure.

88.18 "European agent": One who sees after the
financial interests of an American company in
Europe.

90.19-23 "He paused again, holding the rod . . .
what he needed": Cf. <u>Elmer</u>, in which Elmer is
fascinated by the phallic tubes of paint (p. 5).
(See Note 46.1-3.)

92.4-5 "bullvoiced Druid priest at a sacrifice":
Druidism was the religion of the Celts of ancient
Gaul and the British Isles. Although little is
actually known of their religious rites, popular
belief has it that the Druids performed magic
rituals and employed human sacrifice. (See for
example Sir James Frazer's discussion of the Druids
in <u>The</u> <u>Golden</u> <u>Bough</u> [London: Macmillan & Co.,
Ltd., 1919], XI, 31-44.)

92.13-16 "a tall shape . . . queer shabby Mr.
Gordon": Cf. young Bayard Sartoris in <u>Flags</u>: "a
lean figure in casual easy clothes unpressed and a
little comfortably shabby, and with his air of
smoldering abrupt violence" (p. 64).

93.8 "victrola record": Victrola was the trade
name of one make of phonograph.

94.3 "I don't dance": The image of the dance is
an important one in <u>Mosquitoes</u>, representing the
idea of participation in life, of a sense of
community. Havelock Ellis had used this image in
his book <u>The</u> <u>Dance</u> <u>of</u> <u>Life</u> (1923). Ellis wrote:

We change, and the world changes, in accordance

with the underlying organisation, and
inconsistency, so conditioned by truth to the
whole, becomes the higher consistency of life . . .
there is not only variety, but also unity. The
diversity of the Many is balanced by the stability
of the One. That is why life must always be a
dance, for that is what a dance is: perpetual
slightly varied movements which are yet always held
true to the shape of the whole [(Boston and New
York: Houghton, Mifflin Company, 1923), pp.
vii-viii].

Faulkner was probably familiar with the book, as
Ellis (along with Freud) was a favorite topic of
discussion in <u>The</u> <u>Double</u> <u>Dealer</u> and is, in fact,
mentioned in <u>Mosquitoes</u> (see Note 251.22). That
Gordon does not dance illustrates his removal from
society. As Ellis put it, "The man who
consistently--as he fondly supposes `logically'--
clings to an unchanging opinion is suspended from a
hook which has ceased to exist" (p. vi). One might
also note Faulkner's similar presentations of
dances in <u>Soldiers'</u> <u>Pay</u> and <u>Sanctuary</u>. (See Note
284.17-26.)

94.6-7 "Run along, Aunt Pat . . . . We're talking
about art": Cf. "In the room the women come and
go/Talking of Michelangelo" ("Prufrock," <u>Poems</u>,
p. 11).

96.7-8 "You are a widow only by courtesy . . .
sixteenth century literature": The use of the word
"widow" to refer to an unmarried mother or
discarded mistress dates to the 16th Century.
However, Lillian Marcus was, in fact, a widow: her
husband Peter Marcus, an artist, had committed
suicide.

96.20-21 "The moon . . . hand on the dark water":
Cf. Oscar Wilde, <u>Salome</u>: "Oh! How strange the
moon looks. You would think it was the hand of a
dead woman who is seeking to cover herself with a
shroud" (p. 46). Cf. <u>The</u> <u>Marble</u> <u>Faun</u>:

    The ringed moon sits eerily
    Like a mad woman in the sky,
    Dropping flat hands to caress
    The far world's shaggy flanks and breast

[p. 33].

Cf. Pierrot to the Moon in <u>Marionettes</u>: "plunge
your fingers in her hair/Spin and weave moon
madness there" (p. 27). (See Note 99.33-100.5.)

99.20-21 "lee shore": The shore off a ship's
leeward side (the side opposite the windward),
toward which the ship would be blown in a storm.

99.33-100.5 "But the moon . . . ancient geographical woodcut": Cf. <u>Salome</u>: "The moon has a
strange look tonight. . . . She is like a mad
woman who is seeking everywhere for lovers. She is
naked too. She is quite naked. The clouds are
seeking to clothe her nakedness, but she will not
let them. . . . She reels through the clouds like
a drunken woman" (p. 64).

101.5 "waves . . . endless battalions": Cf.
"assaulting gray battalions of rain" (<u>SP</u>, p. 119).

101.22-26 "She considered a moment . . . waves on
her beam": Cf. "A Justice": "Herman Basket told
how one day during the high water, about three
years after Doom went away, the steamboat came and
crawled up on a sand-bar and died" (<u>Collected
Stories</u>, p. 346).

102.5 "Greenwich Village": Located in Manhattan,
south of 14th Street and west of Broadway, this
section of New York City became known as a haven
for artists, actors, and free spirits, especially
between 1910 and 1925. Faulkner had lived in the
Village during his stay in New York in 1921, while
working at Lord & Taylor's (see Blotner, I,
318-19).

102.16 "experimenting with the conventional tonal
scale": Such experiments with the tonal scale were
pioneered in America by Charles Edward Ives (1874-
1954), who used complex polytonal harmonies,
dissonances, and fragments of other compositions in
his work. Ives wrote most of his work before 1916,
although it had received only limited performance
by the time of <u>Mosquitoes</u> (see <u>Contemporary
American Composers</u>: <u>A Biographical Dictionary</u>,

compiled by Ruth Anderson [Boston: G. K. Hall,
1976], p. 215). Faulkner could also have been
familiar with the atonalism of Europeans Arnold
Schonberg (1874-1951), Anton von Webern
(1883-1945), or Alban Berg (1885-1935).

103.24-25 "She had had one husband, practically
discarded him": See Note 96.7-8.

103.31-104.2 "Of the niece Patricia . . . doesn't
even read": Helen Baird, according to Blotner,
"had early shown a talent for sculpture" (I, 509).
Although she was at one time "an avid reader" (I,
511), she no longer had much interest in books when
Faulkner met her (I, 438, 511). Cf. Linda Condon:
"I don't read, and I can't stand being--well,
loved" (p. 117). Cf. Elmer: "Myrtle simply
couldn't bear books" (p.53).

105.11 "opaque yellow-flecked eyes": Cf. Maurice
in The Wishing Tree: "His eyes had queer golden
flecks in them, like sparks" (p. 6). Cf. Pete in
"Once Aboard the Lugger (I)": "when we spoke to
him he'd glare at us with his yellow cat's eyes
. . ." (Uncollected Stories, p. 352). (See Note
296.20.)

106.29-30 "Romanesque architecture": A style of
building prevalent in western and southern Europe
during the early Middle Ages, marked by heavy
masonry construction, utilizing the round arch and
stone vaults. Most churches built in this style
were constructed in the shape of a Latin cross: a
central nave flanked by lower side aisles.

107.16-17 "A man don't want to be a fish,
though": One easily taken advantage of or fooled;
i.e., a sucker.

108.14-15 "Ah, Pete . . . for all your
experience": Cf. Mayday: The Princess Aelia tells
the knight, "Ah, Galwyn, Galwyn, why are you so
abysmally truthful? If you knew anything about
women, you'd have learned better. But how can you
have learned anything about women, poor dear,
having been so successful with them?" (p. 34).

109.10-16 "'Losing your pants' . . . picking it

up":   Robert M. Slabey has suggested a link between
this episode and the song "Mairy lost the pin of
her drawers" in the "Nausicca" section of <u>Ulysses</u>
(see "Faulkner's <u>Mosquitoes</u> and Joyce's <u>Ulysses</u>,"
436).   This may be, but Slabey is incorrect when he
places the event at 8 p.m., "the time of the Gerty
episode" (436).   Patricia loses her drawers between
7 and 8 o'clock in the morning.

109.24 "German spies":   According to Blotner, "In
mid-October [1917] Governor Theodore Bilbo startled
several thousand of his fellow citizens with a
speech in Meridan which gave them a new view of the
war.   `Did you know that Mississippi today is
covered with German spies?' he asked.   `Did you
know that in the last thirty days a dozen or more
have been arrested in the state, and that one man
had in his grip blueprints of every saw mill in
Missis- sippi?'" (I, 192).   Cf. <u>SP</u>:   "They think we
are trying to poison them.   They think we are
German spies, I guess" (p. 18).   Fear of Germans--
and of foreigners in general--was commonplace
during the years of World War I.

111.10   "`Sleepytime Gal'":   "Sleepy Time Gal" was
a popular song of 1925, words by Joseph R. Alden
and Raymond B. Egan, music by Ange Lorenzo and
Richard A. Whiting (see <u>American</u> <u>Popular</u> <u>Songs</u>, ed.
David Ewen [New York: Random House, 1966], p.
354).

112.23-29   "I don't mean with words . . . they are
interested in what you're going to do":   Cf. <u>SP</u>:
Margaret Powers tells Januarius Jones: "Let me
give you some advice . . . the next time you try to
seduce anyone, don't do it with talk, with words.
Women know more about words than men ever will.
And they know how little they can ever possibly
mean" (p. 250).   Cf. Addie Bundren in <u>AILD</u>:   "I
would think how words go straight up in a thin
line, quick and harmless, and how terribly doing
goes along the earth, clinglng to it, so that after
a while the two lines are too far apart for the
same person to straddle from one to the other
. . ." (p. 165).   (See Notes 130.20-21; 130.22-33.)

112.30-31   "How do you mean, be bold?   What must I
do to be bold?":   Cf. "And indeed there will be

time/To wonder, `Do I dare?' and `Do I dare?'"
(Eliot, "Prufrock," _Poems_, p. 10). Cf. _SP_, in
which Januarius Jones is "a disciple of the cult of
boldness with women" (p. 76).

113.28 "it's a pipe": Blotner writes that Josh
Baird was, in fact, experimenting with a homemade
pipe while Faulkner knew him in New Orleans (see
Blotner, I, 510; also see Note 46.1-3).

114.24 "Yale college": The second oldest
educational institution in the United States,
founded in 1701 and established in New Haven,
Connecticut, since 1716. Faulkner's friend Phil
Stone had attended Yale, and Faulkner had visited
there on at least two occasions. The first was at
the time of Estelle Oldham's marriage to Cornell
Franklin (18 April 1918) before Faulkner entered
the RAF in June (see Blotner, I, 201-07).
According to Carvel Colllins, Faulkner made a
second trip in 1921, one "which apparently is
unknown to his biographers" (see Afterward to
Mayday, p. 9).

115.5 "racehorse colt": Anderson used similar
words to describe Faulkner in a letter to Horace
Liveright: "He may be a little bit like a
thorough- bred colt who needs a race or two before
he can do his best" (_Letters of Sherwood Anderson_,
p. 155). (See Note 24.27-30.)

115.10-14 "Maybe that's the value of Yale . . .
can go there": See Note 41.24-42.2.

115.15-17 "Still, ninety out of a hundred . . .
ain't anything else": A likely reference to Phil
Stone, Faulkner's friend and self-appointed mentor,
who attended Yale. (See Note 114.24.)

115.21-22 "It was a kind of funny college I went
to . . . turned out preachers": Anderson briefly
attended The Lewis Institute (now part of the
Illinois Institute of Technology) in the fall of
1897, taking a business course. After serving in
the army, he entered, on 16 September 1899,
Wittenberg Academy in Springfield, Ohio, which he
described as the equivalent of a senior year of
high school (information for this and following

notes taken from William A. Sutton, <u>The Road to
Winesburg</u>: <u>A Mosaic of the Imaginative Life of
Sherwood Anderson</u> [Metuchen, N.J.: The Scarecrow
Press, 1972], p. 87).

115.22-23 "I was working in a mowing machinery
factory in Indiana": During the summer of 1899,
after being mustered out of the army and before
entering Wittenberg, Anderson worked on a farm
running a threshing machine (Sutton, p. 87). As a
teenager, he had also worked in a bicycle factory
"as an assembler" (<u>A Story Teller's Story</u>, p. 198).

115.24-31 "owner . . . won it, that year": I have
found no record that Anderson attended Wittenberg
on any sort of scholarship such as this. He did do
part-time work as a "house man" at the boarding
house where he lived, "tending stoves, filling and
cleaning kerosene lamps, mowing grass, and running
errands" (Sutton, p. 93). There are, however,
interesting parallels between Fairchild's story and
that of Labove in <u>The Hamlet</u> (pp. 115-28).

116.3-5 "They were a bunch of brokendown preachers
. . . big meaningless words": Actually, according
to Sutton, Anderson was quite fond of his teachers
and kept in touch with some of them throughout his
lifetime (p. 93).

116.5-10 "English literature course . . . the
ocean": William Shakespeare (1564-1616), English
dramatist and poet; John Milton (1608-1674),
English poet who published <u>Paradise Lost</u> in 1666;
Charles Darwin (1809-1882), English naturalist who
argued, in <u>On the Origin of Species by Means of
Natural Selection</u> (1859), the theory of evolution;
George Gordon, Lord Byron (1788-1824), English
poet, renown and often condemned for his satiric
and sensual poetry; Algernon Charles Swinburne
(1837-1909), English poet known as "the laureate
of libidinous- ness and the apostle of despair."
Cf. Swinburne's "The Triumph of Time": "I will go
back to the great sweet mother,/Mother and lover of
men, the sea" (<u>The Complete Works of Algernon
Charles Swinburne</u>, ed. Sir Edmund Bosse and Thomas
James Wise [London: William Heinemenn Ltd.; New
York: Gabriel Wells, 1925], I, 177). Cf.
Faulkner's comment on Swinburne: "Whatever it was

that I found in Swinburne, it completely satisfied
me and filled my inner life" ("Verse Old and
Nascent: A Pilgrimage," EP&P, p. 115).

116.12-13 "But in spite of it, I kind of got
interested in learning things": Anderson was
remembered by his teachers as a student whose
"eagerness to get everything possible out of school
would cause him to ask questions when the time for
dismissal of the class was near" (Sutton, p. 93).

116.16 "And I joined a fraternity, too, almost":
Anderson was active in the Academic Athletic
Association, of which he was elected secretary, and
was a member of the Athenian Literary Society
(Sutton, p. 94). Faulkner himself was a member of
the Sigma Alpha Epsilon fraternity at Mississippi
and included this information in his biographical
sketch sent to the Four Seas Company in connection
with the publication of The Marble Faun (see
Letters, p. 7).

116.21-24 "Senior Club . . . three years": At
Yale, the greatest prestige is reserved for those
few men selected for the Senior Societies, the most
noted of which are Skull and Bones and Scroll and
Key. The invitations are given on Tap Day, held in
the Spring of the students' Junior Year.

116.32 "boarding house": Anderson shared a room
with his brother Karl at "The Oaks," a boarding
house run by Mrs. Louise S. Folger, where he worked
as a "house man" (see Sutton, p. 93; see also Note
115.24-31).

117.18-19 "secret pirates' gang": A possible
reference to Mark Twain's Adventures of Tom Sawyer
(1876) and Adventures of Huckleberry Finn (1881),
both of which are echoed several times in
Mosquitoes (see Note 144.23).

117.32-33 "This had to be night work . . . college
power plant": This description of Fairchild's job
anticipates Faulkner's later well-known account of
having written AILD while working in the university
power plant: "I got a job in the power plant, on
the night shift, from 6 P.M. to 6 A.M., as a coal
passer. I shoveled coal from the bunker into a

wheelbarrow and wheeled it in and dumped it where
the fireman could put it into the boiler" (see
Faulkner's Introduction to the Modern Library issue
of <u>Sanctuary</u> [1932] in <u>ES&PL</u>, p. 177).

118.5-6 "But I learned how to sleep in a cinder
pile or a coal bunker, anyway": A possible
allusion to the fairy tale "Cinderella." There are
a number of references to children's tales in
<u>Mosquitoes</u> (see Notes 9.16; 128.31; 235.13-16 for
other examples) and Fairchild's tale may be read,
in fact, as an ironic retelling of the Cinderella
story.

119.29-30 "So I went . . . already late": See the
account of Anderson's dream in Note 50.17-20.

120.23 "she gazed down into the restless water":
Another example of the Narcissus image in the book
(see Note 47.29-48.21).

121.16-23 "swinging the glass further . . .
extending her hand": Cf. Joseph Conrad, <u>Heart</u> <u>of</u>
<u>Darkness</u>:

I directed my glass to the house. There were no
signs of life, but there were the ruined roof, the
long mud wall peeping above the grass, with three
little square window-holes, no two of the same
size; all this brought within reach of my hand, as
it were. And then I made a brusque movement, and
one of the remaining posts of that vanished fence
leaped up in the field of my glass. . . . These
round knobs were not ornamental but symbolic; they
were expressive and puzzling, striking and
disturbing--food for thought and also for vultures.
. . . I put down the glass, and the head that had
appeared near enough to be spoken to seemed at once
to have leaped away from me into inaccessible
distance [<u>Works</u> <u>of</u> <u>Joseph</u> <u>Conrad</u>, V, 158-60].

122.14 "David West": As Carvel Collins has noted,
Faulkner several times used the name "David" for "a
psychologically autobiographical character" in his
work (see Introduction to <u>Mayday</u>, p. 11). The
David character appears in the typescript version
of "Carcassonne" (written about the time of
<u>Mosquitoes</u>) and in the story "The Leg" (<u>Collected</u>

<u>Stories</u>, pp. 823-42). The Faulkner character in
Anderson's "A Meeting South" (<u>The</u> <u>Dial</u>, 38 [April
1925], 269-79) was named David. In "Out of
Nazareth" (<u>NOS</u>, pp. 101-110) the young man who very
much resembles David West is referred to as
"David," although the reference seems to be to the
Biblical David in this case: "One could imagine
young David looking like that" (p. 102).

122.28-123.8 "It was Mr. Fairchild got me this job
. . . quiet pride": Cf. a surviving fragment,
which possibly came from a manuscript version of
<u>Mosquitoes</u> now lost:

It was Fairchild had found David, a tramp, in
Jackson Park one afternoon, lying on his stomach
reading a dog-eared book. David was a native of
Indiana also, his eyes were calm and gray, his body
was young and splendid; he had done a little of
everything and had just completed a voyage as
messman on a Freighter, and Fairchild had got Mrs.
Maurier to take him on a[s] steward for the
cruise. The book turned out to be a western novel
by Zane Grey.

This morning, David mounted the galley companionway
to the deck and into a quiet fathomless mist. It
was upon the world, unstirred;

(Quoted from Carl Petersen, <u>Each</u> <u>In</u> <u>Its</u> <u>Ordered</u>
<u>Place</u>: <u>A</u> <u>Faulkner</u> <u>Collector's</u> <u>Notebook</u> [Ann Arbor,
Michigan: Ardes Publications, 1975), p. 28).

It is worth speculating how much Faulkner could
have been influenced by F. Scott Fitzgerald's <u>The</u>
<u>Great</u> <u>Gatsby</u> (1925) in his protrayal of David:
both Gatsby and David are from the mid-West; both
work as stewards on yachts--Gatsby (nee Gatz) on
Dan Cody's <u>Tuolomee</u>; both are linked with western
novels--David with Zane Grey and Gatsby with
<u>Hopalong</u> <u>Cassidy</u>, in which he has copied the
"Schedule" for his life; and both are "innocents."

123.17 "to the Mediterranean ports": David's
description of his trip to Europe parallels in part
Faulkner's own trip in the summer and fall of 1925
(see Blotner, I, 443-83 and following Notes).

123.23-24 "I never seemed to get to Paris":
Faulkner did visit Paris and stayed there in August
and September of 1925 (see Blotner, I, 450-73).

123.33 "balloon pants": The large baggy style of
trousers popular at this time among sophisticated
young men.

124.5 "old gray walls and ruined castles": Cf.
Faulkner's letter to his mother (6 August 1925)
from Pavia, Italy: "all around are old, old walls
and gates through which mailed knights once rode,
and where men-at-arms scurried over cobble stones"
(Letters, p. 9). (See Note 335.4-6.)

124.13-24 "The Alps . . . against the blue": Cf.
Faulkner's description in a letter to his mother
(13 August 1925): "I found Stresa full of American
tourists, so I took my pack and typewriter and lit
out for the mountains above Lake Maggiore. It is
in the Italian Alps and I lived in a little village
stuck on the side of a mountain. . . . Below was
the lake, blue, and across it the Swiss Alps. You
could see 4 or 5 towns, and trains and boats like
toy ones" (Letters, p. 10).

124.29-31 "And that's what you get for being a
woman . . . bunch of kids": See Notes 18.27-28;
139.24-25.

125.17-21 "her spirit lay on its belly above
Maggiore . . . taller than God": Maggiore is the
second largest lake in italy, 41 miles long and 7
miles wide at its greatest width. Stresa is
located on the western shore. (See Note 124.
13-24.)

126.10-13 "You see, I--I haven't got a bathing
suit . . . you can wear it": Cf. "The Off-Shore
Pirate," in which Ardita Farnam talks Curtis
Carlyle into swimming with her: "You can use my
uncle's bathing suit, only it'll fit you like a
gunny sack, because he's a very flabby man. I've
got a one-piece affair that's shocked the natives
all along the Atlantic coast from Biddeford Pool to
St. Augustine" (Flappers and Philosophers, pp.
34-35).

127.5-6 "Blonde and pink and soft in sleep was
Jenny":   Cf. Rossetti's poem "Jenny":

> Why, Jenny, as I watched you there,--
> For all your wealth of loosened hair,
> Your silk ungirdled and unlac'd
> And warm sweets open to the waist,
> All golden in the lamplight's gleam,--
> You know not what a book you seem,
> Half-read by lightning in a dream!

(The Poetical Works of Dante Gabriel Rossetti,
Introduction by William M. Rossetti [New York:
Thomas Y. Crowell & Company, 1886], p. 71).

127.29-33 "he stood before the mirror . . . sag of
that deckchair":   Another example of the Narcissus
image (see Notes 47.29-48.21; 120.23).   Cf. Myrtle
Monson in Elmer, who sits "yawning in her deck
chair" (p.53).

128.25 "her red soft mouth where little teeth but
showed":   Cf. Elmer: "a full red mouth never quite
completely closed" (see Note 55.10-11).   Cf. the
description of Eula Varner in Father Abraham: "a
softly ample girl with eyes like cloudy hothouse
grapes and a mouth always slightly open" (p. 16).
(See Note 56.14.)

128.31 "Wake sleeping princess Kiss":   An ironic
reference to the story of Sleeping Beauty, in which
the Prince awakens Beauty in this manner (see Iona
and Peter Opie, The Classic Fairy Tales, pp. 81-
92).

129.6-11 "'Watcher doing, you old--' . . . like a
cablegram":   Cf. Eula Varner to Labove in The
Hamlet: "Stop pawing me. . . .   You old headless
horseman Ichabod Crane" (p. 138).

129.10 "Phillida":   Cf. James Branch Cabell's
Jurgen, in which Jurgen speaks of a "Phyllida":   "I
borrow for my dear love the appellation of that
noted but by much inferior lady who was beloved by
Ariphus of Belsize. . . .   You will remember
Poliger suspects she was a princess of the house of
Scleroveus: and you of course recall Pisander's
masterly summing-up of the probabilities, in his

Heraclea" (p. 96).

130.15 "the Great Illusion, par excellence": A
possible reference to the romantic stage and screen
actor John Barrymore (1882-1942), who was popularly
known as the "Great Profile" at this time.

130.17-19 "The illusion that you can seduce women
. . . Gold help you": Cf. Elmer: "he wondered why
it was that certain girls chose you while others
did not. Elmer at one time thought that you could
seduce them. But now he wasn't sure: he believed
now that they just elected you. And then God help
you" (p. 19). The typescript version of Mosquitoes
reads "God help you" (p. 167).

130.20-21 "ˋAnd with words' . . . he repeated
savagely": Cf. Sherwood Anderson, Marching Men:
"It is a terrible thing to speculate on how man has
been defeated by his ability to say words . . . and
we continuously say words, worn-out words, crooked
words, words without power or pregnancy in them"
([New York: John Lane Company, 1917], p. 123).
(See Note 210.5-6; see also Notes 130.22-31;
210.12- 17 for descriptions of Anderson's love for
words.)

130.22-31 "Well, why not with words . . . starve
to death": Cf. "Words and colors might be
combined. . . . Words might be thrown together and
sentences made and the sentences had uncanny
powers. With a sentence one might destroy a
friendship, win a woman, make a war" (Tar, p. 48).
Cf. "I have not lost my faith in words" (A Story
Teller's Story, p. 291).

131.14-18 "Mussolini . . . fertilizing the
earth": Benito Mussolini (1883-1945), Italian
leader of the Facist movement, served ostensibly as
Prime Minister of Italy from 1922 to 1943, but was,
in fact, made dictator in January 1925. He joined
forces with Hitler in 1939 and was executed by
Italian partisans in 1945.

131.20-21 "Henry Ford": Ford (1863-1947) is
credited with the introduction of modern mass
production in his organization of the assembly line
method of automobile construction. (See Anderson's

comments on Ford and mass industrialization in _A Story Teller's Story_, pp. 187-90.)

131.28-32 "And so do you . . . sweet stupidity of young flesh": Cf. Sherwood Anderson in _Windy McPherson's Son_: "Left to themselves the children played kissing games and young men and tall half-formed girls sat on the front porches in the darkness, thrilled and half frightened, getting through their instincts, crudely and without guidance, their first peep at the mystery of life" (p. 72). Cf. Jurgen in "the garden between dawn and sunrise" (p. 18): "And all the faces that Jurgen saw were young and glad and very lovely and quite heart-breakingly confident, as young persons beyond numbering came toward Jurgen and passed him there . . . in the glory of their youth, and foreknowing life to be a puny antagonist from whom one might take very easily anything which one desired" (_Jurgen_, p. 20). Cf. "Moonlight": "But they--he, anyway--had lost time somewhere in that summer's dark scented with the sweet young smell of invisible girlflesh, somewhere between her lips and the fumbling diffidence of his half-repulsed hands . . ." (_Uncollected Stories_, p. 497).

133.15 "fade out": To disappear from the scene. This expression dates from c. 1924.

134.1-2 "Try it on your saxophone, Pete": To "try it on" means to experiment, to make an attempt. "Saxophone" was often used in a vaguely obscene manner.

134.33-135.1 "the moon . . . pallid and boneless hand": Cf. Poem XIX in _GB_, entitled "Drowning" in the typescript version and dated "2 April 25" (Butterworth, "Census . . . of William Faulkner's Poetry," 338):

> Green is the water, green
> The grave voluptuous music of the sun;
> The pale and boneless fingers of a queen
> Upon his body stoop and run [_MF_, p. 41].

135.5-6 "But there was nothing for it . . . she added aloud": A possible ironic reference to the theme of cannibalism in Conrad's _Heart of_

<u>Darkness</u>. There are a number of other more
specific allusions to the work (see Notes
82.28-83.9; 121.16-23; 164.5-6; 169.19-30;
262.21-22).

136.12-13 "She sat holding a handglass . . . the
handglass was bland": Another example of the
Narcissus image in <u>Mosquitoes</u>. Cf. <u>Marionettes</u>, in
which Marietta stares at herself in a mirror in the
final illustration.

137.20-21 "The only man who could walk on water is
dead": See Matthew 14:25-33: "And in the fourth
watch of the night he came to them, walking on the
sea" (Matthew 14:25). Actually Peter also walks on
the water for a brief time before losing his faith,
but it is the image of the world without Christ
that Faulkner stresses here. Cf. "Jesus walking on
Galilee and Washington not telling lies" (<u>TS&TF</u>,
p. 99).

139.13-15 "I mean, you are kind of thick through
the middle . . . big behind for them": Cf. Myrtle
Monson in <u>Elmer</u>, who has "short legs" and "soft
palpable thighs" (p. 47) and is often shown staring
at herself in the mirror, much as does Jenny.

139.24-25 "So do I . . . do you want one for?":
Cf. <u>Linda Condon</u>: "I'm perfectly sure I'll never
care for babies, they are so mussy" (p. 117). Cf.
<u>Elmer</u>: "Elmer had a bastard son in Houston, and at
one time he had been quite attached to the thing's
mother" (p. 92).

141.23 "petting"; To hug, fondle, kiss, or caress
in a sexual manner. "Heavy petting" stops just
short of coitus.

144.20 "the Market": The French Market, located
along Decatur and North Peter streets from Barricks
to St. Anne's street, consists of five buildings
divided into stalls from which fruits, vegetables,
and other items are sold. According to the <u>New
Orleans City Guide</u>, "The French Quarter is alive
with disciples of the night, from the coming of
darkness until dawn, when many of the devoted can
be found at the French Market. Here society
matrons and truck drivers, night-club entertainers

and tourists sit on stools and drink coffee and eat doughnuts in friendly proximity" (p. xxxvii).

144.23 "there was a man drowned at Mandeville that day": The motif of the drowned man is central to the Narcissus image in Mosquitoes, but Faulkner may have been influenced in his use of the image by a number of other sources. Cf. the "Proteus" section of Ulysses, in which Stephen Dedalus refers to "the man that was drowned nine days ago off Maiden's rock. They are waiting for him now" (p. 45); the "Death by Water" section of The Waste Land: "Phllebas the Phoenician, a fortnight dead,/. . . A current under sea/Picked his bones in whispers" (p. 46); even Tom Sawyer: Gordon's supposed drowning and "resurrection" is not unlike that of Tom, Huck, and Joe. The idea of drowning is central to many of Faulkner's early works, including "Nympholepsy," The Marionettes, Mayday, several poems in A Green Bough (including Poem XIX entitled "Drowning" in typescript), and, most notably, The Sound and the Fury.

144.32-145.8 "A kind of little man . . . just crazy": The description Faulkner gives of himself in the following lines, although obviously self-mocking, was also relatively accurate. Blotner describes the Faulkner of 1925 in the following way: "He usually wore a white shirt and white duck trousers with a rope tied at the waist. His shock of dark brown hair with its red glint was usually uncombed. He had a good meerschaum pipe that summer, which contrasted oddly with the beachcomber effect of his simple dress and unkempt appearance. The mustache was full but neat, and though he shaved the rest of his face, he would sometimes skip a day or two or wait until evening, so that often there would be a dark stubble on the thin cheeks" (I, 437-38). Gordon is also referred to as a "black" man: "why are you so black?" Pat asks him at their first meeting (see Note 25.17). Another possible source is Cabell's Jurgen, in which the god Koshchei, who "made things as they are" (p. 300), is constantly referred to as a "black gentleman" (p. 10).

145.5-6 "He said he was a liar by profession": Cf. Oscar Wilde, "The Decay of Lying": "As one

knows the poet by his fine music, so one can
recognize the liar by his rich rhythmic utterance,
and in neither case will the casual inspiration of
the moment suffice. Here, as elsewhere, practice
must precede perfection" (<u>Intentions</u>, vol. V of <u>The</u>
<u>Complete</u> <u>Works</u> <u>of</u> <u>Oscar</u> <u>Wilde</u>, p. 14). Cf.
Sherwood Anderson in <u>Tar</u>: "All tale telling is, in
a strict sense, nothing but lying. That is what
people cannot understand. To tell the truth is too
difficult. I long since gave up the effort" (p.
xiv). Cf. Faulkner's sketch "The Liar," published
in <u>The</u> <u>Times</u>-<u>Picayune</u>, 26 June 1925 (<u>NOS</u>, pp.
171-84).

145.7-8 "I think he was crazy . . . just crazy":
Cf. Helen Baird's comment on Faulkner: "He was one
of my screwballs" (quoted in Blotner, I, 438).

147.28-149.30 "Jenny . . . are you a virgin . . .
Hell": This scene anticipates the similar,
although more serious, discussion of virginity held
among the college girls in <u>Sanctuary</u> (pp. 181-82).

148.15 "girl scout": Organization for girls
founded in the United States by Juliette Low in
1912. Its original purpose was to develop health,
character and homemaking abilities.

150.9 "Tulane": Tulane University in New Orleans,
founded in 1834.

150.13 "jerkwater": A term of deprecation
indicating rusticity or provincialism, derived from
the term "freshwater" to describe people, towns, or
institutions from the inland regions, away from the
coast.

152.8-9 "red dog": A card game involving betting;
also the name of a 19th century U. S. bank note.

152.16-17 "In the yet level rays of the moon . . .
haughty and inhuman almost": Cf. Salome's description of Jokanaan: "It is his eyes above all that
are terrible. They are like black holes burned by
torches in a Tyrian tapestry. They are like black
caverns where dragons dwell. They are like the
black caverns of Egypt in which the dragons make
their lairs. They are like black lakes troubled by

fantastic moons" (<u>Salome</u>, pp. 50-51).

152.18-19 "It's like a silver faun's face":   Cf.
the marble faun:

> About his cloudy head it curls
> The endless sorrow of all worlds,
> The while he bends dry stricken eyes
> Above the throngs; perhaps he sighs
> For all the full world watching him
> As seasons change from bright to dim [<u>MF</u>, p.36].

Cf. Donald Mahon in <u>SP</u>, who is "thin faced, with
the serenity of a wild thing, the passionate serene
alertness of a faun . . ." (pp. 82-83).

152.33-153.8 "To live within yourself . . . an end
in itself, I think":   Cf. Eliot's "Portrait of a
Lady":

You are invulnerable, you have no Achilles' heel.
You will go on, and when you have prevailed
You can say: at this point many a one has failed.
But what have I, but what have I, my friend,
To give you, what can you receive from me?
Only the friendship and the sympathy
Of one about to reach her journey's end
                              [<u>Poems</u>, pp. 17-18]

Cf. "The Artist":   "But to create! Which among ye
who have not this fire, can know this joy, let it
be ever so fleet?" (<u>NOS</u>, p. 48).

153.8-12 "To know that one had given her mite
. . . gods have trod":   Cf. Mark 12:41-44:

    And there came a certain poor widow: and she
cast in two mites, which make a farthing.
    And calling his disciples together, he saith
to them: Amen I say to you, this poor widow hath
cast in more than all they who have cast into the
treasury.
    For all they did cast in of their abundance;
but she of her want cast in all she had, <u>even</u> her
whole living.

See also Luke 21:1-4.   There is obvious irony that
the wealthy widow Mrs. Maurier should be comparing

herself to this poor woman (see Note 26.30-27.3).

153.24-25 "to regard the antics of man as one
would a puppet show": Cf. <u>The</u> <u>Marionettes</u>. See
Noel Polk's introduction for further discussion of
this image.

153.27-28 "Sufficient unto himself . . . marble
tower of his loneliness and pride": Cf. the
description of Satan in <u>Paradise</u> <u>Lost</u>:

                    He above the rest
In shape and gesture proudly eminent
Stood like a tow'r; his form had yet not lost
All her original brightness, nor appeared
Less than Archangel ruined, and th' excess
Of glory obscured . . . .

                    Darkened so, yet shone
Above them all th' Archangel; but his face
Deep scars of thunder had intrenched, and care
Sat on his faded cheek, but under brows
Of dauntless courage, and considerate pride
Waiting revenge

[Book I, ll. 589-94, 599-604 of <u>Paradise</u> <u>Lost</u> in
<u>The</u> <u>Complete</u> <u>Poetical</u> <u>Works</u> <u>of</u> <u>John</u> <u>Milton</u>].

153.30 "O bitter and new": Cf. Faulkner's letter
to Helen Baird on verso of p. 269 of <u>Mosquitoes</u>
typescript: "Bitter and new as fire" (see Note
48.12).

156.15 There is at this point in the typescript a
four page section (ts. pp. 204-207) which is
omitted from the published book. It is a
continuation of the scene in the book between Pat
and Jenny which occurs on pages 137 to 151 of the
novel. In this earlier scene, Faulkner has hinted
at the attraction Pat feels for Jenny as she
"slowly stroked the back of her hand along the
swell of Jenny's flank. Slowly, back and forth,
while Jenny lay supine and receptive as a cat" (p.
147). Pat's actions do not go beyond this caress
in the book, however. But in the typescript the
scene continues for several pages more at the point
corresponding to line 14 on page 156 of the
published novel, following the description of Eva

Wiseman about to open the door to the cabin in
which Pat and Jenny are together. Faulkner's plan
was to freeze the action, leaving Mrs. Wiseman
outside the door, her hand on the knob, while
developing the scene between the girls. It would
thus have been an early example of the suspended
moment technique which Faulkner would use to such
effect in later works. As published, the novel
gives no indication that anything is taking place
beyond the door at which Mrs. Wiseman pauses. In
the typescript continuation of the scene, Pat's
stroking of Jenny's flank results in Jenny's
turning almost instinctively to Pat and kissing
her: "Jenny made again her drowsy moaning sound,
and without seeming to move at all she came to the
other with a boneless enveloping movement, turning
her head until their mouths touched. Immediately
Jenny went lax, yet she still seemed to envelop the
other, holding their bodies together with her
mouth" (ts. p. 205). Pat reacts violently to
Jenny's kiss, not to the act itself but to the
manner in which Jenny performs it. Spitting in
disgust, she accuses Jenny of kissing like a
"common" person: Pat then proceeds to teach Jenny
the way "nice" people kiss, and it is at this point
that they are interrupted by Mrs. Wiseman. This is
one of four major excisions from the typescript to
which Faulkner strenuously objected in a letter to
Horace Liveright (see Blotner, I, 539; also see
Note 177.19). A possible inspiration for this
scene can be found in Gautier's <u>Mademoiselle De
Maupin</u> (pp. 224-32, 249-60). In these two
episodes, Magdalen de Maupin, disguised as Theodore
de Serannes, and the Lady Rosette participate in
sexual dallyings, and in each case they are
interrupted by Rosette's brother Alcibiades "like a
god in his machine" (p. 233). However, Pat and
Jenny's adventurings remain much more innocent than
do Magdalen and Rosette's.

160.4-5 "This water is different from seawater":
Lake Pontchartrain is a land-locked salt-water bay
which is fed by the Mississippi and merges into the
Gulf of Mexico.

162.15-163.2 "It was like one morning . . . .
Simple, like that": Cf. "Frankie and Johnny,"
which contains an earlier version of this section

(_Uncollected_ _Stories_, p. 341). Cf. "The Kid
Learns": "he kissed her cold mouth, and it was as
though dawn had come among the trees where the
birds were singing" (_NOS_, p. 166).

162.16 "Bulls": Slang term for police or, in this
case, railroad guards.

163.13-14 "a long pencil of moonlight . . .
shattering upon the floor": Cf. Poem III of
_GB_: ". . . spears of starlight/Shatter and
break among them" (p. 18). (See Note 46.9-10.)

163.20-21 She lay in bed . . . without a sound":
Cf. _Elmer_:

> Mrs. Monson's body was never restless,
regardless of how chaotic her thoughts might be,
and she lay flat on her back motionless, with the
placidity of a paralytic, in her darkened room.
Even the sea here seemed ancient and weary of
restlessness and commotion, as if, having seen what
it had seen, it knew there was nothing new to
interest it, no reason for sweeping landward in
waves to peer and topple and fall. Even the sky
seems a little tired here Mrs. Monson thought
regarding the pale rectangle of her window where
within the weary bowl of the sky the rumor of the
sea was like the echo of a void that Paul hushing
for a moment two thousand years ago his beautiful
fatuity of conviction, might have heard spoken, and
which all the Pauls since have not heard die away
> [p. 70].

(See also Note 10.30-31.)

164.5-6 "the yacht was a thick jewel swaddled in
soft gray wool": Cf. _Heart_ _of_ _Darkness_, in which
the ship is "buried miles deep in a heap of cotton-
wool" (_Works_ _of_ _Joseph_ _Conrad_, V, 131). (See ms.
fragment, Note 122.28-123.8.)

164.10-11 "It is well: let there be light":
Genesis 1:3: "And God said, `Let there be light':
and there was light."

166.6-9 "as her grave simple body . . . sped
across the deck and out of the ken of his dog's

eyes": Cf. <u>Mayday</u>: Sir Galwyn comes across Iseult
bathing in a stream. She later tells him: "I
blush to think of it, but for some reason--though
it is not at all like myself--I feel no sense of
immodesty whatever in being naked with you . . ."
(p. 25). Cf. Juliet Bunden and Lee Hollowell in
"Adolescence," who swim naked together without
embarrassment (<u>Uncollected</u> <u>Stories</u>, pp. 461-66).
Cf. Charlotte and Harry in <u>WP</u>: She swam each
morning, the three bathing suits still undisturbed
in the locker. He would rise from breakfast and
return to the porch and lie on the cot and hear
presently her bare feet cross the room and then the
porch; perhaps he would watch the steadily and
smoothly browning body cross the porch"
(p. 110).

167.4-5 "His hand . . . had not felt it": Cf.
<u>Linda</u> <u>Condon</u>: "Throughout her life she had
rebelled against any profanation of her person, she
had hated to be touched" (p. 265). Cf. <u>Elmer</u>:
"Just to touch her, withdrawing his hand
immediately. Perhaps she doesn't understand what
just to touch is, he thought with longing" (p. 9).

167.5-14 "She turned suddenly . . . then released
him": Cf. <u>Linda</u> <u>Condon</u>: "I don't believe I'll
ever like being kissed. Can you tell me why? No
one ever has; they all think they can bring me
around to it" (p. 149). Cf. Margaret Powers and
Cadet Julian Lowe in <u>SP</u>:

    She offered her face coolly and he kissed her
as she wished: coldly, remotely. She put her
hands on his cheeks. "Dear boy," she said, kissing
him again, as his mother kissed him.
    "Say, that's no way for engaged people to
kiss," he objected.
    "How do engaged people kiss?" she asked. He
put his arms around her, feeling her shoulder
blades, and drew her mouth against his with the
technique he had learned. She suffered his kiss a
moment, then thrust him away.
    "Is that how engaged people kiss?" she asked,
laughing. "I like this better." She took his face
in her palms and touched his mouth briefly and
coolly [p. 54].

(See also Note 156.15.)

168.5-19 "When he returned . . . skiff back to the
yacht": In the typescript (p. 223), Pat displays
more understanding of, is more in control of these
details and directs David in each action.
Faulkner's revisions reflect more realistically
David's and Pat's respective knowledge.

169.1-2 "That's the name of it--Mandeville. Which
way is Mandeville from here?": According to
Blotner, Faulkner and Virginia Parker Nagle left
the <u>Josephine</u> when she was stranded during their
lake voyage and made a similar mosquito-ridden trip
to Mandeville to visit the amusement area (see
Blotner, I, 418). However, the journey in
<u>Mosquitoes</u> takes on greater importance and seems to
have been influenced by Marlow's adventures in
<u>Heart</u> <u>of</u> <u>Darkness</u> and also perhaps by the episode
in Hergesheimer's <u>Cytherea</u> in which Lee Randon runs
away with Savina Grove to Cuba, hoping to find a
paradise but encountering instead disillusionment
and defeat. One might also note similarities
between Pat and David's adventure and that of
Curtis Carlyle (or Toby Moreland, his real name)
and Ardita Farnam, who also slip away from a yacht
to a nearby island in Fitzgerald's "The Off-Shore
Pirate," although their escape leads to romance
rather than disappointment. And, finally, there
are interesting connections between these passages
in <u>Mosquitoes</u> and the story of Ike Snopes and the
cow in <u>The</u> <u>Hamlet</u>; cf. pp. 204-13. (See following
Notes.)

169.19-30 "Trees heavy . . . small voice": Cf.
<u>Heart</u> <u>of</u> <u>Darkness</u>:

Trees, trees, millions of trees, massive, immense,
running up high. . . .   It made you feel very
small, very lost, and yet it was not altogether
depressing, that feeling. . . .   We were wanderers
on a prehistoric earth, on an earth that wore the
aspect of an unknown planet. We could have fancied
ourselves the first of men taking possession of an
accursed inheritance, to be subdued at the cost of
profound anguish and of excessive toil [<u>Works</u> <u>of</u>
<u>Joseph</u> <u>Conrad</u>, V, 115-16].

169.21-24 "No, this mist . . . beginning of things
fecundated": Cf. <u>Cytherea</u>, in which Lee Randon and
Savina Grove find in Cuba a primitive and
frightening world, an "incomprehensible state of
life a million years beyond their grasp. . . . Was
he, Lee Randon, instead of advancing, falling back
into a past more remote than coherent speech?
Nothing, he asserted, could be further from his
intention and hope. Yet, without doubt, he was
surrounded by the denial of order, of disciplined
feeling; and, flatly, it terrified him" (pp. 336-
37).

169.24-30 "these huge and silent trees . . . in a
small voice": Cf. <u>Mayday</u>: "In a while they came
to a forest. This was a certain enchanted forest
and the trees in this forest were more ancient than
any could remember. . . . The trees of this forest
were not as ordinary trees, for each bore a living
eye and these eyes stared without winking at young
Sir Galwyn as he rode beneath them" (pp. 8-9). Cf.
<u>AILD</u>: "Above the ceaseless surface they stand--
trees, canes, vines--rootless, severed from the
earth, spectral above a scene of immense yet
circumscribed desolation filled with the voice of
the waste and mournful water. . . . He [Cash]
looks about quietly, at the position of the trees,
leaning this way and that . . . as if the road too
had been soaked free of earth and floated upward,
to leave in its spectral tracings a momument to a
still more profound desolation than this above
which we now sit, talking quietly of old security
and old trivial things" (p. 136).

171.11-12 "They hadn't found the road . . .
distance from the lake": The Tchefuncte State
Park, located along Lake Pontchatrain between Cane
Bayou and Bayou Castine, is a 1000-acre
heavily-forested tract; a white sand beach covered
with cypress, cedar, palmetto and other growths
borders the lake shore. This area seems to be that
in which David and Pat make their journey.

171.32-172.11 "Don't look at me like that . . .
Not like David": Cf. "The Off-Shore Pirate":

        "Don't talk to me like that!" fired up
Ardita. "I won't tolerate the parental attitude

from anybody! Do you understand me?"
     He chuckled and then stopped, rather abashed,
as her cold anger seemed to fold him about and
chill him.
     "I'm sorry," he offered uncertainly.
     "Oh, don't apologize! I can't stand men who
say `I'm sorry' in that manly, reserved tone. Just
shut up!" [<u>Flappers</u> <u>and</u> <u>Philosophers</u>, p. 34].

Cf. <u>Elmer</u>, in which Myrtle Monson has a romance
with a man on board ship: "His beautiful eyes look
exactly like a dog's Myrtle told herself with a
mild bored satisfaction. Like a lady dog's she
added pleased at the simile" (p. 82). Cf.
Charlotte Rittenmeyer to Harry Wilbourne in <u>WP</u>:

"Stand up. . . . Stand up like a man." He rose,
she put her hard arms around him, wrestling him
against her with restrained savage impatience. . .
She held him hard against her, leaning back, her
hips against him and moving faintly while she
stared at him, the yellow stare inscrutable and
derisive and with that quality which he had come to
recognize--that ruthless and almost unbearable
honesty. "Like a man, I said," holding him hard
and derisive against her moving hips though that
was not necessary [pp. 108-09].

172.18-22 "She moved again . . . tiny splash of
crimson": Cf. "Once Aboard the Lugger (I)": "I
killed a mosquito on the back of my hand. It left
a huge, warm splash, like a raindrop. I wiped my
hands on my flanks" (<u>Uncollected</u> <u>Stories</u>, p. 355).

174.5-11 "Huge cypress roots . . . in his mother's
arms": Cf. "Nympholepsy":

     He had thought of trees as being so much
timber but these silent ones were more than that.
. . . These trees gazed on him impersonally,
taking a slow revenge. The sunset was a fire no
fuel had ever fed, the water murmured in a dark and
sinister dream . . . . And above all brooded some
god to whose compulsions he must answer long after
the more comfortable beliefs had become out-worn as
a garment used everyday.
     And this god neither recognized him nor
ignored him: this god seemed to be unconscious of

him entirely, save as a trespasser where he had no
business being [<u>Uncollected</u> <u>Stories</u>, pp. 333-34].

176.11 "Sing Sing": Well-known prison in
Ossining, New York.

177.19 The typescript version (pp. 235-37)
continues after this point, but this section was
omitted from the published book. In it Jenny
attempts to teach Pete how to "kiss refined." The
removal of the earlier scene between Jenny and Pat
(see Note 156.15) necessitated the cutting of this
one, which would not make sense without the earlier
episode.

179.2-21 "When he reached her . . . `I'm dying, I
tell you'": Cf. <u>Cytherea</u>, in which the doomed
Savina Grove suffers horribly from the heat
(p. 346). Cf. "Once Aboard the Lugger (I)": the
narrator is "surrounded always by a soundless and
vicious needling which I could not brush even
temporarily off, [in which] that sense of nightmare
returned ten fold--a sense of hopeless enslavement
to an obscure compulsion, in which the very
necessity for striving was its own derision"
(<u>Uncollected</u> <u>Stories</u>, p. 357).

180.13-14 "like a thin voice cursing in a
cathedral": Cf. <u>Light</u> <u>in</u> <u>August</u> (New York: Random
House, 1932): "It is like listening in a cathedral
to a eunuch chanting in a language which he does
not even need to not understand" (p. 301).

180.22-27 "`Let's put the shirt on you . . . I
don't need it,' he repeated": Cf. "Once Aboard the
Lugger (I)":

    "Skeeter bad here," the nigger said.
    I killed another on my forearm, and two bit me
on the ankles at the same time, and one on the
neck, and I rolled my sleeves down and buttoned my
collar.
    "They'll eat you up, without any shirt on," I
said.
    "No, sir," he said. "Skeeter dont bother me.
Cant nothing off the land bother me. I got
medicine" (<u>Uncollected</u> <u>Stories</u>, pp. 355-56).

181.19   "The race hasn't degenerated that far":
This emphasis on the weakening of the white race
was a popular topic in intellectual circles in the
1920's, inspired in large part by Oswald Spengler's
<u>The</u> <u>Decline</u> <u>of</u> <u>the</u> <u>West</u> (trans. by Charles Francis
Atkinson [London: G. Allen, 1922; New York: A. A.
Knopf, 1926-28]).   Excerpts from the book appeared
in <u>The</u> <u>Dial</u> under the title "The Downfall of
Western Civilization" (November 1924-January
1925).   Spengler (1880-1936) was a German
philosopher who described a "life cycle" through
which all civilizations passed.   The Western
Civilization had, he felt, moved beyond its
creative stage into one of reflection and material
comfort.   Thus, only the decline remained.
Although Spengler's work was attacked, it remained
highly influential nonetheless.   Cf. Tom Buchanan
in <u>The</u> <u>Great</u> <u>Gatsby</u>:   "Civilization is going to
pieces. . . if we don't look out the white race
will be--will be utterly submerged.   It's all
scientific stuff; it's been proved" (p. 13).   (See
Note 328.6-7.)   Cf. Januarius Jones in <u>SP</u>:   "The
race is weakening, degenerating: we cannot stand
nearly as much sleep as our comparatively recent
(geologically speaking of course) forefathers could
. . ." (p. 64).

181.20-27   "In a book, now, it would be kind of
terrible . . . events must never flout credulity":
Cf. Faulkner's 1925 essay "On Criticism," in which
he quotes Gerald Gould in the (English) <u>Saturday</u>
<u>Review</u>:   "It will not do to set down ordinary
speech of ordinary people; that would generally be
dull . . . .   To give the deadly detail is
misleading" (<u>EP&P</u>, p. 111).   Cf. Oscar Wilde:
"What Art really reveals to us is Nature's lack of
design, her curious crudities, her extraordinary
monotony, her absolutely unfinished condition.
. . .   Art is our spirited protest, our gallant
attempt to teach Nature her proper place" ("The
Decay of Lying" in <u>Intentions</u>, vol. V of <u>The</u>
<u>Complete</u> <u>Works</u> <u>of</u> <u>Oscar</u> <u>Wilde</u>, pp. 7-8).   Cf.
Sherwood Anderson: "[People] do not converse in
the book world as they do in life.   Scenes of the
imaginative world are not real scenes. . . .   The
life of reality is confused, disorderly, almost
always without apparent purpose, whereas in the
artist's imaginative life there is purpose" (<u>A</u>

<u>Story</u> <u>Teller's</u> <u>Story</u>, p. 291; quoted in Kreiswirth,
<u>The</u> <u>Making</u> <u>of</u> <u>a</u> <u>Novelist</u>, p. 93).

182.5 "handful of dust": Cf. "I will show you
fear in a handful of dust" (Eliot, <u>The</u> <u>Waste</u> <u>Land</u>,
1. 30).

182.20 "Grieg": Edvard Grieg (1843-1907),
Norwegian composer who wrote the incidental music
to Henrik Ibsen's <u>Peer</u> <u>Gynt</u> (1876). (See following
Note.)

182.22-23 "Ibsen and the Peer Gynt legend":
Henrik Johan Ibsen (1828-1906), Norwegian dramatist
and poet, considered the father of modern realistic
prose drama. He based <u>Peer</u> <u>Gynt</u> on a popular
Norwegian legend.

182.23-25 "a sonnet of Siegfried Sassoon's about
Sibelius that he had once read in a magazine":
Siegfried Lorraine Sassoon (1886-1967) was an
English writer and poet, best noted for his
anti-war poetry arising from his experiences in
World War I. Jean Sibelius (1865-1957) was a
Finnish composer. Cf. Faulkner's letter to his
mother from Paris (22 September 1925) in which he
refers to having heard performed "a short tone poem
of the Scandinavian composer Sibelius. It was
beautiful" (<u>Letters</u>, p. 24). Martin Kreiswirth, in
"William Faulkner and Siegfried Sassoon: An
Allusion in <u>Mosquitoes</u>" (<u>Mississippi</u> <u>Quarterly</u>, 29
[Summer 1976], 433-34), suggests that Faulkner is
referring to Sassoon's "Finn Fanatasia" in <u>The</u>
<u>Bookman</u> ([June 1921], 305), although, as he notes,
the poem is not a sonnet.

182.29 "Chopin": Frederic Francois Chopin (1810-
1849), Polish composer and pianist, whose music has
the reputation of being romantic and emotional.
(See Note 185.26-28.) Cf. Faulkner's letter to his
mother (22 September 1925) referring to the music
heard in the Luxembourg Gardens: "It's lovely, the
way the music sounds. . . . The bands play
Massenet and Chopin and Berlioz and Wagner, and the
kids are quiet, listening, and taxi drivers stop
their cars to hear it . . ." (Letters, p. 23).

183.1-2 "art also depends on population, on the

herd instinct": Cf. Elsie Clews Parsons' essay on
"Sex" in Civilization in the United States: "May
not some such theory of sex failure account also
for the herd sense which is so familiar a part of
Americanism, and which is not incompatible with the
type of self-seeking or pseudo-individualism of
which American individualism appears to be an
expression?" (p. 311).

183.10-11 "Ask any man on the street what he
understands by the word art: he'll tell you it
means a picture": Cf. Clive Bell in Art:

We live in a nice age. With the man-in-the-street
"beautiful" is more often than not synonymous with
"desirable"; the word does not necessarily connote
any aesthetic reaction whatever . . . . We are all
familiar with pictures that interest us and excite
our admiration, but do not move us as works of
art. To this class belongs what I call
"Descriptive Painting"--that is, painting in which
forms are used not as objects of emotion, but as
means of suggesting emotion or conveying
information. . . . They interest us; they may move
us too in a hundred different ways, but they do not
move us aesthe- tically. According to my
hypothesis they are not works of art [pp. 21-22].

183.13-19 "Art means anything consciously done
well . . . Art's greatest function": Cf. Sherwood
Anderson in Windy McPherson's Son, in which John
Telfer announces, "I do not paint pictures; I do
not write books; yet am I an artist. . . . I am an
artist practising the most difficult of all arts--
the art of living" (p. 14). Cf. Ludwig Lewisohn's
essay "Literature and Life" in A Modern Book of
Criticism (pp. 174-86):

. . . a civilized man reads books not to find in
them the illustration of a ready-made theory of
living which has his antecedent approval, nor that
shallow emotional stimulus to his public morality
which is known as "uplift"; nor, finally, the
optimism that comes from seeing things as they are
not. He goes to literature for life, for more life
and keener life, for life as it crystallizes into
higher articulateness and deeper significance. . .
Literature, so used, will not make men "better."

. . . But it will make them wiser and, above all,
deeper [p. 183].

183.21-24 "As rabidly American as you are . . .
the function of creating art depends on
geography": Cf. Clive Bell: "It is the mark of
great art that its appeal is universal and eternal"
(<u>Art</u>, p. 33). Cf. Joel Elias Spingarn, "The Seven
Arts and the Seven Confusions" in <u>A</u> <u>Modern</u> <u>Book</u> <u>of</u>
<u>Criticism</u> (pp. 159- 66): "Not what the poet's
environment may have been, but what he has made of
it, is what interests us in a poem. . . . To look
for a poet's power outside of his work rather than
in it, to assume that his relation to his
environment is of any concern whatever to a lover
or critic of poetry, is to confuse criticism and
sociology" (p. 161). Cf. Faulkner's 1925 essay
"Sherwood Anderson": "I can not understand our
passion in America for giving our own productions
some remote geographical significance. `Maryland'
chicken! `Roman' dressing! The `Keats' of Omaha!
Sherwood Anderson, the `American' Tolstoi! We seem
to be cursed with a passion for geographical
cliche" (<u>NOS</u>, p. 139).

183.25-30 "You can't grow corn without something
to plant it in . . . it will still grow corn":
Cf. Faulkner's 1925 essay "Sherwood Anderson," in
which he uses the symbol of corn as literature to
explain Anderson (see Note 52.7).

184.5-7 "Dawson clings to his conviction . . .
comfortable to die with": Cf. "Home": "Yours is a
comfortable belief to die with, but I am not
interested in death . . ." (<u>NOS</u>, p. 77).

184.10-15 "Clinging spiritually to one little spot
of the earth's surface . . . as trivialities in
quantities will": Although this judgment appears
to condemn the local color school of writing,
Faulkner was very early aware of the importance of
his "spot of the earth's surface." See, for
example, "Verses Old and Nascent," in which he
writes of "the beauty of being of the soil" (<u>EP&P</u>,
p. 117). Also see the 1925 "Sherwood Anderson"
essay in which he writes of Anderson's getting "his
fingers and toes . . . into the soil . . ." (<u>NOS</u>,
p. 134).

184.20 "Souls? . . . I hate that word": Cf.
Michael Arlen, <u>The</u> <u>Green</u> <u>Hat</u>: "They are so certain
about their souls, your carnal idealists! Soul,
soul, soul! May their punishment be to meet their
souls face to face in the afterworld!" (p. 102).

184.26-29 "I always did want to be one of those
old time eunuchs . . . those sultans and things
would come visiting": Cf. the Preface to
<u>Mademoiselle</u> <u>De</u> <u>Maupin</u>, in which Gautier compares
the critic to a eunuch:

He is admitted into the most sacred depths of the
Oda; he conducts the Sultanas to the bath; he sees
their beautiful bodies glistening beneath the
silver water of the great reservoirs, streaming
with pearls and smoother than agates; the most
hidden beauties are unveiled to him. His presence
is no restraint--he is a eunuch. The Sultan
caresses his favorite before him, and kisses her on
her pomegranate lips. His position is, in truth, a
very false one, and he must feel greatly
embarrassed [p. xi].

185.8-10 "It's not lovely ladies . . . disfigures
our foreheads": An allusion to the figuratively
horned forehead of the cuckold. Cf. William
Shakespeare, <u>Othello</u>, <u>the</u> <u>Moor</u> <u>of</u> <u>Venice</u>: "A
horned man's a monster and a beast" (IV, i, 64).

185.11-13 "There'd sure be a decline in population
if a man were twins . . . making love": Another
reference to both the Narcissus and the
Hermaphrodite images in the novel. (See Notes
46.1-3; 46.24-26; 46.27-29; 47.29-48.21; 251.29-30;
252.17; 252.17-19.)

185.14 "Mister Fairchild!": In the typescript,
Fairchild pursues the subject of lovemaking. He
says that women would not look so foolish in the
act as men because "there wouldn't be so much of
them in sight. And anyway, it's your backside
that's ridiculous, that gives you away, you know."
Mark Frost suggests that women could get "a
mechanical contrivance to do the work." "A small
one," Fairchild says, and then amends, "not too
small." Finally he concludes, "Yes sir, I'll
always vote for the old orthodox way: what was

good enough for my father is good enough for me"
(p. 247 of typescript.)   Cf. Januarius Jones in
<u>SP</u>: "Do you know how falcons make love?   They
embrace at an enormous height and fall locked, beak
to beak, plunging: an unbearable ectasy.   While we
have got to assume all sorts of ludicrous postures,
knowing our own sweat." (p. 227).   (See Notes
156.15; 177.19.)

185.26 "Verdi":   Guiseppe Fortunino Francesca
Verdi (1813-1901), Italian composer.

185.26-28 "Chopin . . . Snow rotting under a dead
moon":   Cf. Oscar Wilde, "The Critic as Artist":
"After playing Chopin, I feel as if I had been
weeping over sins that I had never committed, and
mourning over tragedies that were not my own"
(<u>Intentions</u>, vol. V of <u>The Complete Works of Oscar
Wilde</u>, p. 112).   Cf. "A Portrait of Elmer":
"Chopin, that sick feminine man like snow rotting
under a dead moon" (<u>Uncollected Stories</u>, p. 640).

185.32 "Debussy, George Gershwin, Berlioz":
Claude Debussy (1862-1918), French composer noted
for his impressionistic music, often based on
poetic themes such as Mallarme's <u>L'Apres-midi d'un
faune</u> (1894);   George Gershwin (1898-1937),
American composer of <u>Rhapsody in Blue</u>, which
combined elements of the classical and jazz and was
first performed in 1924; Louis Hector Berlioz
(1803-1869), French composer, critic and conductor,
associated with the Romantic movement.

186.2 "Swedenborg":   Emanuel Swedenborg (1688-
1772), Swedish scientist, philosopher, and
theologian who considered himself in touch with God
and the spirit world and felt that all creation
originated in divine love and wisdom.

186.21-24 "Talk, talk, talk: . . . sounds to be
bandied about until they were dead":   Cf. Sherwood
Anderson: "There was the voice that said words.
Words came forth from lips.   They conformed, fell
into a certain mold.   For the most part the words
had no life of their own. . . .   They had once
expressed living truth.   Then they had gone on
being said, over and over, by the lips of many
people, endlessly, wearily" ("Out of Nowhere Into

Nothing," <u>The Triumph of the Egg</u>, pp. 196-97).
(See Notes 112.23-29; 130.20-21; 130.22-31;
210.5-6; 210.12- 17.)

186.25-187.1 "Noon was oppressive as a hand . . .
soundless brazen wings rushed westward":   Cf. <u>MF</u>:

> There is no sound in all the land,
> There is no breath in all the skies.
> . . . .
> The silent noon waits over us,
> The feathers stir not on his breast
> . . . .
> Then the blackbirds wheeling through
> By Pan guarded in the skies,
> Piercing the earth with remorseless eyes
> Are burned scraps of paper cast
> On a lake quiet, deep, and vast [pp. 22-24].

Cf. the description of noon in <u>Flags</u> (pp. 94-95).
(See Note 188.8-10.)

187.11-12 "strangle your heart o israfel winged
with loneliness feathered bitter with pride":
Israfel had four wings: "one in the west, one in
the east, one with which he covers his body, and
one as a protection against the majesty of God."
He is also "covered with hair, mouths and tongues"
(<u>Shorter Encyclopedia of Islam</u>, p. 184). (See Note
48.14-15.)

187.17-19 "The road ran on . . . no escape":   See
Note 190.18-19.

188.8-10 "The sunlight was beginning to slant
. . . unheard golden wings across the sky":   Cf.
"The Priest": "How like birds with golden wings
the measured bell notes fly outward and upward
. . ." (<u>NOS</u>, p. 39).   Cf. "lights were shimmering
birds on motionless wings, bell notes in arrested
flight" (<u>SP</u>, p. 22).

189.24-28 "Then she became utterly static . . . as
young girls can":   Cf. <u>Mademoiselle De Maupin</u>:

Her easy, supple body modelled itself on mine like
wax, following its external outline with the
greatest possible accuracy. . . .   Only with a

woman in love can there be such undulations and
entwinings. Ivy and willow are a long way behind.
    The soft warmth of her body penetrated through
her garments and mine; a thousand magnetic currents
streamed around her; her whole life seemed to have
left her altogether and to have entered into me
[p. 230].

Cf. also "Rosette clasped me more and more tightly
in her arms and covered me with her body" (p. 254).
Cf. <u>Elmer</u>, in which Elmer's first sexual experience
is described as "a sort of mesmerism of enveloping
breast and a surreptituous cloudiness of thighs"
(p. 94).

190.14-15 "Her legs twinkled on ahead in the
shimmering forgotten road": Cf. Temple Drake in
<u>Sanctuary</u>: "She watched her legs twinkle against
the sand . . ." (p. 109).

190.18-19 "the shimmering endless ribbon of the
road": Cf. Alfred Noyes, "The Highwayman": "The
road was a ribbon of moonlight over the purple
moor" (<u>Collected</u> <u>Poems</u> <u>of</u> <u>Alfred</u> <u>Noyes</u>, vol. 1 [New
York: Frederick A. Stokes Co., 1913], 192). Cf.
"The road was straight and white as a swift
unrolling ribbon . . ." ("Country Mice," <u>NOS</u>,
p. 194). Cf. "the unrolling monotonous ribbon of
road" (<u>Flags</u>, p. 129).

190.29 "My heart's going too fast": Cf. Savina
Grove in <u>Cytherea</u>, who dies in Cuba of "an acute
dilation of the heart" (p. 346). (See Note
169.1-2.)

193.14 "O immaculate cherubim": The plural of
cherub, one of the second order of the angels; also
refers to a beautiful or innocent child; hence, as
his name suggests, to Fairchild's essential
innocence.

193.23 "voices without; alarums and excursions,
etc.": Typical stage directions in Elizabethan
drama. Faulkner experimented with the use of
dramatic dialogue in his earlier sketch "Peter"
(see <u>Uncollected</u> <u>Stories</u>, pp. 491-93). Gautier
also used the dramatic form in <u>Mademoiselle</u> <u>De</u>
<u>Maupin</u> on occasion. One might also note Herman

Melville's use of stage directions in _Moby-Dick_
(see Chapter 40: "Midnight, Forecastle").
Faulkner's experiment here anticipates his more
adventurous attempt to combine the dramatic and
novel forms in _Requiem for a Nun_ (New York: Random
House, 1951).

193.30-31 "Shelley could row a boat . . . what
happened to him, too":   Percy Bysshe Shelley
(1792-1822), English romantic poet, was drowned
during a storm while sailing near Leghorn, Italy, 8
July 1822.

196.12 "trimmed the boat":   To adjust the sails or
weight, or to change directions of a boat to
restore balance.

197.5 "caught a crab at every stroke":   In rowing,
to miss or skim the top of the water with a stroke
of the oar.

200.8 "All but his buttocks, that is":   Cf. the
Tall Convict in _WP_: ". . . and he scrambling still
on the bottom, still trying to scream even before
he regained his feet and still all submerged save
his plunging unmistakable buttocks, the outraged
screaming bubbling from his mouth and about his
face since he merely wanted to surrender" (pp. 173-
74).

200.23 "He--he sc-scared me so bad":   Cf. "Moonlight":   "`You sc-scared me so bad,' she said,
clinging to him" (_Uncollected Stories_, p. 503).
Cf. "The Kid Learns":   "`O-o-o-oh, he sc-scared me
s-o,' she wailed, clinging to him (_NOS_, p. 165).
Cf. Narcissa Benbow in _Flags_: "`You scared me,'
she moaned.   `You scared me so bad'" (p. 238).

202.11 "Jesus H.":   A condensation of "Jesus H.
Christ," a blasphemous oath.

202.30 "Jenny's little soft wormlike fingers":
Cf. the little Italian girl in _TS&TF_: "Her fingers
closed about them [the coins], damp and hot, like
worms" (p. 157).

204.1-2 "Dorothy Mackaill's":   Dorothy Mackaill
(1903-   ), British actress, former Ziegfeld chorine

and leading lady in American silent films.

204.20-26 "Their shapeless, merged shadow moved on
. . . a fading ghost of a forgotten passage": Cf.
"Nympholepsy": "Soon the sharp line of the hill-
crest had cut off his shadow's head; and pushing it
like a snake before him, he saw it gradually become
nothing. And at last he had no shadow at all. His
heavy shapeless shoes were gray in the dusty road,
his overalls were gray with dust: dust was like a
benediction upon him and upon the day of labor
behind him (Uncollected Stories, p. 331). (See
Note 231.23.)

205.4-206.23 "Trees without tops passed him . . .
One. Two. Three": Cleanth Brooks suggests that
this scene be compared to the "Proteus" section of
Ulysses, in which Stephen Dedalus walks along the
beach (see WF: TYB, pp. 370-71). Cf. also "Once
Aboard the Lugger (I)": The description of the
men's digging up of the contraband whiskey and that
of David's exhaustion are quite similar. See
especially the following:

My back and arms and loins ached, and whenever I
closed my eyes it seemed immediately that I was
struggling through sand that shifted and shifted
under me with patient derision, and that I still
heard the dark high breath of the sea in the pines.
     Out of this sound another sound grew, mounted
swiftly, and I raised my head and watched a red
navigating light and that pale wing of water that
seemed to have a quality of luminousness of its
own. . . . Then it was gone, the sound too died
away, and I lay back again while my muscles jerked
and twitched to the fading echo of the old striving
and the Hush   Hush   of the sea in my ears
[Uncollected Stories, p. 358].

207.8 "his fatuous Frankenstein": A reference to
the novel by Mary Wollstonecraft Shelley, Frankenstein, or the Modern Prometheus (1818). Victor
Frankenstein, a scientist, gives life to a creature
made from the parts of dead bodies. The creature
later turns against him, as Fairchild's "crew"
threatens to do here. In the novel, the monster
has no name; Faulkner mistakenly gives him the name
of his creator, a very common error.

208.5-7 "The ones that produce it . . . a whole
lot to expect in this world": Cf. Sherwood
Anderson, A Story Teller's Story:

In the movies signs were put up: "Best place in
town to kill time."
     Time then was a thing to be killed. It would
seem an odd notion, I fancy, to a Frenchman or an
Italian [p. 389].

Anderson was perhaps thinking of Charles
Baudelaire's "The Courteous Marksman":

As the carriage drove through the wood, he told the
driver to stop near a shooting gallery, remarking
that he would like to take a shot or two, to kill
Time. To kill that monster: isn't that everyone's
most usual and legitimate occupation? [Baudelaire,
Prose and Poetry, p. 73].

208.27 "Sandhurst": Sandhurst Royal Military
Academy, located in Berkshire, England, equivalent
to the U.S. Military Academy at West Point.

209.15-16 "Just because the New Republic gives him
hell--": Actually the New Republic was quite kind
to Anderson, frequently printing his articles and
usually giving him favorable book reviews. (See,
for example, the reviews of A Story Teller's Story
[5 November 1924], 255-56; Triumph of the Egg [4
March 1925], 45; and even the negative yet
sympathetic review of Many Marriages [11 April
1923], 6-8.) The harshest criticism I found of
Anderson in the magazine was a letter by Gorham
Munson concerning Anderson's article "Four American
Impressions" ([11 October 1922], 171-73). The
letter was published in the 1 November 1922 issue
and referred to Anderson's article as an
"exhibition of cerebral fat" (252). Still, the
standard judgment of Anderson in the New Republic
is typified by "The All-Star Literary Vaudeville"
([30 June 1926], 158-63), anonymously written by
Edmund Wilson, which admits Anderson's weaknesses
as a technician, seen most clearly in his novels,
but concludes that "Anderson's artistic instinct in
his best stories is almost perfect and the visions
which fill his imagination have a freshness and a
slightly discomforting strangeness which seem to be

derived from some more intimate stratum of being
than our novelists usually explore" (159).

209.17 "But the _Dial_ once bought a story of his":
In fact, the _Dial_ bought a number of Anderson's
stories, including "The Triumph of the Egg" ([March
1920], 295-304), "I'm a Fool" ([February 1922],
119-29), and "A Meeting South" ([April 1925],
269-79).   Faulkner may have been referring to this
last story, in which Anderson used him as a model
for the character David (see Note 122.14), or he
might have had the serial version of _Many Marriages_
in mind, which appeared in six consecutive issues
of the magazine (October 1922-March 1923) and which
Faulkner mistakenly thought won the _Dial_ prize (see
"Sherwood Anderson," _NOS_, p. 135).

209.20-21 "old young ladies of either sex":   Cf.
Faulkner's letter to his mother from Tunbridge
Wells, England: "This is a funny place I have got
to now.   It is a watering place where the water
tastes like hell and where earls and dukes that had
too much fun while they were young, and old women
of both sexes . . . come to drink the water"
(_Letters_, p. 30).   Cf. the dance in _SP_: "Boys of
both sexes swayed arm in arm . . ." (p. 170).   (See
Note 52.1.)

210.5-6 "Well, it's a kind of sterility--Words
. . . substitute words for things and deeds":   Cf.
Sherwood Anderson's _Marching Men_: "Why has thought
never succeeded in replacing action. . . .   Why are
the men who write books in some way less full of
meaning than the men who do things?" (p. 129).
Also, "Words mean nothing but when a man marches
with a thousand other men and is not doing it for
the glory of some king, then it will mean
something" (p. 150).   Cf. Faulkner, "American
Drama: Inhibitions":   "As a nation, we are a
people of action . . . even our language is action
rather than communication between minds . . .
employed only as a means of relief, when physical
action is impossible or unpleasant . . ." (_EP&P_,
pp. 96-97).   (See Notes 130.20-21; 186.21-24;
210.12-17.)

210.6-8 "like the withered cuckold husband that
took the Decameron to bed with him every night":

The _Decameron_ (1353) was a collection of a hundred
tales, often ribald, written by the Italian author
Giovanni Boccaccio (1313-1375). Cf. _SP_: "Who was
the old pagan who kept his Byzantine goblet at his
bedside and slowly wore away the rim kissing it?"
(p. 61). Faulkner's source for the _SP_ allusion was
Henryk Sienkiewicz's _Quo Vadis_ (1895). I have not
found a source for the similar allusion in
Mosquitoes.

210.12-17 "But words brought into a happy
conjunction . . . a tree sooner or later": Cf.
Sherwood Anderson, _Dark Laughter_: "Words--the
beginning of poetry, perhaps. The poetry of seed
hunger" (p. 60). Cf. _A Story Teller's Story_: "I
spent days going about with a tablet of paper in my
pocket and making new and strange combinations of
words. . . . Perhaps it was then I really fell in
love with words, wanted to give each word I used
every chance to show itself at its best" (p. 362).

210.18-19 "If you just talk long enough . . . the
right thing some day": Cf. Joe Gilligan in _SP_:
"It ain't knowing, it's just saying things. I
think I done it through practice. . . . I talk so
much I got to say the right thing sooner or later"
(p. 41).

211.22 "Evening came sad as horns among the
trees": Cf. _MF_: "The horns of sunset slowly
sound/Between the waiting sky and ground" (p. 28).
Cf. "A Portrait of Elmer": "Out of the secret dusk
the grave brazen notes come, overtaking the people.
. . . Yet still within the formal twilight of the
trees the bugle sounds, measured, arrogant, and
sad" (_Uncollected Stories_, p. 641). Cf. _Flags_:
"For there is death in the sound of it [the name
Sartoris], and a glamorous fatality, like silver
pennons downrushing at sunset, or a dying fall of
horns along the road to Roncevaux" (p. 370).

212.2, 9: "timeless twilight of trees"; "twilight
of their beards": The reiteration of the word
"twilight" in connection with the god-like trees in
their timeless environment is perhaps an allusion
to Ragnarok, or the "Twilight of the Gods," the day
of doom in Scandinavian mythology. After the final
battle between the gods of good and evil, during

which all will die, a regeneration will occur, a
new world repopulated. Faulkner knew Norse
mythology (see his reference to the mythical tree
Ygdrasil in _The Wishing Tree_), but he could also
have gotten this idea from Richard Wagner's epic
Der Ring des Nibelungen, the fourth opera of which
is _Gotter-_ dammerung (_The Twilight of the Gods_),
composed in 1876. The title "Twilight" was also a
working title of _The Sound and the Fury_. (See
Notes 169.19-30; 169.24-30;174.5-11.)

215.7 "flivver": A term of disparagement, usually
for a cheap, small, delapidated automobile,
although it may denote other things small of their
kind.

218.30-31 "Love itself is stone blind": Cupid,
the Roman god of love, is sometimes pictured as
blind. Cf. William Shakespeare, _The Merchant of
Venice_: "But love is blind, and lovers cannot
see/The pretty follies they themselves commit" (II,
vi, 36).

219.4-12 "Gretna Green . . . homes were
destroyed": Gretna Green is a village in Scotland
just across the English border, noted for the
runaway marriages performed there. Since parental
consent was not required, couples in England could
elope to Gretna Green until an act of Parliment
abolished the practice in 1856 by declaring any
marriage illegal unless one of the partners had
lived in the village for 21 days. In 1940 all such
irregular marriages were declared illegal. The
term "Gretna Green" came to apply to any town which
allowed easy marriages. Cf. Faulkner's poem
"Co-Education At Old Miss":

       An lov'st thou me
       As I love thee,
Let's off to Gretna Green--O [_EP&P_, p. 77].

219.23 "Yokohama": The capitol of Kanagawa on the
island of Honshu, Japan. It lies on Tokyo Bay and
serves as an international seaport. Yokohama was
almost completely destroyed by an earthquake and
fire in 1923.

219.25-27 "Like whitebait . . . sardines": There

is apparently a good deal of nonsense talk going on
in this passage, to the bewilderment of the reader
as well as Talliaferro.

221.13-14 "Virginity don't make any difference as
far as the body's concerned": Cf. "The Priest":
"And he wondered how many priests leading chaste
lives relieving human suffering, were virgin, and
whether or not the fact of virginity made any
difference" (<u>Uncollected</u> <u>Stories</u>, p. 350). Cf.
<u>TS&TF</u>: "Purity is a negative state and therefore
contrary to nature. It's nature is hurting you not
Caddy and I said That's just words and he said So
is virginity . . ." (p. 143).

222.4-6 "They are such practical creatures . . .
hold to conventions for moral reasons": Cf. <u>SP</u>:
"Men are the ones who worry about our good names,
because they gave them to us. But we have other
things to bother about, ourselves. What you mean
by a good name is like a dress that's too flimsy to
wear comfortable" (pp. 104-105). Cf. <u>TS&TF</u>:
"Because it means less to women, Father said. He
said it was men invented virginity not women"
(p. 96).

226.2 "Golconda of her hair": Golconda was a
fortress in India, built of concentric walls. It
was celebrated for the diamonds which were cut
there, and the word came to represent a place or
thing of wealth.

228.1 "But people do not die of love": Cf.
Michael Arlen, <u>The</u> <u>Green</u> <u>Hat</u>: "If people died of
love I must have risen from the dead to be driving
this car now" (p. 268). Cf. <u>SP</u>: "Men have died
and worms have eaten them, but not for love"
(p. 318).

228.6-13 "Lucky he who believes that his heart is
broken. . . . You write a book": Faulkner is
almost certainly commenting here on his own
relationship with Helen Baird (see Note to
Dedication and Note 145.7-8). According to Carvel
Collins, he went so far as to propose marriage to
her, although she apparently cared little for him
(see Introduction to <u>Mayday</u>, p. 10). The irony of
their relationship was underlined when Helen

married Guy Lyman on 4 May 1927, the same week in
which _Mosquitoes_ was published (30 April 1927).
(See Blotner, I, 549.) Also, her reaction to
Mosquitoes would not have given Faulkner a sense of
satisfaction: Blotner records that Helen told her
friend Ann Farnsworth, "Don't read it. . . . It's
no good" (I, 549).

228.22-24 "No excuses . . . postwar young folks
have taught us": Cf. Harold E. Stearns, "The
Intellectual Life":

The most hopeful thing of intellectual promise in
America to-day is the contempt of the younger
people for their elders; they are restless, uneasy,
disaffected. It is not a disciplined contempt; it
is not yet kindled by any real love of intellectual
values--how could it be? Yet it is a genuine and
moving attempt to create a way of life free from
the bondage of an authority that has lost all
meaning, even to those who wield it.

(_Civilization_ in _the_ _United_ _States_, p. 149).

228.24-229.7 "Only old folks . . . hold each
other's hands": Cf. Michael Arlen, _The_ _Green_ _Hat_:

Above all things in this world I love the love that
people have for each other, the real, immense,
unquestioning, devouring, worshipful love that now
and then I have seen in a girl for a boy, that now
and then I have seen in a boy for a girl, that
playmate love. It isn't of this world, that
playmate love, it's of a larger world than ours, a
better world, a world of dreams which aren't
illusions but the very pillars of a better life.
But in our world all dreams are illusions, and that
is why the angels have crowsfeet round their eyes,
because they are peering to see why all dreams in
our world should be illusions [p. 142].

Cf. _SP_: "It is jealousy, I think, which makes us
wish to prevent young people doing the things we
had not the courage or the opportunity ourselves to
accomplish once, and have not the power to do now"
(p. 59).

229.27-28 "squads of K. K. K.'s beating the

surrounding copses": The Ku Klux Klan was
originally a secret organization formed in Pulaski,
Tennessee, in 1867, by a small group of Southern
veterans to resist Northern reconstruction
policies. It became known as the "Invisible Empire
of the South." In the 1920's, it experienced a
strong resurgance of popularity nationwide, by
which time its policies were largely associated
with racial and religious bigotry. (See David
Chalmers, <u>Hooded</u> <u>Americanism</u>: <u>The</u> <u>First</u> <u>Century</u> <u>of</u>
<u>the</u> <u>Ku</u> <u>Klux</u> <u>Klan</u> <u>1865-1965</u> [Garden City, N. Y.:
Doubleday & Company, Inc., 1965], pp. 8-21, 28-38.)

230.10 "John Held": John Held, Jr. (1889-1958),
American cartoonist and illustrator whose drawings
of the 1920's helped to establish the stereotype of
the jazz age "flappers" and "jelly beans." His
work often appeared in <u>Liberty</u> and <u>The</u> <u>New</u> <u>Yorker</u>.
The style of Faulkner's early drawings shows Held's
strong influence.

231.13-15 "Sex and death . . . shadow is life":
Cf. <u>SP</u>: "Sex and death: the front door and the
back door of the world. . . . In youth they lift
us out of the flesh, in old age they reduce us
again to the flesh; one to fatten us, the other to
flay us, for the worm" (p. 295).

231.23 "life is a kind of antic shadow": Possible
reference to William Shakespeare's <u>Macbeth</u>:
"Life's but a walking shadow, a poor player/That
struts and frets his hour upon the stage/And then
is heard no more" (V, v, 24-26).

231.25-26 "I have a kind of firm belief that life
is all right": Cf. "Out of Nazarath": "But seeing
him [the David character] in his sorry clothes,
with his clean young face and his beautiful faith
that life, the world, the race, is somewhere good
and sound and beautiful, is good to see" (<u>NOS</u>,
p. 110).

231.29-234.28 "I was spending the summer . . .
youth and love, and time and death": Fairchild's
story apparently had its source in a childhood
adventure of William Spratling, which he recounts
in his autobiography <u>File</u> <u>on</u> <u>Spratling</u> (pp. 14-15).
Cleanth Brooks feels that the story is assigned to

Fairchild because "such an anecdote fits the
character of Fairchild much better than it fits the
character of Gordon" (<u>WF</u>: <u>TYB</u>, p. 140). However,
Faulkner may also have had in mind Anderson's fine
story of Judge Turner in <u>A</u> <u>Story</u> <u>Teller's</u> <u>Story</u>
(pp. 159-83), specifically the episode of the
outhouse (pp. 168-69), which presents an effective
counterpoint to the Spratling story.

232.23 "burdocks": Coarse, weedy plants with
large leaves and prickly burs.

234.1-2 "Arcturus, Orion . . . an electirc
lobster": Arcturus, named for the son of Poseidon,
is a star of the first magnitude in the constellation Bootes. Orion is the name of another constellation which is represented as a hunter. The
"electric lobster" apparently refers to Scorpius, a
constellation in the southern part of the heavens.
Cf. T. S. Eliot's "Sweeney Among the
Nightingales": "Gloomy Orion and the Dog/Are
veiled; and hushed the shrunken seas" (<u>Poems</u>, pp.
61-62). Cf. also "The Priest": "Orion through the
starry meadows strays, the creaking Wain breaks
darkly through the Milky Way's faint dewed grass"
(<u>NOS</u>, p. 39). Cf. "Once Aboard the Lugger (I)":
"Though I had not seen him moving, Orion was down
beyond the high pines and the moon was gone"
(<u>Uncollected</u> <u>Stories</u>, p. 358). Cf. Poem III in <u>GB</u>:

     The sleeping gate wakes yawning back upon
     Where gaunt Orion, swinging by his knees,
     Crashes the arcing moon among the stars [p. 19].

235.13-16 "It was a slipper . . . that hard and
sexless graveness of hers": The image of the lost
or castaway slipper is a recurring one in early
Faulkner works. Cf. Pierrot in <u>The Marionettes</u>,
who is found asleep as the play opens, "a bottle
and an overturned wine glass upon the table, a
mandoline and a woman's slipper lie at his feet"
(p. 2). Cf. Benjy in <u>TS&TF</u>: "<u>In the corner it was
dark, but I could see the window. I squatted
there, holding the slipper. I couldn't see it, but
my hand saw it, and I could hear it getting night,
and my hands saw the slipper but I couldn't see
myself, but my hands could see the slipper, and I
squatted there, hearing it getting dark</u>" (pp. 88-

89). Cf. Tommy in <u>Sanctuary</u>, who is fascinated by
Temple Drake's shoe (pp. 106, 109). Faulkner could
very likely have had the story of Cinderella in
mind for this important image (see Note 118.5-6).

236.9-15 "Dear Mr. Fairchild . . . David West":
Cf. the prose poem given the narrator by the David
figure in "Out of Nazareth": "And this is what he
gave me. There is bad punctuation here, and mis-
spelling: there is one word I have never deci-
phered. But to correct it would ruin it" (<u>NOS</u>,
pp. 105-106).

237.21-239.5 See Note 193.23.

238.30 "Her screams . . . among her chins": Cf.
"Mrs. Marders sat now with her slack chins in a
raised teacup" (<u>Flags</u>, p. 174).

239.20-21 "Chastity . . . lack of opportunity":
See Notes 221.13-14; 222.4-6.

239.24-240.1 "Maybe we all have different ideas of
sex . . . to an American, a horserace": Cf.
Faulkner's letter from Paris to his mother (22
September 1925):

After having observed Americans in Europe I believe
more than ever that sex with us has become a
national disease. The way we get it into our
politics and religion, where it does not belong
anymore than digestion belongs there. All our
paintings, our novels, our music, is concerned with
it, sort of leering and winking and rubbing hands
on it. But Latin people keep it where it belongs,
in a secondary place. Their painting and music and
literature has nothing to do with sex. Far more
healthy than our way [<u>Letters</u>, p. 24].

240.8-11 "Do you remember . . . Anna Held and Eva
Tanguay with shapes like elegant parlor lamp
chimneys?": Eva Tanguay (1878-1947) and Anna Held
(1865-1918) were leading musical comedy stars in
the <u>Ziegfeld</u> <u>Follies</u>. Anna Held married Florenz
Ziegfeld (1867-1932), the man most responsible for
the growth of the musical theater in America. She
is said to have given him the idea for the <u>Follies</u>,
and she starred in the first of them, the <u>Follies</u>

<u>of</u> <u>1907</u>. Marjorie Farnsworth, in <u>The</u> <u>Ziegfeld</u>
<u>Follies</u> (London: Peter Davies, 1956), described
Held as follows: "Actually Anna was not a striking
beauty. She had a plump little figure laced in at
the waist until the hips jutted out horizontally.
Her hand-spanned eighteen-inch waist was later to
become the envy of the ladies in the audience
. . . To Americans she was the epitome of Gallic
spice and naughtiness" (quoted in William C. Young,
<u>Famous</u> <u>Actors</u> <u>and</u> <u>Actresses</u> <u>on</u> <u>the</u> <u>American</u> <u>Stage</u>
[New York: R. R. Bowker Company, 1975], I, 497).
Cf. Carl Sandburg's poem "An Electric Sign Goes
Dark," which deals with the death of Anna Held and
which contains images echoed in <u>Mosquitoes</u>:

> A voice, a shape, gone.
> A baby bundle from Warsaw . . . legs, torso, head
>   . . . on a hotel bed at The Savoy.
> . . . .
> She belonged to somebody, nobody.
> No one man owned her, no ten nor a thousand.
> She belonged to many thousand men, lovers of the
>   white chiselling of arms and shoulders, the
>   ivory of a laugh, the bells of song.

(<u>Selected</u> <u>Poems</u> <u>of</u> <u>Carl</u> <u>Sandburg</u>, ed. Rebecca West
[New York: Harcourt, Brace and Company, 1926], pp.
232-33. See also Gorham B. Munson, "The Single
Portent of Carl Sandburg," <u>The</u> <u>Double</u> <u>Dealer</u>, VII
[October 1924], 17-26, which discusses this poem
and could possibly have brought it to Faulkner's
attention.)

240.19 "cambric drawers": Underwear made of fine
white linen.

240.26-241.10 "Not stupid . . . you can give all
your attention to their bodies": Cf. d'Albert in
<u>Mademoiselle</u> <u>De</u> <u>Maupin</u>:

I consider women, after the manner of the ancients,
as a beautiful slave designed for our pleasure.
Christianity has not rehabilitated her in my eyes.
To me she is still something dissimilar and
inferior that we worship and play with, a toy which
is more intelligent than if it were of ivory or
gold, and which gets up of itself if we let it
fall. I have been told, in consequence of this,

that I think badly of women; I consider, on the
contrary, that it is thinking very well of them
                                        [p. 137].

Cf. Faulkner's letter to Anita Loos concerning
<u>Gentlemen</u> <u>Prefer</u> <u>Blondes</u>: "I am still rather
Victorian in my prejudices regarding the
intelligence of women, despite Elinor Wylie and
Willa Cather and all the balance of them" (<u>Letters</u>,
p. 32). Cf. his letter to Horace Liveright quoted
in Note to Dedication: "You can lie to women, you
know, but you cant break promises you make 'em.
That infringes on their own province" (<u>Letters</u>,
p. 34). Cf. <u>SP</u>: "As far as the kiss itself goes,
women do not particularly care who does the
kissing. All they are interested in is the kiss
itself" (p. 75).

241.26-28 "There's a man . . . sophisticated
emotions": This criticism of Fairchild is typical
of those made of Anderson. Cf. "Anderson himself
is frequently inarticulate, adolescent. There is
no possibility of clearness, of coherence, where
the thoughts themselves are incoherent . . .
everywhere the baffled expression, the
acknowledgement of limitation. And at the same
time the urge to comprehend" (N. Bryllion Fagin,
"Sherwood Anderson and Our Anthropological Age,"
<u>The</u> <u>Double</u> <u>Dealer</u>, VII [January-February 1925],
94-95). Cf. Rexford Guy Tugwell's review of <u>Dark</u>
<u>Laughter</u> (<u>New</u> <u>Republic</u>, 45 [9 December 1925], 88):
"This fellow Anderson, it seems, has written
another book. . . . What would it be that he would
make or do with those ruthless, fumbling, inept
hands of his this time? Something that must be
attended to, so much had always been, somehow,
known . . . challenging, dumb, inert, but not for
an instant to be ignored." Faulkner himself
referred to Anderson's "halting questioning manner"
in his 1925 essay "Sherwood Anderson" (<u>NOS</u>, p.
136); and, indeed, Anderson admitted to this
quality in his work: "There were in my head
certain tales I knew but could not yet tell and
certain others I had told but felt I had told badly
or haltingly. Was there a certain formula one
could learn that might help one out of the
difficulty?" (<u>A</u> <u>Story</u> <u>Teller's</u> <u>Story</u>, p. 351).
(See Note 209.15-16.)

241.32-33 "having been born . . . lower middle
class family": Anderson was born in Clyde, Ohio,
and gives a lengthy account of his childhood in _A
Story Teller's Story_. William Sutton has written
of Anderson's family: "The soundest view of the
position of the Anderson family in Clyde seems to
be that conditions, though at times difficult, were
seldom if ever desperate. . . . It was assuredly a
hard life, but it was not so hard that Sherwood's
imagination could not harden it still more" (_Road
to Winesburg_, p. 20).

242.12-13 "Emersons and Lowells": Ralph Waldo
Emerson (1803-1882) and James Russell Lowell
(1819-1891), used as examples of the genteel New
England literary tradition. Anderson wrote of
these men and their school of thought in _A Story
Teller's Story_:

A few English came and settled in that far-away
frozen northeast corner--New England--and their
sons did the book-writing and the school-teaching.
They did not get themselves--physically--as
breeders--very deeply into the new blood of the
land, but they made their notion of what we are and
of what we are to be stick pretty well.
     In time, however, the basic cultural feeling
of the land must change too. Mind cannot persist
without body. Blood will tell.
     And in my own time I was to see the grip of
the old New England, the Puritanic culture, begin
to loosen. The physical incoming of the Celts,
Latins, Slavs, men of the Far East, the blood of
the dreaming nations of the world gradually flowing
thicker and thicker in the body of the American,
and the shrewd shop-keeping money-saving blood of
the northern men getting thinner and thinner [p.
101].

242.14-18 "who `seated on chairs' . . . ubiquitous
watchfulness": I have been unable to find the
source of these quotations. However, George
Santayana expressed a very similar idea in much the
same terms in "The Genteel Tradition in American
Philosophy" and Faulkner may have had this thought
in mind: "Emerson had no system; and his coveting
truth had another exceptional consequence: he was
detached, unworldly, contemplative. When he came

out of the conventicle or the reform meeting, or
out of the rapturous close atmosphere of the
lecture-room, he heard nature whispering to him:
`Why so hot, little sir?'" (<u>Winds</u> <u>of</u> <u>Doctrine</u>,
p. 199).

243.4-13 "He need only let himself go . . . it
will become eternal and timeless despite him": Cf.
Clive Bell: "It is the mark of great art that its
appeal is universal and eternal" (<u>Art</u>, p. 33). Cf.
Joel E. Spingarn, "Scholarship and Civilization" in
<u>Civilization</u> <u>in</u> <u>the</u> <u>United</u> <u>States</u> (pp. 93-108):

To the creative writers of America . . . I should
say . . .: "Express what is in you, all that
serene or turbulent vision of multitudinous life
which is yours by right of imagination, trusting in
your own power to achieve discipline and mastery,
and leave the discussion of `American ideals' to
statesmen, historians, and philosophers, with the
certainty that if you truly express the vision that
is in you, the statesmen, historians, and
philosophers of the future will point to your work
as a fine expression of the `American ideals' you
have helped to create" [p. 105].

(See Note 243.14-22.)

243.11 "Balzac": Honore de Balzac (1799-1850),
French novelist famed for his <u>La</u> <u>Comedie</u> <u>Humaine</u>, a
series of inter-related novels, novellas and short
stories. Balzac had been a favorite author of
Faulkner's since childhood and was an important
influence on him as a writer. (See Blotner, I,
110, 160, 192.)

243.14-22 "Life everywhere is the same . . .
pleasures which we probably will not achieve": Cf.
Randolph Bourne, "A Literary Radical" in <u>A</u> <u>Modern</u>
<u>Book</u> <u>of</u> <u>Criticism</u> (pp. 206-10):

The American has to work to interpret and portray
the life he knows. He cannot be international in
the sense that anything but the life in which he is
soaked with its questions and its colors, can be
the material for his art. But he can be
international--and must be--in the sense that he
works with a certain hopeful vision of a "young

world," and with certain ideal values upon which
the younger men, stained and revolted by war, in
all countries are agreeing [pp. 209-10].

Cf. Faulkner's comments in "American Drama:
Inhibitions":

Sound art, however, does not depend on the quality
or quantity of available material: a man with real
ability finds sufficient what he has to hand.
Material does aid that person who does not possess
quite enough driving force to create living figures
out of his own brain; wealth of material does
enable him to build better than he otherwise could
[<u>EP&P</u>, p. 94].

(See Note 243.4-13.)

245.4-5 "<u>Satyricon</u> <u>in</u> <u>Starlight</u>": The <u>Satyricon</u>,
written by Petronius Arbiter (?-65 A.D.), was a
bawdy, satirical, picaresque tale of the adventures
of Encolpius and Ascyltus. The most famous episode
of the work was the "Banquet of Trimalchio," which
ridiculed the ways of the rich, an idea echoed in
<u>Mosquitoes</u>. In naming Mrs. Wiseman's book,
Faulkner may have intended a connection between the
sexual proclivities described in Petronius's work
and those suggested in <u>Mosquitoes</u>.

245.20-29 "Nowadays the gentle art . . . dine with
whoever will invite you": Cf. Conrad Aiken,
"Poetry" in <u>Civilization</u> <u>in</u> <u>the</u> <u>United</u> <u>States</u> (pp.
215-26):

Lawlessness has seemed at times to be the
prevailing note; no poetic principle has remained
unchallenged. . . . Ugliness and shapelessness
have had their adherents among those whom aesthetic
fatigue had rendered momentarily insensitive to the
well-shaped; the fragmentary has had its adherents
among those whom cynicism had rendered incapable of
any sevice, too prolonged, to one idea. But the
fetichists of the ugly and the fragmentary have
exerted, none the less, a wholesome and fructifying
influence. Whatever we feel about the ephemerality
of the specifically ugly or fragmentary, we cannot
escape a feeling that these, almost as importantly
as the new realism or the new colourism, have

enlarged what we might term the general "poetic
consciousness" of the time [p. 224].

(See Note 321.26-30.)

246.5-8 "I'd intersperse my book with photographs
. . . across their middles": Cf. Anderson's <u>The
Triumph</u> <u>of</u> <u>the</u> <u>Egg</u>, which is introduced by a series
of photographs by Eugene Hutchinson of grotesque
clay figures made by Anderson's second wife,
Tennessee Mitchell. Cf. Charlotte Rittenmeyer in
<u>WP</u>: "It was one of the men whom McCord had
brought, a photographer. She was to make puppets,
marionettes, and he to photograph them for magazine
covers and advertisements . . ." (p. 90).

246.22-24 "to have your infancy darkened . . .
Great American Novel": Cf. an omitted section of <u>A
Story</u> <u>Teller's</u> <u>Story</u>: "I am sure there is not a
scribbler in America but that, upon seeing in print
his publisher's announcement that he has just
written The Great American Novel, is first glad and
then strangely sick inside himself" (<u>A Story
Teller's</u> <u>Story</u>: <u>A Critical</u> <u>Text</u>, ed. Ray Lewis
White, p. 285). Cf. Joel E. Spingarn, "Scholarship
and Criticism" in <u>Civilization</u> <u>in</u> <u>the</u> <u>United
States</u>: "The idea that great national energy must
inevitably flower in a great literature, and that
our wide-flung power must certainly find expression
in an immortal poem or in the `great American
novel,' is merely another example of our mechanical
optimism" (p. 93).

246.31-247.13 "On rose and peach their droppings
bled . . . To another sing, and close--": Cf. Poem
XXVII in <u>GB</u>. Butterworth lists typescript versions
of this poem dated "February 26, 1925" and "1 March
1925" (see "Census of . . . William Faulkner's
Poetry," 347). There are slight variants between
the poem in the <u>Mosquitoes</u> typescript and that in
the published novel. Cf. T. S. Eliot's "Sweeney
Among the Nightingales":

   The nightingales are singing near
   The Convent of the Sacred Heart,

   And sang within the bloody wood
   When Agamemnon cried aloud,

    And let their liquid siftings fall
    To stain the stiff dishonoured shroud
         [_Poems_, pp. 61-62, 11. 35-40].

247.6 "Philomel": In Greek mythology, the
daughter of Pandion, a king of Athens. She is
raped by Tereus, her brother-in-law, who then cuts
out her tongue and hides her in a forest to prevent
her telling of the outrage. In the Roman version
of the myth, she is turned into a nightingale (see
Ovid's _Metamorphoses_, Book VI). Cf. Eliot's _The
Waste Land_:

    Above the antique mantel was displayed
       . . . .
    The change of Philomel, by the barbarous king
    So rudely forced . . .[pp. 69-70].

247.16-26 "Mostly words . . . love and death":
See Note 245.20-29.

247.29-248.4 "But women have done some good things
. . . the vagaries of the child?": Cf. "The
Ephemeral Sex" (_The Double Dealer_, I [March 1921],
84-85): "We have, dear girls, no contention to
make with your sex. As a sex you are a delight and
a necessity. As mothers, wives and mistresses, you
are beyond compare, but, as creative artists, we
reaffirm, complete failures, pathetic nonentities"
(85).

248.5 "Tom o' Bedlam's": A fool or madman. In
King Lear, a disguise taken by Edgar to be near his
father, the Earl of Gloucester.

248.14-16 "It's a kind of dark thing. . . . Will
you enter that room, or not?": Cf. _A Story
Teller's Story_: "There is a world into which no
one but myself has ever entered and I would like to
take you there; but how often when I go, filled
with confi- dence, to the very door leading into
that strange world, I find it locked!" (p. 121).

248.20-21 "There are rooms, dark rooms . . . .
Freud and these other--": Sigmund Freud (1856-
1939), the founder of psychoanalysis, which
emphasizes the effect of the unconscious and the
force of instinctive drives on conscious actions

(see Note 9.4 "The sex instinct"; 250.3-6; 251.29-30).

249.5-7 "we all wrote poetry . . . all of us wrote it": Cf. <u>Mademoiselle</u> <u>De</u> <u>Maupin</u>: "The best part of us is that which remains within us, and which we cannot bring forth. It is so with poets. Their finest poem is the one that they have not written; they carry away more poems in their coffins than they leave in their libraries" (p. 102).

249.10-18 "˘. . . O spring O wanton O cruel . . . perplexed with pleasure . . .'": Cf. Poem IV of <u>GB</u>:

                    o spring
above unsapped convolvulae of hills april
a bee sipping perplexed with pleasure o spring
o wanton o cruel [p. 21].

Butterworth identifies one typescript of this poem under the title "Guidebook," dated "Paris/27 Aug 1925" (see "Census . . . of William Faulkner's Poetry," 340).

249.25 "It's a kind of fire, you know": Cf. <u>Cyrano</u> <u>de</u> <u>Bergerac</u>:

   Yes, that is Love--that wind
   Of terrible and jealous beauty, blowing
   Over me--that dark fire, that music . . .
[p. 169].

Cf. Walter Pater's "hard, gemlike flame" (see Note 48.12). Cf. "The Artist": "A dream and a fire which I cannot control, driving me without those comfortable smooth paths of solidity and sleep which nature has decreed for man. A fire which I inherited willy-nilly, and which I must needs feed with talk and youth and the very vessel which bears the fire . . ." (<u>NOS</u>, p. 47).

250.3-6 "I believe that every word . . . the nature of women": Cf. Freud, "The Development of the Symptoms":

The artist is an incipient introvert who is not far from being a neurotic. He is impelled by too

powerful instinctive needs. He wants to achieve
honor, power, riches, fame and the love of women.
But he lacks the means of achieving these satisfac-
tions. So . . . he turns away from reality, and
transfers all his interests, his libido, too, to
the elaboration of his imaginary wishes . . .

(A General Introduction to Psychoanalysis, trans.
by G. Stanley Hall [New York: Boni & Liveright,
1920], p. 326)

(See Notes 228.6-13; 248.20-21; 251.29-30.)

250.6-12 "Well, maybe she ain't always a flesh and
blood creature . . . you can only generalize from
results": Cf. d'Albert in Mademoiselle De Maupin:

How could a real woman, eating and drinking,
getting up in the morning and going to bed at
night, however adorable and full of charms she
might otherwise be, compare with a creature such as
this? It could not reasonably be expected, and yet
it is expected and sought. What strange blindness!
It is sublime or absurd. How I pity and how I
admire those who pursue their dream in the teeth of
all reality, and die content if they have but once
kissed the lips of their chimera! But what a
fearful fate is that of a Columbus who has failed
to discover his world, and of a lover who has not
found his mistress! [p. 23].

250.28-31 "The trouble with modern verse . . . the
poet himself has recently passed": Cf. Crome
Yellow, in which Scogan discusses the necessity to
"feel the same emotions as the authors felt when
they were writing" in order to understand the work
(p. 260). Cf. Faulkner's comment that "I have
written a poem so modern that I dont know myself
what it means" (Letters, p. 17). (See Note 245.20-
29.)

251.9-10 "esthetic Israelites . . . pink sea of
dullness and security": Cf. Exodus 14:26-31: "But
the children of Israel walked upon dry land in the
midst of the sea; and the waters were a wall unto
them on their right hand, and on their left"
(Exodus 14:29).

251.22 "Dr. Ellis": Havelock Ellis (1859-1939),
English psychologist and author who was best known
for his writings on sexual psychology in <u>Studies</u> <u>in</u>
<u>the</u> <u>Psychology</u> <u>of</u> <u>Sex</u>, 7 vols. (1897-1928). (See
Arthur Symons, "An Appreciation of Havelock Ellis,"
<u>The</u> <u>Double</u> <u>Dealer</u>, III [February 1922], 78-83.)
(See Note 94.3.)

251.25 "Ashur-bani-pal's stallion": Ashurbanipal
ruled as the greatest warrior-king of Assyria
(669-626 B.C.) and led his people in two attempted
conquests of Egypt. He was also noted as a patron
of letters, and his library at Neneveh has formed
the basis of what is now known about ancient
Assyria. In Greek literature he was known as
Sardanapalus and was pictured as an effeminate
debaucher, a womanish king who dressed in female
attire and secluded himself with concubines,
unmindful of his country's safety. However, when
finally forced to fight an invading army, he threw
off this attire and bravely but futilely led his
men against the enemy. To avoid capture, he
ordered himself and his concubines burned alive on
a great pyre. This legendary view of Ashurbanipal
is recounted in Frazer's <u>The</u> <u>Golden</u> <u>Bough</u> (IX,
387-88), and it is this image that Faulkner seems
to suggest to support his theme of "Emotional
bisexuality." A reference to Sardanapalus appears
in <u>Mademoiselle</u> <u>De</u> <u>Maupin</u>: "I am as weary as if I
had gone through all the prodigalities of
Sardanapalus . . ." (p. 90). Faulkner could have
also known the story from Byron's poetic drama
<u>Sardanapalus</u>: <u>A</u> <u>Tragedy</u> (1821).

251.29-30 "A book is the writer's secret life, the
dark twin of a man": Cf. Freud's "The Development
of the Symptoms": "If one is a real artist . . .
he understands how to elaborate his day dreams so
that they lose their essentially personal element,
which would repel strangers, and yield satisfaction
to others as well. He also knows how to disguise
them so that they do not easily disclose their
origin in their despised sources" (<u>A</u> <u>General</u>
<u>Introduction</u>, p. 327). (See Notes 9.4 "The sex
instinct"; 248.20- 21; 250.3-6.)

252.3-16 "ˋLips that of thy weary all . . . it
cannot break'": Cf. Poem XXXVII in <u>GB</u> (p. 61).

There is a slightly different version of this poem
in the typescript of Mosquitoes. Butterworth lists
several typescript copies of this poem entitled
"Hermaphroditus" (see "Census . . . of William
Faulkner's Poetry," 341). (See following Note.)

252.17 "Hermaphroditus": In Greek mythology, the
son of Hermes and Aphrodite. He was fused with the
nymph Salmakis into a creature with both male and
female attributes (see Note 46.27-29). The figure
of the Hermaphrodite became a favorite subject of
Greek sculptors from the 4th Century B.C. onwards
(see H. J. Rose, A Handbook of Greek Mythology [New
York: E. P. Dutton & Co., Inc., 1959], p. 148).
Cf. Mademoiselle De Maupin, in which d'Albert
describes the feminine Theodore in terms of the
Hermaphrodite, a description Faulkner may have
remembered in composing the poem:

Since the time of Christ there has not been a
single human statue in which adolescent beauty has
been idealised and represented with the care that
characterises the ancient sculptors. Woman has
become the symbol of moral and physical beauty:
man has really fallen from the day that the infant
was born at Bethlehem. . . . Previous to the
gentle and worthy narrator of parables, it was
quite the opposite; gods or heroes were not made
feminine when it was wished to make them charming;
they had their own type, at once vigorous and
delicate, but always male, however smooth and
destitute of muscles and veins the workman might
have made their divine legs and arms. He was more
ready to bring the special beauty of woman into
accordance with this type. . . . There is scarcely
any difference between Paris and Helen. And so the
hermaphrodite was one of the most eagerly cherished
chimeras of idolatrous antiquity.
This son of Hermes and Aphrodite is, in fact,
one of the sweetest creations of Pagan genius.
Nothing in the world can be imagined more ravishing
than these two bodies, harmoniously blended
together and both perfect, these two beauties so
equal and so different, forming but one superior to
both, because they are reciprocally tempered and
improved. To an exclusive worshipper of form, can
there be a more delightful uncertainity than that
into which you are thrown by the sight of the back,

the ambiguous loins, and the strong, delicate legs,
which you are doubtful whether to attribute to
Mercury ready to take his flight or to Diana coming
forth from the bath? [pp. 143-44].

Cf. also Oscar Wilde, <u>The</u> <u>Burden</u> <u>of</u> <u>Itys</u>:

Who is not boy or girl and yet is both,
        Fed by two fires and unsatisfied
Through their excess, each passion being loath
        For love's own sake to leave the other's side,
Yet killing love by slaying, memories
Of Oreads peeping through the leaves of silent
                                        moonlit trees

(<u>Poems</u>, Vol. I of <u>The</u> <u>Complete</u> <u>Works</u> <u>of</u> <u>Oscar</u>
<u>Wilde</u>, p. 90. Noted by Michael Millgate in <u>The</u>
<u>Achievement</u> <u>of</u> <u>William</u> <u>Faulkner</u>, p. 300.) (See
Following Note.)

252.17-19 "It's a kind of dark perversion . . .
lives on its own heat": Cf. J. K. Huysmans,
<u>La-Bas</u>, in which Durtal has discovered a "new sin":
"Pygmalionism, which embraces at the same time
cerebral onanism and incest." As Durtal explains
it, Pygmalionism occurs when "the father violates
the child of his soul, of that which alone is
purely and really his, which alone he can
impregnate without the aid of another. . . . This
cerebral hermaphrodism, self-fecundation, is a
distinguished vice . . . being the privilege of the
artist--a vice reserved for the elect, inaccessable
to the mob" (trans. by Keene Wallace [New York:
Dover Books Inc., 1972], pp. 171-72). (See Notes
26.24-26; 46.24-26; 252.17.)

252.22-26 "Kind of like men nowadays are not
masculine and lusty enough . . . men too feminine
to beget": Cf. Sherwood Anderson, <u>A</u> <u>Story</u> <u>Teller's</u>
<u>Story</u>: "In the factories so many of the workers
spent so large a part of their time boasting of
their sexual effectiveness. Was that because they
felt themselves every year growing more and more
ineffectual as men? Were modern women going more
and more toward man's life and man's attitude
toward life because they were becoming all the time
less and less able to be women?" (p. 376). Cf. the
"Circe" section of <u>Ulysses</u>, in which Leopold Bloom

is declared "bisexually abnormal" and becomes "a
finished example of the new womanly man" (p. 493).
Cf. Harold E. Stearns, in his essay "The
Intellectual Life" (Civilization in the United
States, pp. 135-50): He argues that "the things of
the mind and the spirit have been given over in
America, into the almost exclusive custody of
women. This has been true certainly of art,
certainly of music, certainly of education. . . .
Where men and women in America to-day share their
intellectual life on terms of equality and perfect
understanding, closer examination reveals that the
phenomenon is not a sharing but a capitulation.
The men have been feminized" (pp. 141-42). (See
Notes 52.1; 209.20-21.)

255.1-2 "I'm so unlucky . . . things--things
happen to me, you see": An early version of Temple
Drake's disclaimer of responsibility in Sanctuary:
"Something is happening to me!" (p. 122).

257.28 "Dwight or Osborne hall": Dwight and
Osborne Halls are buildings on the Yale campus.
Osborne was the location of the student YMCA and
used as headquarters for incoming freshmen to meet
upperclassmen.

258.5 "you can haul out the family sock on it":
You can bet money, kept in the family sock, on it.

258.10-11 "like a stereopticon slide flashed on
the screen": A stereoptican is a hand-held optical
instrument in which a slide with two almost
identical pictures parallel on it is placed before
a lens, resulting in the appearance of three-
dimensionality. Cf. "But as if a magic lantern
threw the nerves in patterns on a screen" (Eliot,
"Prufrock," Poems, p. 11).

262.21-22 "the negro sat . . . eating of a large
grayish object": Cf. the fireman in Heart of
Darkness: "He was an improved specimen; he could
fire up a verticle boiler. He was there below me,
and, upon my word, to look at him was as edifying
as seeing a dog in a parody of breeches and a
feather hat, walking on his hind legs" (p. 118) In
the story, the natives eat "a few lumps of some
stuff like half-cooked dough, of a dirty lavender

colour, they kept wrapped in leaves, and now and
then swallowed a piece of. . . ." (See <u>Works of
Joseph Conrad</u>, V, 127.) (See Notes 82.28-83.9;
83.17; 121.16-23; 164.5-6; 169.19-30 for other
references to this work.)

267.23-24 "Gordon ought to celebrate his own
resurrection, anyway": Another example of the use
of the Christ figure in relationship to Gordon (see
Notes 47.31-48.4).

267.32-268.1 "your name is like a little golden
bell hung in my heart": Cf. <u>Cyrano de Bergerac</u>:

>   Your name is like a golden bell
>   Hung in my heart; and when I think of you,
>   I tremble, and the bell swings and rings--
>   <u>Roxane</u>! . . .
>   <u>Roxane</u>! . . . along my veins, Roxane!
>   [Act III, pp. 168-69].

Faulkner used a similar phrase--"Helen Helen its
like a golden bell hung in my heat [<u>sic</u>]"--in a
letter to Helen Baird which he never sent and on
the back of which he typed page 269 of the
typescript of <u>Mosquitoes</u> (see Blotner, I, 519).
Cf. Poem XXIV in <u>GB</u>: "Wherein thy name like muted
silver bells/ Breathed over me . . ." (p. 46).

268.6-7 "a bright silver joy like wings": Cf.
<u>Cyrano de Bergerac</u>:

>   And what is a kiss, when all is done?
>   . . . .
>   . . . . a moment made
>   Immortal, with a rush of wings unseen
>   [Act III, p. 174].

268.19-22 "We're sure the herrings on this boat.
. . . Guts, you know": Faulkner's use of the term
"herrings" is unclear here. To be "herring-gutted"
means to lack courage, to be "gutless" (see <u>Dictio-
nary of Slang and Unconventional English</u>, p.
1195). Perhaps the idea is that Pat and Gordon had
courage, the "guts," to leave the boat but betrayed
that courage in returning.

269.21 "Cyrano": Savinien Cyrano de Bergerac

(1619-1655), French soldier, author, playwright;
the inspiration for Edmond Rostand's play _Cyrano de
Bergerac_ (1897). I have found nothing in Cyrano's
works or in Rostand's play which resembles the
italicized story counterpointing Gordon's
discussion with Pat. There is some minor revision
in this tale from the typescript to the published
version which suggests that the story is original
to Faulkner. However, see following Notes for
possible influences.

270.8-20 "That's what you've done . . . like a dog
with a dry bone": Cf. Gustave Flaubert, _The
Temptation of St. Anthony_:

Apollonius. "At Cnidos, I cured the man that had
             become enamored of Venus."
Damis.   "Aye! a fool who had even vowed to
             espouse her. To love a woman is at
             least comprehensible; but to love a
             statue--what madness!"

(trans. by Lafcadio Hearn [New York and Seattle:
The Alice Harriman Company, 1910], p. 141. For
further references to this work, see Notes 335.2-
340.22; 337.26-27; 338.18-19.) Cf. _Cytherea_:

    "It was then," Lee [Randon] specified, "that
all my loose ends were gathered up in Cytherea. I
have, I think, explained her. She was a doll, but
it is more useful, now, to picture her as a
principle. . . . That's her secret, what she's
forever smiling at--her power, through man's
vanity, to conquer the earth. She's the reward of
all our fineness and visions and pleasure, the idol
of our supreme accomplishment: the privilege of
escaping from slavery into impotence, the doubtful
privilege of repaying the indignities of our
longing and discontent, an idol of silk and gilt
and perverse fingers, and put her above the other,
above everything. She rewarded us, oh, yes--with
promises of her loveliness. Why shouldn't she be
lovely eternally in the dreams of men? [pp.365-67].

Cf. _Elmer_: "Somewhere a fierce proud Dianalike
girl, small and dark and impregnably virginal,
waiting to cast him through the window of her
arrogance, a bone as though he were a dog . . ."

(p. 38). (See Note 26.24-26.)

271.16-23 "He raised her from the floor . . .
spanked her, good": Cf. Poem XLIII in <u>GB</u>: "the
hand that once did short to sighs her breast/now
slaps her white behind to rosy fire" (p. 66). This
poem is identified by Butterworth as "In the Spring
a Young Man's Fancy-----" and dated "1 Aug 1925" on
one typescript version (see "Census . . . of
William Faulkner's Poetry," 342).

271.30 "you've got the genders backward": Cf.
<u>Portrait</u> <u>of</u> <u>the</u> <u>Artist</u> <u>as</u> <u>a</u> <u>Young</u> <u>Man</u>, in which
Stephen Dedalus' father calls him a "lazy bitch of
a brother" and Stephen answers, "He has a curious
idea of genders if he thinks a bitch is masculine"
(p. 203).

272.17-22 "<u>I</u> <u>desire</u> <u>a</u> <u>thing</u> . . . <u>sounds</u> <u>of</u>
<u>paradise</u>": Cf. Stephen Dedalus in <u>Portrait</u> <u>of</u> <u>the</u>
<u>Artist</u> <u>as</u> <u>a</u> <u>Young</u> <u>Man</u>: "Michael Robartes remembers
forgotten beauty and, when his arms wrap her round,
he presses in his arms the loveliness which has
long faded from the world. Not this. Not at all.
I desire to press in my arms the loveliness which
has not yet come into the world" (p. 297). Cf.
<u>Mayday</u>: Galwyn tells Iseult: "Ah, lady . . . what
boots it who I am, who have now found all beauty
and despair and all delight in an inaccessible
place to which living I can never attain and which
dead I can never forget?" (pp. 23-24). (See Notes
11.19-30; 11.25- 29.)

272.24 "Learning your face": Cf. <u>Portrait</u> <u>of</u> <u>the</u>
<u>Artist</u> <u>as</u> <u>a</u> <u>Young</u> <u>Man</u>: "Her image had passed into
his soul for ever and no word had broken the holy
silence of his ecstasy. . . . A wild angel had
appeared to him, the angel of mortal youth and
beauty, an envoy from the fair courts of life, to
throw open before him in an instant of ecstasy the
gates of all the ways of error and glory" (p. 200).

273.5-20 "<u>Now</u>, <u>this</u> <u>Halim</u> <u>was</u> <u>an</u> <u>old</u> <u>man</u> . . . .
<u>But</u> <u>that</u> <u>was</u> <u>long</u> <u>ago</u>, <u>and</u> <u>she</u> <u>is</u> <u>dead</u>": The
Georgian hills are located in Russia, near the
Black Sea. The land was under Turkish and Persian
rule in the 16th and 17th centuries. Lines from
two plays of Christopher Marlowe are echoed in this

section. Cf. _Tamburlaine the Great_, Part _I_:

Then having past Armenian desarts now,
And pitcht our tents under the Georgean hilles,
Whose tops are covered with Tartarian thieves,
That lie in ambush, waiting for a pray
                    [II, ii, 537-40].

Cf. _The Jew of Malta_:

Thou hast committed--
Fornication? but that was in another Country!
And besides, the Wench is dead
                    [IV, 11. 1549-51].

These last lines are also found as the epigraph to
Eliot's "Portrait of a Lady," a poem already echoed
often in _Mosquitoes_ (see Notes 16.21-17.1; 28.8-9;
30.20-22). The character of Halim is quite similar
to the speaker in Ezra Pound's poem "La Fraisne,"
which was included in his _Personae_: _The Collected
Poems of Ezra Pound_ (New York: New Directions
Books, 1926). Cf.:

For I was a gaunt, grave councillor
Being in all things wise, and very old,
But I have put aside this folly and the cold
That old age weareth for a cloak.
          . . . .
Once when I was among the young men
And they said I was quite strong, among the young
    men,
Once there was a woman . . .
. . . but I forget . . . she was . .
. . . I hope she will not come again.

. . . I do not remember . . . . .

I think she hurt me once, but . .
That was very long ago.

I do not like to remember things any more
                    [11. 1-4, 41-49].

Cf. T. S. Eliot, "Gerontion" (1920): "I am an old
man/A dull head among windy spaces" (_Poems_, p.
39). Cf. Gordon Lawrence, "An Encounter in Hades,"
The Double Dealer, VII (April 1925), 126:

I had forgotten, lady, long ago
Whether you lived, or I loved any maid
Now passionless, a thousand years a shade
Beside the river where dark waters flow,
You, little ghost, but half-remembered yet,
Have wakened old sweetness, and an old infinite
                                        regret.

Cf. "The Cobbler": "I am very old: I have
forgotten much" (<u>NOS</u>, p. 131).

273.33 "vamp me": To seduce or influence through
sexual means. <u>Vamp</u> (derived from "vampire") came
to mean a <u>femme</u> <u>fatale</u> who uses her sexual charms
to captivate men c. 1918, inspired by the bizarrely
threatening sexuality of silent film star Theda
Bara (1890-1955). Bara was publicized as the "love
child" of a French artist and his Egyptian
mistress, born in the Sahara Desert. She was often
photographed surrounded by symbols of death and was
sometimes accompanied by "Nubian slaves." Among
her screen roles were Salome and Cleopatra. The
verb form, as Faulkner uses it, would have been
very contemporary to <u>Mosquitoes</u>: the OED dates the
use to 1927.

275.8-10 "My first is an Indian princess . . .
it's a little early to play charades yet, isn't
it?": In the game of charades, an actor gives
clues by which a title or identification may be
guessed by the members of his team. "My first"
would be the first syllable or word in the answer:
the name of a specific Indian princess--Pocahontas,
for example--would in some way identify that part
of the answer.

277.4-282.2 The Jackson Tale: Anderson and
Faulkner swapped tall tales concerning a fictitious
"Al Jackson" while they were in New Orleans in 1925
(see Note 66.22). Although this specific tale is
attributed to Fairchild, and thus to Anderson, in
fact it was written by Faulkner and is superior to
any Anderson wrote himself. Compare this version
of the Jackson story to that found in <u>Uncollected
Stories</u> ("Al Jackson," pp. 474-79).

279.15-16 "he just took off his clothes and went
right in the water and grappled for 'em": Claude

Jackson prefigures the Tall Convict in <u>WP</u> in his
willingness to wrestle alligators (see <u>WP</u>, pp. 258-
59).

281.19-20   "Go on, go on . . . about the one that
stole the money, you know":   There is no extant Al
Jackson tale about stolen money.   However, in his
next novel, <u>Flags in the Dust</u>, Faulkner did present
the character of Byron Snopes, a member of a family
which appeared in the <u>Father Abraham</u> material
(1926) and which has some similarities to the
Jackson clan.   Byron does rob the bank at which he
works.   Perhaps Faulkner was looking forward to
this episode while writing <u>Mosquitoes</u>.

282.13-23   "That Englishman. . . .   anything at
all":   Cf.   "Yo Ho and Two Bottle of Rum" (<u>NOS</u>, pp.
201-23), in which a Freddie Ayers is a mate on
board the <u>Diana</u>, a British boat which "did her six
knots, rolling and groaning her stinking way
through Eastern waters from Canton to the Straits,
anywhere the ingenuity of man might send a cargo.
She might be seen anywhere; tied rolling heavily to
a wharf in Singapore, weathering a typhoon in an
anchorage known only to admiralty charts, next year
in Bangkok or the Dutch Indies" (p. 212).   (See
Note 61.29 and following Notes.)

282.19-20   "pidgin English":   A jargon of English
words, generally mispronounced and arranged in
Chinese idiom, largely used for communication
between Chinese and English traders, especially at
seaports in the East.

282.20   "Hindustani":   A mixture of the Hindi,
Arabic, and Persian languages, used as a kind of
<u>lingua franca</u> throughout India.

282.21   "Singapore":   Located at the southern end
of the Malay Peninsula, in 1824 the island of
Singapore was ceded to the British.   In 1867 it and
surrounding islands were made a Crown Colony.   The
waterfront of the city of Singapore had a
reputation as a place of intrigue and sinister
adventure.

282.22   "the Straits":   This may refer to the
Singapore Straits to the south of Singapore Island

or the Johore Straits which separate the Island
from the Malay Peninsula.

284.17-28   "Gordon had come up . . .   `New.   Like
bark when the sap is rising'":   Cf. the dance in
<u>MF</u>.   Note especially the similarities between the
Faun's and Gordon's reactions to the dance:

> But now we, who would dream at night,
> Are awakened by the light
> . . . .
> . . . in a loud extravagance
> And reft of grace, yet called a dance,
> Dancers in a blatant crowd
> To brass horns horrible and loud.
> . . . .
> . . . Must I see
> Always this unclean heated thing
> Debauching the unarmed spring
> While my back I cannot turn,
> Nor may not shut these eyes that burn? [p. 46].

Cf. "The Cobbler":   "She often chided me on my
backwardness in the dance or with girls--how I
labored and saved, and at the dance looked by
diffidently on while others danced and wooed her
. . ." (<u>NOS</u>, p. 108).   Cf. another view of the
dance in "Out of Nazareth":   "At the dance no
introductions are necessary.   We are all brothers
and sisters" (<u>NOS</u>, p. 95).   Cf. the dance in <u>Crome
Yellow</u> (pp. 93-97).   (See Note 94.3.)

285.1   "a saxaphone was a wailing obscenity":   Cf.
"He heard the rhythmic troubling obscenities of
saxophones" (<u>SP</u>, p. 95).   (See Note 134.1-2.)

285.25   "the hoi polloi":   The mass, the rabble.
Fairchild commits an error of repetition here in
that "hoi" means "the."

287.25   "Got over it without leaving a scar, didn't
you?":   Pete here refers to Jenny's earlier desire
to "kiss polite," as Pat had taught her to do.
Since this episode was omitted from the published
version, Pete's comment makes no sense (see Note
156.15).

290.13-14   "But . . . suppose she isn't expecting

me. Suppose she were to call out-- No, no": Cf.
Eliot, "Prufrock":

And would it have been worth it, after all,
                . . . .
If one, settling a pillow by her head,
     Should say: "That is not what I meant at all.
     That is not it, at all" [<u>Poems</u>, p. 13].

291.11-13 "The moon . . . like a coin after too
much handling": See Note 48.31-32.

291.23-31 "`It had come, at last' . . . harbored
unaware": Cf. Mary Webster in Sherwood Anderson's
<u>Many</u> <u>Marriages</u> (New York: B. W. Huebsch, 1923):

If one lived behind a wall one preferred life
behind the wall. Behind the wall the light was dim
and did not hurt the eyes. Memories were shut
out. The sounds of life grew faint and indistinct
in the distance. There was something barbaric and
savage in all this business of breaking down walls,
making cracks and gaps in the wall of life [p.
153].

Cf. the Doctor in <u>WP</u>:

He spoke aloud quite carefully; the veil was going
now, dissolving now, it was about to part now and
now he did not want to see what was behind it; he
knew that for the sake of his peace of mind forever
afterward he did not dare and he knew that it was
too late now and that he could not help himself
. . ." [p. 16].

292.11 "the Charleston": A dance popular in the
1920's, named after Charleston, S.C.

294.9-10 "Canal street": The main street of New
Orleans which divides the old and new sections of
town. In the 1920's all street cars, with one
exception, began and ended their lines on Canal.

294.11-12 "clutching the dime . . . in her little
soiled hand": Cf. the Italian girl in <u>TS&TF</u>: "She
extended her fist. It uncurled upon a nickel,
moist and dirty, moist dirt ridged into her flesh.
The coin was damp and warm. I could smell it,

faintly metallic" (p. 157). (See Notes 55.10-11;
87.13-14; 202.30.)

294.26 "old iron lovely as dingy lace":   Cf. Ralph
Waldo Emerson, Nature:

Not only resemblances exist in things whose analogy
is obvious . . . but also in objects wherein there
is great superficial unlikeness. Thus architecture
is called "frozen music" by De Stael and Goethe.
Vitruvius thought an architect should be a
musician. "A Gothic church," said Coleridge, "is a
petrified religion" [Works of Ralph Waldo Emerson,
vol. IV, 31].

Cf. Faulkner's description of the Cathedral at
Piazza del Duomo: "Can you imagine stone lace? or
frozen music?" (Letters, p. 9). Cf. "Mirrors of
Chartres Street": "Later, from a railed balcony--
Mendelssohn impervious in iron--I saw him for the
last time" (NOS, p. 54). Cf. Elmer: "And for a
background those hushed colored walls like an old
fairy tale, domed, spired like voluptuous lace"
(p. 73).

295.12 "Her father was on the night force": Cf.
"The Cop" (NOS, pp. 45-50). Although there is
little similarity between these two policemen, the
sketch does show how Faulkner was incorporating
earlier character types into Mosquitoes.

296.6 "a statutory impediment": The Eighteenth
Amendment to the U. S. Constitution, which
instituted Prohibition, was adopted in January
1919.

296.12 "Ginotta": Faulkner experimented with
several other names--Minelli, Mancini, and
Maccocelli--before settling on Ginotta, which he
used in the published version (see Blotner, I,
523). Cf. "Father Gianotti" in "The Priest"
(Uncollected Stories, p. 349).

296.20 "queer golden eyes": Cf. Faulkner's letter
to Helen Baird: "Pete with his queer golden eyes."
(See Notes 105.11; 267.32-268.1.)

298.21-23 "But Joe . . . tight embryonic paunch":

Cf. "Country Mice":   "My friend the bootlegger
. . . . His shirt is of silk and striped
viciously, and collarless . . ." (NOS, p. 194).
Cf. "Once Aboard the Lugger (I)": "Joe was his
[Pete's] older brother. He was about thirty-five.
He had some yellow diamonds big as gravel"
(Uncollected Stories, p. 352).

301.29 "St. Charles": St. Charles Street runs
uptown from Canal Street.

304.17-21 "Major Ayers . . . two cities": See
Collins' Introduction to NOS (pp. 22-23). (See
Note 61.29.)

304.20-21 "the Armistice": Signed in France on 11
November 1918 at 5 a.m. World War I officially
ended at 11 p.m.

304.28-29 "a typewriter was being hammered by a
heavy and merciless hand": Cf. Sherwood Anderson's
description of the young Faulkner: "I used to hear
his typewriter rattling away as I went through the
passageway. I heard it in the morning, in the
afternoon and often late at night. He was always
at it, pounding away" (We Moderns: 1920-1940,
Catalogue No. 42 of the Gotham Book Mart, 51 West
47th Street; compiled by Frances Steloff and Kay
Steele, p. 29). Cf. Roger Howes in "Artist at
Home": "He came back down to the office and put
some paper into the typewriter and began to write.
He didn't go very fast at first, but by daylight he
was sounding like forty hens in a sheet-iron corn-
crib, and the written sheets on the desk were
piling up . . ." (Collected Stories, p. 638).

305.5-312.31 "Then he saw and recognized Mr.
Talliaferro . . . Fairchild rose and stood on the
balcony and watched him out of sight": Cf. the
earlier version with the characters Herbie and
Morrison in "Don Giovanni" (Uncollected Stories,
pp. 481-84).

305.8 "pennyroyal": A species of mint; also a
kind of minty aromatic spray. One of its many uses
is that of a mosquitoe repellent.

305.32-33 "gazing at stars . . . open coffin of

the street":   Cf. "Home":   "Jean-Baptiste leaned
motionless in a dark area-way, feeling the darkness
flow past him down the street, watching the quiet
roof-tops cutting the sky, watching the stars like
cast roses arranged above an open coffin" (NOS,
p. 18).   Cf. Elmer: "They passed to a measured
rythmic thrust, borne on a quiet liquid sound between high walls broken by sparse mellow lighted
windows above which in a soft vague sky stars were
large as roses being cast into a narrow coffin"
(p. 79).

307.13-15 "There is also the fable . . . change
the gender, by Jove":   Aesop's fable of "The Wind
and the Sun," in which the wind and the sun argue
as to which is stronger.   They agree to decide in
favor of the one who can cause a traveller to
remove his cloak.   The wind blows, but the man only
pulls his wrap tighter about him; the sun blazes
and the man removes the cloak for relief.   Faulkner
may have known the version of the fable by the Rev.
Thomas James (Aesop's Fables: A New Version,
illustrations designed by John Tenniel [London:
John Murray, 1848], pp. 59-60), which concludes:
"Thus the Sun was declared the conqueror; and it
has ever been deemed that persuasion is better than
force; and that the sunshine of a kind and gentle
manner will sooner lay open a poor man's heart than
all the threatenings and force of blustering
authority" (p. 60).   Talliaferro will "change the
gender" by having Jenny in the cloak, which he will
remove from about her by persuasion rather than
force.

312.10 "Napoleon said something about the heaviest
artillery, too":   Napoleon Bonaparte (1769-1821),
military leader and Emperor of France, 1804-14,
1815.   I have not identified any quote attributed
to Napoleon concerning the "heaviest artillery";
however, a similiar quote appears in one of
Voltaire's letters: "It is said that God is always
on the side of the heaviest battalions" (John
Bartlett, Familiar Quotations [Garden City, N.Y.:
Garden City Publishing Company, 1944], p. 1053).
In his essay "Napoleon; or, The Man of the World,"
Ralph Waldo Emerson wrote: "The art of war was the
game in which he exerted his arithmetic.   It consisted, according to him, in having always more

forces than the enemy, on the point where the enemy
is attacked, or where he attacks . . . ." "He
never economized his ammunition, but, on a hostile
position, rained a torrent of iron,--shells, balls,
grape-shot,--to annihilate all defense. On any
point of resistance, he concentrated squadron on
squadron in overwhelming numbers, until it was
swept out of existence" (<u>Works</u> <u>of</u> <u>Ralph</u> <u>Waldo</u>
<u>Emerson</u>, vol. II, pp. 373, 378).

315.4-25 "˄Look out, Josh' . . . lay rigidly on
her back": Cf. the myth of Salmakis and
Hermaphroditos in Ovid, in which the nymph attacks
the boy and wrestles with him until they are merged
(see Notes 46.27-29; 252.17). Cf. <u>Elmer</u>, in which
Jo-Addie allows her brother Elmer to touch her as
they lie in bed: "His hand went out with quiet joy
touching his sister's side where it curved briefly
and sharply into the mattress" (p. 13). Cf. <u>WP</u>, in
which Charlotte tells Harry about the scar: "I
liked my oldest brother the best but you cant sleep
with your brother . . . and when I was seven years
old I fell in the fireplace, my brother and I were
fighting, and that's the scar" (p. 40).

318.20 "Leda clasping her duck between her
thighs": In Greek mythology, Leda is raped by
Zeus, who has taken the shape of a swan. She later
gives birth to twin sons, Castor and Pollux.
Although the myth was surely known to Faulkner from
many sources, important possibilities are William
Butler Yeats' "Leda and the Swan" (1923) and Aldous
Huxley's <u>Leda</u> (1920). Cf. "Leda lurking in the
bushes, whimpering and moaning for the swan . . ."
(<u>TS&TF</u>, p. 207).

318.25-26 "Or udders and a fig leaf . . . as it
stands": Cf. Gautier's Preface to <u>Mademoiselle</u> <u>De</u>
<u>Maupin</u>:

For my own part, not being accustomed to look at
statues in certain places, I thought, like other
people, that the vine leaf carved by the chisels of
the superintendent of the fine arts was the most
ridiculous thing in the world. It appears that I
was wrong, and that the vine leaf is among the most
meritorious of institutions. . . . The great
affectation of morality which reigns at present

would be very laughable, if it were not very
tiresome [pp. i-ii].

(See Note 321.16-24.)

319.12-13 "it's a kind of Battle Creek, Michigan,
for the spirit": A famous health center and headquarters of the Seventh Day Adventist Church in the
latter half of the 19th century. John Harvey
Kellogg also developed a cereal food industry there
and it has become the breakfast food capital of the
world. Thus, for Faulkner, Battle Creek
represents, in a very ironic sense, both physical
and spiritual healthiness.

319.16-18, 24-28 "But one who spends his days
trying to forget time . . . forgetting death and
digestion." "Time? Time? . . . utterly unaware of
it": Cf. Mr. Compson in TS&TF: "I give it [the
watch] to you not that you may remember time, but
that you might forget it now and then for a moment
and not spend all your breath trying to conquer it"
(p. 93). "Father said that constant speculation
regarding the position of mechanical hands on an
arbitrary dial which is a symptom of mind-function.
Excrement Father said like sweating" (p. 94).

320.9-15 "Women can do it without art . . . . But
in art, a man can create without any assistance at
all: what he does is his": Cf. "The Book of the
Grotesque" in Winesburg, Ohio, in which Anderson
describes the writer: "He was like a pregnant
woman, only that the thing inside him was not a
baby but a youth" (p. 2). Cf. A Story Teller's
Story: "Having . . . got the tone of a tale, I was
like a woman who has just become impregnated.
Something was growing inside me. At night when I
lay in my bed I could feel the heels of the tale
kicking against the walls of my body" (p. 358).

320.15-17 "A perversion, I grant you, but . . . a
pretty good thing": Chartres Cathedral in
Chartres, France, one of the greatest examples of
High Gothic architecture. Anderson called the
cathedral "the beauty shrine of my life" (A Story
Teller's Story, p. 185) and used it as a central
image in this book (see pp. 398-410). Anderson, in
turn, had been influenced by Henry Adams' The

<u>Education</u> <u>of</u> <u>Henry</u> <u>Adams</u> (privately printed in
1907, published in 1918) and probably took the
image of Chartres from him. (See <u>A</u> <u>Story</u> <u>Teller's</u>
<u>Story</u>, pp. 377-79. Also see Notes 76.7-10;
252.17-19.)

320.16 "Lear": <u>King</u> <u>Lear</u> (1605) by William
Shakespeare. (See Note 248.5.)

320.20-22 "There is a kind of spider . . . she
devours him during the act of conception": This is
not an unusual practice among spiders of all kinds,
but Faulkner may have had the Black Widow spider in
mind.

320.27-33 "Listen . . . I had to work all the time
to earn a living, when I was a young man": Cf.
Faulkner's 1925 essay "Sherwood Anderson":

I do not mean to imply that Mr. Anderson has no
sense of humor. . . . But only recently has he got
any of it into his stories, without deliberately
writing a story with a humorous intent. I wonder
sometimes if this is not due to the fact that he
didn't have leisure to write until long after these
people had come to be in his mind; that he had
cherished them until his perspective was slightly
awry [<u>NOS</u>, p. 138]. Anderson worked as an
advertising copywriter and then as a mail-order
businessman before publishing his first novel at
the age of forty.

321.16-24 "When the statue is completely nude . . .
I require in my sculpture": Cf. <u>Mademoiselle</u> <u>De</u>
<u>Maupin</u> (see Note 318.25-26). Cf. <u>Sanctuary</u>: "The
worst one of all said boys thought girls were ugly
except when they were dressed. She said the Snake
had been seeing Eve for several days and never
noticed her until Adam made her put on a fig leaf"
(p. 181).

321.26-30 "The same food nourishes everybody's
convictions alike. . . . There's your perversion,
I think": Cf. John McClure, "Notes on the Theory
of Beauty" (<u>The</u> <u>Double</u> <u>Dealer</u>, VI [July 1924],
139-46):

Natural objects, which lack proportion, balance or

consummated gradation (completed sequence in
contour or color) are not beautiful except to
individuals for whom they are a fetish or for whom
they serve as symbols. All objects of desire are
symbols, representing a consummation of a sequence
or balance of ideas. An ugly woman seems lovely to
a sailor and a vivacious one seems beautiful even
to a philosopher. . . . Fishermen see beauty in
fish. Ambitious jurists see beauty in wigs. And
this is as it must be. Perverted minds . . . see
beauty in the most absurd fetishes [144-45].

(See Notes 252.17-19; 320.15-17.)

322.1-2 "But if I earned my bread by means of sex
. . . good honest whore": Cf. Charlotte
Rittenmeyer in <u>WP</u>: "I would be a good whore.
That's what I would try to be" (p. 179).

322.13-23 "It was clay . . . `Well, I'll be
damned,' he said again": Cf. Dodge Pleydon's bust
which indicates his growth as an artist in <u>Linda
Condon</u>:

It was the head and part of the shoulders of a very
old woman, infinitely worn, starved by want and
spent in brutal labor. There was a thin wisp of
hair pinned in a meager knot on her skull; her
bones were mercilessly indicated, barely covered
with drum-like skin; her mouth was stamped with
timid humility; while her eyes peered weakly from
their sunken depths [p. 207].

When Linda sees the work, she says, "I--I suppose
it's perfectly done. . . . It's true, certainly.
But isn't it more unpleasant than necessary?"
Pleydon then answers, "Beauty . . . Pity,
<u>Katharsis</u> --the wringing out of all dross" (p.
207). Later Pleydon explains his artistic growth,
which has been a direct result of his disappointed
love for Linda: "Do you suppose I was able then to
understand the sheer tragic fortitude to live of a
scrubwoman . . . to experience that in your spirit
and put it into durable metal, hard stone--is to
hold beauty in your hands" (p. 208).

323.19-326.25 "The story is, that her people
forced her to marry old Maurier. . . . But I see

something thwarted back of it all, something
stiffled, yet which won't quite die":   Blotner
states that the story of Mrs. Maurier's marriage
was suggested by local Oxford history (I, 520).
Cf. also the story of Thomas and Ellen Sutpen in
Absalom, _Absalom_! ([New York: Random House, 1936],
pp. 31-58).   Other variations on Mrs. Maurier's
story can be found in the marriage of Flem Snopes
and Eula Varner in _Father Abraham_ and _The Hamlet_,
and in the story of Melisandre Backus Harriss in
Knight's Gambit (New York: Random House, 1949).

324.6-7   "General Butler's assumption of the local
purple":   Benjamin Franklin Butler (1818-1903),
known as "Beast" Butler, Union military commander
of New Orleans after its capture in 1862.   Butler's
rule was almost totally dictatorial, and he was
despised by the populace as a tyrant. "Purple" is
the color of royal robes and represents power of
authority.

325.20-21   "Her name was a byword . . . Antoine's
or the St. Charles":   Antoine's, established in
1868, is located at 713 St. Louis Street and is one
of the most famous restaurants in America.   The St.
Charles Hotel, at 211 Chartres Street, was the
leading New Orleans "society" hotel in the last
half of the 19th century.

325.33-326.1   "horseless Lochinvar":   Cf. Sir
Walter Scott, _Marmion_, in which Lochinvar is the
subject of the Lady Heron's song.   The young lord,
on horse- back, rescues his loved one from an
enforced marriage to a "laggard in love and a
dastard in war" (Canto V, XII, 1. 323).   Cf. "Young
Lochinvar rode out of the west a little too soon,
didn't he?" (_TS&TF_, p. 115).

328.1-2   "Prohibition for the Latin, politics for
the Irish, invented He them":   Word play on Genesis
1:27:   "So God created man in his own image, in the
image of God created he him; male and female
created he them."   Cf. _Crome Yellow_: "Male and
female created He them" (p. 284).   Cf. _SP_: "Male
and female created He them, young" (p. 314).

328.6-7   "Italians and Irish.   Where do we
homegrown Nordics come in?   What has He invented

for us?":   Cf. Tom Buchanan in <u>The Great Gatsby</u>:
"It's up to us, who are the dominant race, to watch
out or these other races will have control of
things. . . . This idea is that we're Nordics
. . . . And we've produced all the things that go
to make civilization--oh, science and art, and all
that" (pp. 13-14). (See Notes 52.10; 181.19.)

328.32-329.1 "you'd like to watch her from a
distance . . . in a pool where there were a lot of
poplar trees": Cf. <u>MF</u>:

> While I lie in the leafy shade
> Until the nymphs troop down the glade.
>   . . . .
> To comb and braid their short brown hair
> Before they slip into the pool--
> Warm gold in sliver liquid cool [p. 26].

Cf. <u>Mayday</u>, when Galwyn discovers Iseult in a
stream bathing (pp. 20-24). Cf. Huxley's <u>Leda</u>, in
which Zeus spies Leda naked by the stream ([New
York: George H. Doran Company, 1920], pp. 10-11).
(See Note 318.20.)

329.9-11 "Marble, purity . . . some way to make it
unpure. They would if they could, God damn them!":
Cf. Gerald March in <u>The Green Hat</u>, who is described
as the "dark knight of purity" (p. 66). He writes
a book, the opening lines of which read:

The history of Felix Burton is the history of an
ideal and a vision. They had nothing to do with
one another except that the pursuit of the vision
hardened him and bloodied him for the attainment of
the ideal. . . . The ideal was, of course,
defeated: the vision, of course, defeated him.
The ideal was purity: the vision had something to
do with pain . . .[p. 63]

329.14-16 "Only an idiot has no grief . . . sharp
enough to stick to your guts?": Cf. Harry
Wilbourne's final pronouncement in <u>WP</u>: "<u>Yes</u> . . .
<u>between</u> <u>grief</u> <u>and</u> <u>nothing</u> <u>I</u> <u>will</u> <u>take</u> <u>grief</u>"
(p. 324). Faulkner sometimes used variations of
this line to describe his own view of life.

333.33 "Snipe": The unsmoked portion of a cigar

or cigarette.

334.9-19 "So, after a while he did look . . . from
the light at the head of the stairs": Sam Gilmore
has been described as "Fastidious to the point of
effeminacy" (see Bowen, <u>The New Orleans Double
Dealer</u>, p. 235). (See Notes 54.25-29; 54.29-55.2;
65.3-4.)

335.2-340.22 Section 9: The italicized lines
interspersed in this section of <u>Mosquitoes</u> are
reworkings of pp. 79-82 of <u>Elmer</u> (pp. 81-85 of the
<u>Elmer</u> typescript) which describe Elmer's drunken,
nightmarish spree in Italy. It is probable that
Faulkner modeled this section on the Circe episode
in <u>Ulysses</u>; however, there are also striking
similarities between it and Flaubert's <u>The
Temptation of St. Anthony</u> (see Brooks' discussion
in <u>WF</u>: <u>TYB</u>, pp. 127-28, and following Notes).

335.2 "<u>Three gray, softfooted priests</u>": Cf. Poem
III of <u>GB</u>: "And silence like a priest on thin gray
feet/Tells his beads of minutes on beside" (p. 19).

335.4-6 "<u>Beneath a high stone gate . . . a crust
of bread</u>": Cf. Poem XX of <u>GB</u>:

> Here he stands, while eternal evening falls
> And it is like a dream between gray walls
> . . . .
> Between two walls of gray and topless stone
> Between two walls with silence on them grown
>   [p. 42].

Cf. "The Beggar": "The knight still would ride
forth, but his steed is old and not sure of foot
any more; other warriors on younger and lustier
stallions override and unhorse him, and now he must
whine and snarl with others whose steeds have
failed, over gnawed crusts without the relentless
gates, in the dusty road" (<u>NOS</u>, p. 47).

335.12-13 "<u>Spring is in the world . . . high and
fiery cold</u>": Cf. <u>MF</u>:

> Pan sighs, and raises to his lips
> His pipes, down which his fingertips
> Wander lovingly; then low

And clearly simple does he blow
A single thin clear melody
. . . .
A sudden strain, silver and shrill [p. 16].

335.16-18 "In a doorway slightly ajar were women
. . . odorous and exciting and unchaste": From
1897 to 1917, the restricted but legal red light
district of New Orleans was located in the area
"between North Robertson and North Basin streets,
and from Customhouse (Iberville) to St. Louis
streets" (Al Rose, <u>Storyville</u>, <u>New</u> <u>Orleans</u>
[University of Alabama Press, 1974], p. 38). The
section was known as Storyville, named after Sidney
Story, the alderman who introduced the ordinance
establishing the district. As the <u>New</u> <u>Orleans</u> <u>City</u>
<u>Guide</u> explained: "The women were not permitted to
leave the house, so they solicited vocally from
behind doorways and window blinds" (p. 210). The
district was officially closed in 1917, after which
time prostitution spread throughout the city.

335.18 "hello dempsey": William Harrison (Jack)
Dempsey (1895-1983), world heavyweight boxing
champion, 1919-1926. Cf. the Circe section of
<u>Ulysses</u>, in which the prostitutes beckon to Stephen
Dedalus and Lynch as they walk through Nighttown
(pp. 430-31).

335.24-29 "That's it, that's it! . . . natural and
fecund and foul--you don't stop for it; you pass
on": Cf. Sherwood Anderson, <u>Poor</u> <u>White</u>: "That was
the only answer to the question Hugh could find
within himself. The destruction of what was white
and pure was a necessary thing in life. It was a
thing men must do in order that life go on. As for
women, they must be white and pure--and wait"
(p. 322).

335.31-336.5 "<u>Rats</u> <u>like</u> <u>dull</u> <u>and</u> <u>cunning</u> <u>silver</u>
. . . <u>sniffing</u> <u>his</u> <u>intimate</u> <u>parts</u>": Cf. Eliot, <u>The</u>
<u>Waste</u> <u>Land</u>:

A rat crept softly through the vegetation
Dragging its slimy belly on the bank
While I was fishing in the dull canal [ll.
187-89]

Cf. "Carcassonne": "It was dark, a darkness filled
with a fairy pattering of small feet. stealthy and
intent. Sometimes the cold patter of them on his
face waked him in the night, and at his movement
they scurried invisibly like an abrupt disinte-
gration of dead leaves in a wind, in whispering
arpeggios of minute sound, leaving a thin but
definite effluvium of furtiveness and voracity"
(Collected Stories, p. 898).

336.13-17 "To look into all the darkened rooms in
the world. . . . as you steal in to look at a
sleeping child, not to disturb it": Cf. Sherwood
Anderson, Tar:

As a grown man Tar thought much on the subject of
childhood and houses. . . . He had begun again, as
he was always beginning, on the theme of houses,
places in which people live, into which they come
at night and when it is cold and stormy outside the
house--houses with rooms in which people sleep, in
which children sleep and dream [p. 42].

(See Note 248.14-16.)

337.8-9 "slow as a procession of nuns with
breathing blent": Cf. Poem III in GB:

   Before him as, the priest of Silence by
   And all the whispering nuns of breathing blent
   With Silence's self [p. 19].

337.26-27 "a young naked boy daubed with
vermilion, carrying casually a crown": An image
possibly taken from Macbeth (IV, i): a combination
of the "bloody Child" and "the Child crowned" which
appear to Macbeth. Also a possible reference to
Adonis. Cf. Oscar Wilde's The Burden of Itys:

   Sing on! and I the dying boy will see
      Stain with the purple blood the waxen bell
   That overweighs the jacinth . . .

(Complete Works of Oscar Wilde, vol. I, Poems, 94).
Cf. the "black child who appeared to me [St.
Anthony] in the midst of the sands, who was very
beautiful, and who told me that he was called the
Spirit of Lust" (Flaubert, The Temptation of St.

<u>Anthony</u>, p. 16).

337.28-30 "<u>the headless naked body of a woman</u>
. . . <u>wearing skins of slain beasts and chained one
to another, lamenting</u>": Cf. <u>Mademoiselle De
Maupin</u>:

Thy gilded house, O Nero! is but a miry stable
beside the palaces that I have raised; my wardrobe
is better equipped than thine, Heliogabalus, and of
very different splendour. My circuses are more
roaring and more bloody than yours, my perfumes
more keen and penetrating, my slaves more numerous
and better made; I, too, have yoked naked
courtesans to my chariot, and I have trodden upon
men with a heel as disdainful as yours [p. 91].

Cf. the Oriental woman in <u>Ulysses</u>:

<u>A coin gleams on her forehead</u>. <u>On her feet are
jewelled toerings</u>. <u>Her ankles are linked by a
slender fetterchain</u>. <u>Beside her a camel</u>, <u>hooded
with a turreting turban</u> . . ." (p. 439).

Cf. Gordon Lawrence, "Parade," a poem which
appeared in <u>The Double Dealer</u> (VII [January-
February 1925], 99) and contains many images found
in Faulkner's description:

Of popes, and mitred Heliogabalus,
And eunuchs with great breasts and leaden whips,
And men of stone with yellow shells for eyes.
Of naked queens who pull the chariot,
Their long hair streaming,
    . . . .
Of recent maids who follow chained and stripped,
Of squatty dragons, hastening now, the crew.

Cf. Faulkner's poem "Sapphics":

Before her go cryings and lamentations
Of barren women, a thunder of wings,
White ghosts of outcast Lethean women, lamenting,
    Stiffen the twilight

                                    [<u>EP&P</u>, p. 52].

Cf. Horace Benbow in <u>Flags</u>: "You ought to run in a
cheese-cloth shimmy on hills under a new moon

. . . . With chained ankles, of course. But a
slack chain" (p. 173).

338.17-18 "<u>Amid</u> <u>shadows</u> <u>and</u> <u>echoes</u> . . . <u>clashing</u>
<u>hooves</u> <u>of</u> <u>centaurs</u>": Cf. "Hymn," an unpublished
poem written c. 1916, in which Faulkner presented
the centaur as a sexual image:

Where shall we seek thee, O Beauty? Aloft in the
                                            morning
Where the hooves of the centaurs ring like brass
                                       on the hill,
          . . . .
Glittering leaves are shaken and soundless bells
To the centaur's rush: his hooves are a myriad suns
In the strength of his fire to love, in the fire
                          of his strength to kill.
          . . . .
Shards of light that lance from the centaur's coat
Are spokes in the wheel of the storming rush
                                 of his motion.

(See <u>Man</u> <u>Collecting</u>: <u>The</u> <u>Works</u> <u>of</u> <u>William</u>
<u>Faulkner</u>, compiled by Joan St. C. Crane and Anne E.
H. Freudenberg [Charlottesville: University of
Virginia Press, 1975], p. 126.)

338.18-19 "<u>The</u> <u>headless</u> <u>black</u> <u>woman</u>": Cf. the
"black woman with the putrid teeth, who is the
Ruler of Hell" (<u>The</u> <u>Temptation</u> <u>of</u> <u>St</u>. <u>Anthony</u>, p.
158).

338.31-339.6 "Gordon entered . . . <u>echoes</u> <u>whirl</u>
<u>away</u>": Cf. <u>Elmer</u>, in which Elmer sees "a slim
proud shape virginal as silver and just beyond it
another sweet shortlegged body in a retreating
lemoncolored dress, that almost merged one with the
other, but not quite" (p. 45). Like Elmer, Gordon
cannot quite match his ideal with the real. Cf.
Jurgen's lament at the end of James Branch Cabell's
<u>Jurgen</u>:

    Oh, I have failed my vision! . . . I have
failed, and I know very well that every man must
fail: and yet my shame is no less bitter. For I
am transmuted by time's handling! I shudder at the
thought of living day-in and day-out with my
vision! And so I will have none of you for my

wife. . . . Oh, all my life was a foiled quest of
you, Queen Helen, and an unsatiated hungering. And
for a while I served my vision, honoring you with
clean- handed deeds. Yes, certainly it should be
graved upon my tomb, "Queen Helen ruled this earth
while it stayed worthy." But that was very long
ago [p. 347].

339.8-12 "Dante invented Beatrice . . . impossible
heart's desire": Dante Alighieri (1265-1321)
expressed his impossible love for Beatrice,
daughter of Folco Portinari, in the <u>Vita</u> <u>Nuovo</u> (c.
1293) in which she acts as poetic muse. In the
<u>Divina</u> <u>Commedia</u> (1310-21) Beatrice appears as one
of the "blessed ladies," in company with St. Lucy
and the Virgin Mary. She acts as Dante's spiritual
guide, leading him to Heaven. In both cases, she
is the unattainable woman, the ideal who transcends
the physical.

339.23-24 "Passion Week of the heart, that instant
of timeless beatitude": Cf. James Joyce's idea of
an epiphany in <u>Portrait</u> <u>of</u> <u>the</u> <u>Artist</u> <u>as</u> <u>a</u> <u>Young</u>
<u>Man</u>: "The instant wherein that supreme quality of
beauty, the clear radiance of the esthetic image,
is apprehended luminously by the mind which has
been arrested by its wholeness and fascinated by
its harmony . . . [an] enchantment of the heart"
(p. 250).

339.31-340.1 "Yseult of the White Hands and her
Tristram . . . dullness of his": Faulkner
apparently intends the lovers of the medieval
legend; however, there are two Yseults in the tale
and Yseult of the White Hands is the woman Tristram
marries in order to forget his true love, the first
Yseult, wife of King Mark. Because Tristram
remains faithful to the first Yseult and never
consumates his marriage with Yseult of the White
Hands, she grows to hate him and is finally
responsible for his death. Professor Calvin Brown
has suggested that Faulkner's knowledge of the
Tristram legend came primarily from Swinburne's
<u>Tristram</u> <u>of</u> <u>Lyonesse</u>. Cf. <u>Mayday</u>, in which Galwyn
kills Tristram and makes love to a beautiful but
vapid Yseult.

340.1-3 "that young Lady Something . . . cut her

head off": Faulkner here apparently confuses two
famous historical executions. A likely reference
is to Lady Jane Grey (1537-1554) who was named
Queen of England in 1553 after the death of Edward
VI to prevent Mary, his sister, from becoming ruler
since she was Roman Catholic. When Mary did gain
the throne, she had Jane beheaded, at the age of
16, for treason. A popular, romanticized account
of her death can be found in William Harrison
Ainsworth's <u>The Tower of London</u> (London: George
Routledge and Sons, 1840). It was, however, Sir
Walter Raleigh (1552?-1618) who asked to touch the
blade used to execute him. "Show me the axe," he
is said to have told his executioner. In the
description of his 19th century biographer Edward
Edwards, "Touching its edge with his finger, to
feel its keenness, and then kissing the blade, he
said: `This gives me no fear. It is a sharp and
fair medicine, to cure me of all my diseases'" (<u>The
Life of Sir Walter Raleigh</u> [London: Macmillan &
Co., 1868], p. 705).

340.10-11, 19-20 "I love three things: gold,
marble and purple . . . form solidity color": Cf.
"Wealthy Jew": "I love three things: gold, marble
and purple; splendor, solidity, color" (<u>NOS</u>,
p. 37). The original source for both these quotes
is d'Albert's assertion in <u>Mademoiselle De Maupin</u>:

My rebellious body will not recognise the supremacy
of the Soul, and my flesh does not admit that it
should be mortified. I deem the earth as fair as
heaven, and I think that correctness of form is
virtue. Spiritually does not suit me, I prefer a
statue to a phantom, and noon to twilight. Three
things please me: gold, marble and purple,
splendour, solidity and colour. My dreams are
composed of them, and all my chimerical palaces are
constructed of these materials [p. 133].

(Noted by Michael Millgate, <u>The Achievement of
William Faulkner</u>, p. 300.) Cf. Joyce, <u>Portrait of
the Artist as a Young Man</u>: "<u>Three things are
needed for beauty, wholeness, harmony and radiance</u>"
(p. 248).

340.24-349.5 Section 10. Cf. "Don Giovanni"
(<u>Uncollected Stories</u>, pp. 484-488).

345.4-8 "The other man looked at Mr. Talliaferro
. . . `trying to invent people by means of the
written word!'": Cf. "Artist at Home," in which
Roger Howes' wife taunts him for his failure to
match, in his fiction, the complexities and
surprises of life: "You put him [John Blair] in a
book, but you didn't finish it. . . . God beat
you, that time, Roger." Roger answers, "Ay . . .
God beats me lots of times" (Collected Stories, pp.
645- 46).

345.6-7 "Balzac, chew thy bitter thumb": A sign
of derision, or, as here, of regret and
frustration. Cf. Poem XXXII of GB: "and
paris/tastes his bitter thumbs" (p. 35). Cf.
"Horace sat beside her and watched both Belle in
her self-imposed and tragic role, and himself
performing like the old actor . . . while the
younger men chew their bitter thumbs in the wings"
(Flags, p. 180).

346.3-4 "I wonder if it does show on me?": Cf.
SP: "Mr. George Farr considered himself quite a
man. I wonder if it shows in my face? he thought
. . . . It would be fine if . . . without talking
men who had women could somehow know each other on
sight . . . an automatic masonry" (p. 147).

346.17-19 "his grumbling skeleton . . . I told you
so": Cf. A. E. Housman's "The Immortal Part":

    Wanderers eastward, wanderers west,
    Know you why you cannot rest?
    'Tis that every mother's son
    Travails with a skeleton.

(The Collected Poems of A. E. Housman [New York:
Holt, Rinehart and Winston, 1965], p. 65.) Cf.
"Carcassonne": "His skeleton lay still. Perhaps
it was thinking about this. Anyway, after a time
it groaned. But it said nothing. which is
certainly not like you he thought you are not like
yourself. but I can't say that a little quiet is
not pleasant" (Collected Stories, p. 895).

346.24-25 "that he had been always a firearm
unloaded and unaware of it": Cf. "Moonlight": "He
was like the hunter who finds the game suddenly and

at last and then discovers that he has never
learned how to load his gun . . ." (_Uncollected
Stories_, p. 498).

347.16-17 "Agnes Mabel Becky": A brand of condoms
which bore the picture of these three ladies on the
cover. The brand name was _Three Merry Widows
Agnes Mabel Becky_ (see Calvin S. Brown, _Glossary_,
p. 19). Cf. "Agnes Mabel Becky. . . . Damn if one
of them didn't leave a track" (_TS&TF_, p. 61).

347.21-23 "But must I become an old man . . . have
lived at all": Cf. Eliot, "Prufrock":

I grow old . . . I grow old . . .
I shall wear the bottoms of my trousers rolled
                              [_Poems_, p. 14].

349.5 "You tell 'em, big boy; treat 'em rough":
Faulkner may have been influenced here by
Hergesheimer's ironic ending to _Cytherea_. After
Savina Grove's death, Lee Randon finds himself cut
off from his former life. He talks at length with
his brother Daniel, but on turning to his brother
for encouragement, he finds that "Daniel Randon was
asleep" (p. 371). A similar situation is found in
Fitzgerald's "The Off-Shore Pirate":

    "You see," said Carlyle softly, "this is the
beauty I want. Beauty has got to be astonishing,
astounding--it's got to burst in on you like a
dream, like the exquisite eyes of a girl."
    He turned to her, but she was silent.
    "You see, don't you, Ardita--I mean, Ardita?"
    Again she made no answer. She had been sound
asleep for some time [_Flappers and Philosophers_,
pp. 29-30].

Works by Faulkner:

Absalom, Absalom! New York: Random House, 1936;
    The Modern Library, 1951.

"Adolescence." Uncollected Stories of William
    Faulkner, pp. 459-73.

"Al Jackson." Uncollected Stories of William
    Faulkner, pp. 474-79.

"Appendix: The Compsons, 1699-1945." The Portable
    Faulkner, ed. Malcolm Cowley. New York:
    The Viking Press, 1967, pp. 704-21.

"Artist at Home." Collected Stories of William
    Faulkner, pp. 627-46.

"The Artist--New Orleans." New Orleans Sketches,
    pp. 47-48.

As I Lay Dying. New York: Vintage Books, 1964.

"Books and Things: American Drama: Inhibitions."
    Early Prose and Poetry, pp. 93-97.

"Books and Things: In April Once by W. A. Percy."
    Early Prose and Poetry, pp. 71-73.

"Books and Things: Joseph Hergesheimer." Early
    Prose and Poetry, pp. 101-03.

"Books and Things: Turns and Movies by Conrad
    Aiken." Early Prose and Poetry, pp. 74-77.

"The Brooch." Collected Stories of William
    Faulkner, pp. 647-65.

"Carcassonne." Collected Stories of William
    Faulkner, pp. 895-900.

"The Cobbler." New Orleans Sketches, pp. 129-34.

Collected Stories of William Faulkner. New York:
    Random House, 1950.

"Country Mice." New Orleans Sketches, pp. 191-207.

154   Bibliography

"Don Giovanni." Uncollected Stories of William
      Faulkner, pp. 480-88.

Early Prose and Poetry, ed. Carvel Collins.
      London: Jonathan Cape, 1963.

Essays, Speeches & Public Letters by William
      Faulkner, ed. James B. Meriwether. New York:
      Random House, 1966.

Elmer, ed. Dianne L. Cox. Northport, Alabama:
      The Seajay Press, 1983.

Father Abraham. Introduction by James B.
      Meriwether. New York: Random House, 1983.

Flags in the Dust. New York: Random House, 1973.

"Frankie and Johnny." Uncollected Stories of
      William Faulkner, pp. 338-47.

The Hamlet. New York: Random House, 1940.

Helen: A Courtship and Mississippi Poems. Intro.
      essays by Carvel Collins and Joseph Blotner.
      Published jointly by Tulane University Press
      and Yoknapatawpha Press, 1981.

"Home." New Orleans Sketches, pp. 71-79.

"A Justice." Collected Stories of William
      Faulkner, pp. 343-60.

"The Kid Learns." New Orleans Sketches, pp. 159-
      67.

"The Kingdom of God." New Orleans Sketches,
      pp. 111-19.

Knight's Gambit. New York: Random House, 1949.

"The Leg." Collected Stories of William Faulkner,
      pp. 823-42.

"The Liar." New Orleans Sketches, pp. 169-84.

Light in August. New York: Random House, 1932.

The Marble Faun and A Green Bough. New York:
    Random House, 1965.

The Marionettes, ed. Noel Polk. Charlottesville:
    University Press of Virginia, 1977.

Mayday, ed. Carvel Collins. South Bend, Indiana:
    University of Notre Dame Press, 1977.

"Mirrors of Chartres Street." New Orleans
    Sketches, pp. 51-57.

"Moonlight." Uncollected Stories of William
    Faulkner, pp. 495-503.

Mosquitoes. New York: Boni & Liveright, 1927.

New Orleans Sketches, ed. Carvel Collins. New
    York: Random House, 1968.

"A Note on Sherwood Anderson." Essays, Speeches, &
    Public Letters, pp. 3-10.

"Nympholepsy." Uncollected Stories of William
    Faulkner, pp. 331-37.

"Once Aboard the Lugger (I)." Uncollected
    Stories of William Faulkner, pp. 352-58.

"Once Aboard the Lugger (II)." Uncollected
    Stories of William Faulkner, pp. 359-67.

"On Criticism." Early Prose and Poetry, pp. 109-
    12.

"Out of Nazareth." New Orleans Sketches,
    pp. 99-110.

"Peter." Uncollected Stories of William
    Faulkner, pp. 489-94.

"A Portrait of Elmer." Uncollected Stories of
    William Faulkner, pp. 610-41.

"The Priest." Uncollected Stories of William
    Faulkner, pp. 348-51.

Requiem For a Nun. New York: Random House, 1951.

Sanctuary. New York: Jonathan Cape and Harrison
     Smith, 1931.

Selected Letters of William Faulkner, ed. Joseph
     Blotner. New York: Random House, 1977.

Sherwood Anderson & Other Famous Creoles. Austin
     and London: University of Texas Press, 1966.

Soldiers' Pay. New York: Boni & Liveright, 1926.

The Sound and the Fury. New York: Jonathan Cape
     and Harrison Smith, 1929.

"Sunset." New Orleans Sketches, pp. 145-57.

"The Tourist--New Orleans." New Orleans Sketches,
     pp. 49-50.

Uncollected Stories of William Faulkner, ed. Joseph
     Blotner. New York: Random House, 1979.

"Verse Old and Nascent: A Pilgrimage." Early
     Prose and Poetry, pp. 114-18.

Visions in Spring. Introduction by Judith L.
     Sensibar. Austin: University of Texas Press,
     1984.

"Wealthy Jew--New Orleans." New Orleans Sketches,
     pp. 37-38.

The Wild Palms. New York: Random House, 1939.

The Wishing Tree. New York: Random House, 1964.

"Yo Ho and Two Bottles of Rum." New Orleans
     Sketches, pp. 209-23.

Works About Faulkner:

Adams, Richard P. Faulkner: Myth and Motion.
     Princeton: Princeton University Press, 1968.

Anderson, Sherwood in We Moderns: 1920-1940,

<u>Catalogue</u> <u>No</u>. <u>42</u> <u>of</u> <u>the</u> <u>Gotham</u> <u>Book</u> <u>Mart</u>,
comp. by Frances Steloff and Kay Steele,
p. 29.

Arnold, Edwin T. III. "Faulkner and Huxley: A
Note on <u>Mosquitoes</u> and <u>Crome</u> <u>Yellow</u>."
<u>Mississippi</u> <u>Quarterly</u>, 30 (Summer 1977),
433-36.

Bassett, John, comp. <u>William</u> <u>Faulkner</u>: <u>An</u>
<u>Annotated</u> <u>Checklist</u> <u>of</u> <u>Criticism</u>. New
York: David Lewis, 1972.

Bleikasten, Andre. <u>The</u> <u>Most</u> <u>Splendid</u> <u>Failure</u>:
<u>Faulkner's</u> <u>The</u> <u>Sound</u> <u>and</u> <u>The</u> <u>Fury</u>.
Bloomington: Indiana University Press,
1976.

Blotner, Joseph. <u>Faulkner</u>: <u>A</u> <u>Biography</u>. 2 vols.
New York: Random House, 1974; rev. one-vol.
ed., 1984.

---------------. <u>William</u> <u>Faulkner's</u> <u>Library</u>: <u>A</u>
<u>Catalogue</u>. Charlottesville: University Press
of Virginia, 1964.

Brooks, Cleanth. <u>William</u> <u>Faulkner</u>: <u>Toward</u>
<u>Yoknapatawpha</u> <u>and</u> <u>Beyond</u>. New Haven and
London: Yale University Press, 1976.

Broughton, Pamela Reid. <u>William</u> <u>Faulkner</u>: <u>The</u>
<u>Abstract</u> <u>and</u> <u>the</u> <u>Actual</u>. Baton Rouge and
London: Louisiana State University Press,
1974.

Brown, Calvin. <u>A</u> <u>Glossary</u> <u>of</u> <u>Faulkner's</u> <u>South</u>.
New Haven and London: Yale University Press,
1976.

Brylowski, Walter. <u>Faulkner's</u> <u>Olympian</u> <u>Laugh</u>:
<u>Myth</u> <u>in</u> <u>the</u> <u>Novels</u>. Detroit: Wayne State
University Press, 1968.

Butterworth, Keen. "A Census of Manuscripts and
Typescripts of William Faulkner's Poetry."
<u>Mississippi</u> <u>Quarterly</u>, 26 (Summer 1973), 333-
59.

158   Bibliography

Carey, Glenn O. "Faulkner and _Mosquitoes_: Writing Himself and His Age." _Research Studies_, 39 (December 1971), 271-83.

Collins, Carvel. "Biographical Background for Faulkner's Helen." _Helen: A Courtship and Mississippi Poems._ Tulane University and Yoknapatawpha Press, 1981.

----------. "Faulkner's _Mayday_." _Mayday_, ed. Carvel Collins. South Bend, Indiana: University of Notre Dame Press, 1977, pp. [1]-30.

----------. "The Interior Monologues of _The Sound and the Fury_." _The Merrill Studies in The Sound and the Fury_, comp. James B. Meriwether (Columbus, Ohio: Charles E. Merrill Publishing Company, 1970), pp. 59-79.

Cooley, Thomas W., Jr. "Faulkner Draws the Long Bow." _Twentieth Century Literature_, 16 (October 1970), 268-77.

Cox, Leland H., Jr. "Sinbad in New Orleans: Early Short Fiction by William Faulkner--An Annotated Edition." Dissertation, University of South Carolina, 1977.

Crane, Joan St. C. and Anne E. H. Freudenberg, comps. _Man Collecting: The Works of William Faulkner._ Charlottesville: University Press of Virginia, 1975.

Dunlap, Mary M. "Sex and the Artist in _Mosquitoes_." _Mississippi Quarterly_, 22 (Summer 1969), 207-13.

Franklin, Phyllis. "The Influence of Joseph Hergesheimer Upon _Mosquitoes_." _Mississippi Quarterly_, 22 (Summer 1969), 207-13.

Garrett, George. "An Examination of the Poetry of William Faulkner." _Princeton University Library Chronicle_, 8 (Spring 1957), 124-35.

Gidley, M. "One Continuous Force: Notes on Faulkner's Extra-Literary Reading."

Mississippi Quarterly, 23 (Summer 1970),
299-314.

----------. "Some Notes on Faulkner's Reading."
Journal of American Studies, 4 (July 1970),
299-314.

Gwynn, Frederick L. and Joseph Blotner, eds.
Faulkner in the University: Class Conferences
at the University of Virginia 1957-1958. New
York: Vintage Books, 1958.

Gwynn, Frederick. "Faulkner's Prufrock--And Other
Observations." Journal of English and German
Philology, 52 (January 1953), 63-70.

Hepburn, Kenneth William. "Faulkner's Mosquitoes:
A Poetic Turning Point." Twentieth Century
Literature, 17 (January 1971), 19-28.

----------. "Soldiers' Pay to The Sound and the
Fury: Development of the Poetic in the Early
Novels of William Faulkner." Dissertation,
University of Washington, 1968.

Irwin, John T. Doubling and Incest/Repetition and
Revenge: A Speculative Reading of Faulkner.
Baltimore and London: The Johns Hopkins
University Press, 1975.

Kreiswirth, Martin. William Faulkner: The Making
of a Novelist. Athens: University of Georgia
Press, 1983.

----------. "William Faulkner and Siegfried
Sassoon: An Allusion in Mosquitoes."
Mississippi Quarterly, 29 (Summer 1976),
433-34.

Lind, Ilse Dusoir. "Faulkner's Women." The Maker
and the Myth: Faulkner and Yoknapatawpha
1977, ed. Evans Harrington and Ann J. Abadie.
Jackson: University Press of Mississippi,
1978, pp. 89-104.

McHaney, Thomas L. "The Elmer Papers: Faulkner's
Comic Portraits of the Artist." Mississippi
Quarterly, 26 (Summer 1973), 281-311.

160   Bibliography

----------, comp. William Faulkner: A Reference
    Guide. Boston: G. K. Hall & Co., 1976.

----------. William Faulkner's The Wild Palms.
    Jackson: University Press of Mississippi,
    1975.

Meriwether, James B. "Faulkner's Essays on
    Anderson." Faulkner: Fifty Years After The
    Marble Faun, ed. George H. Wolfe. University,
    Alabama: The University of Alabama Press,
    1976, pp. 159-81.

---------- and Michael Millgate, eds. Lion in the
    Garden: Interviews with William Faulkner,
    1926-1962. New York: Random House, 1968.

----------. The Literary Career of William
    Faulkner. Columbia: The University of South
    Carolina Press, 1971.

Millgate, Michael. The Achievement of William
    Faulkner. New York: Random House, 1966.

Mirabelli, Eugene. "The Apprenticeship of
    William Faulkner: The Early Short Stories and
    the First Three Novels." Dissertation,
    Harvard University, 1963.

Petersen, Carl. Each In Its Ordered Place: A
    Faulkner Collector's Notebook. Ann Arbor,
    Michigan: Ardes Publication, 1975.

Polk, Noel. "Introduction." The Marionettes, ed.
    Noel Polk. Charlottesville: University Press
    of Virginia, 1977.

Putzel, Max. Genius of Place: William Faulkner's
    Triumphant Beginnings. Baton Rouge and
    London: Louisiana State University Press,
    1985.

Richardson, H. Edward. "Faulkner, Anderson, and
    Their Tall Tale." American Literature, 34
    (May 1962), 287-91.

Rideout, Walter B. and James B. Meriwether. "On
    the Collaboration of Faulkner and Anderson."

American Literature, 35 (March 1963), 277-81.

Sensibar, Judith L. _The Origins of Faulkner's Art_.
     Austin: University of Texas Press, 1984.

Serafin, Joan Michael. "Faulkner's Use of the
     Classics." Dissertation, University of Notre
     Dame, 1968.

Slabey, Robert M. "Faulkner's _Mosquitoes_ and
     Joyce's _Ulysses_." _Revue des Langues Vivandes_,
     28 (1962), 435-37.

Spratling, William. "Chronicle of a Friendship:
     William Faulkner in New Orleans." _Texas
     Quarterly_, 9 (Spring 1966), 34-40; rptd. in
     Sherwood Anderson and Other Famous Creoles.
     Austin: University of Texas Press, 1966,
     pp. 11-16.

Vickery, Olga W. _The Novels of William Faulkner_.
     Baton Rouge: Louisiana State University
     Press, 1959.

Volpe, Edmond L. _A Reader's Guide to William
     Faulkner_. Farrar, Straus and Giroux, 1964.

Warren, Joyce W. "Faulkner's `Portrait of the
     Artist.'" _Mississippi Quarterly_, 19 (Summer
     1966), 121-31.

Yonce, Margaret. "_Soldiers' Pay_: A Critical and
     Textual Study of Faulkner's First Novel."
     Dissertation, University of South Carolina,
     1970.

Other Sources:

Adams, Henry. _The Education of Henry Adams_.
     Boston: Massachusetts Historical Society,
     1918.

Aiken, Conrad. "Poetry." _Civilization in the
     United States_: _An Inquiry by Thirty
     Americans_, pp. 215-26.

----------. _Turns and Movies_. New York: Houghton

Mifflin and Company, 1916.

Ainsworth, William Harrison. The Tower of London.
     London: George Routledge and Sons, 1840.

Allen, Hervey. Israfel: The Life and Times of
     Edgar Allan Poe. New York: George H. Doran
     Company, 1926.

"The All-Star Literary Vaudeville." The New
     Republic (30 June 1926), 158-63.

Anderson, Elizabeth and Gerald R. Kelly. Miss
     Elizabeth: A Memoir. Boston: Little, Brown
     and Company, 1969.

Anderson, Ruth, comp. Contemporary American
     Composers: A Biographical Dictionary.
     Boston: G. K. Hall, 1976.

Anderson, Sherwood. Dark Laughter. New York:
     Boni & Liveright, 1925.

----------. Many Marriages. New York: B. W.
     Huebsch, 1923.

----------. Marching Men. New York: John Lane
     Company, 1917.

----------. "A Meeting South." The Dial, 38
     (April 1925), 269-79.

----------. "New Orleans, The Double Dealer and
     the Modern Movement in America." The Double
     Dealer, III (March 1922), 119-26.

----------. Poor White: A Novel. New York:
     B. W. Huebsch, 1920.

----------. A Story Teller's Story. New York:
     B. W. Huebsch, 1924.

----------. A Story Teller's Story: A Critical
     Edition, ed. Ray Lewis White. Cleveland: The
     Press of Case Western University, 1968.

----------. Tar: A Midwestern Childhood. New
     York: Boni & Liveright, 1926.

----------. The Triumph of the Egg: A Book of
    Impressions from American Life in Tales and
    Poems. New York: B. W. Huebsch, 1921.

----------. Windy McPherson's Son. New York:
    John Lane Company, 1916.

----------. Winesburg, Ohio: A Group of Tales of
    Ohio Small Town Life. New York: B. W.
    Huebsch, 1919.

Arlen, Michael. The Green Hat. New York: George
    H. Doran Company, 1924.

Bartlett, John. A Complete Concordance of
    Shakespeare. London: Macmillan & Co., Ltd.,
    1953.

Barton, Bruce. The Man Nobody Knows: A Discussion
    of the Real Jesus. Indianapolis, Indiana:
    Bobbs-Merrill Company, 1925.

Baudelaire, Charles. Baudelaire, Prose and Poetry,
    translated by Arthur Symons. New York:
    Albert & Charles Boni, 1926.

Bell, Clive. Art. New York: Capricorn Books,
    1958.

Bourne, Randolph. "A Literary Radical." A Modern
    Book of Criticism, pp. 206-10.

Bowen, Frances Jean. "The New Orleans Double
    Dealer: 1921-May 1926, A Critical History."
    Dissertation, Vanderbilt University, 1954.

Brooks, Van Wyck. "An External Civilization." A
    Modern Book of Criticism, pp. 194-98.

Bury, J. B., et al. The Cambridge Ancient History.
    New York: The Macmillan Company, 1925.

Cabell, James Branch. Jurgen: A Comedy of
    Justice. New York: Grosset & Dunlap, 1919.

Cather, Willa. The Song of the Lark. Boston and
    New York: Houghton, Mifflin and Company,
    1915.

Chalmers, David. Hooded Americanism: The First
     Century of the Ku Klux Klan 1865-1965. Garden
     City, N.Y.: Doubleday and Company, Inc.,
     1965.

Crane, Stephen. Maggie: A Girl of the Streets.
     New York: D. Appleton and Company, 1896.

----------. The Red Badge of Courage. New York:
     D. Appleton and Company, 1895.

Cohen, J. M. and M. J. The Penguin Dictionary of
     Quotations. New York: Antheneum, 1962.

The Compact Edition of the Oxford English
     Dictionary. 2 vols. Oxford University Press,
     1971.

Conrad, Joseph. Heart of Darkness. Vol. V of The
     Works of Joseph Conrad. London: William
     Heinemann, 1921.

Cumberlege, Geoffery, comp. The Oxford Dictionary
     of Quotations. 2nd ed. London: Oxford
     University Press, 1953.

Davidson, Gustav. A Dictionary of Angels. New
     York: The Free Press, 1967.

Dictionary of American Biography, ed. Dumas Malone.
     New York: Charles Scribner's Sons, 1961.

Dos Passos, John. Three Soldiers. New York: The
     Modern Library, 1932.

Dupuy, R. Ernest and Trevor H., eds. The
     Encyclopedia of Military History. Rev. ed.
     New York: Harper & Row, 1970.

Edwards, Edward. The Life of Sir Walter Raleigh.
     London: Macmillan & Co., 1868.

Eidelburg, Ludwig, ed.-in-chief. Encyclopedia of
     Psychoanalysis. New York: The Free Press,
     1968.

Eldridge, Paul. "The Carnival." The Double
     Dealer, V (January 1923), 4-29.

Eliot, T. S. Poems: 1909-1925. London: Faber
     and Gwyer, 1925.

----------. The Waste Land. Richmond, Surrey:
     Hogarth Press, 1923.

Ellis, Havelock. The Dance of Life. Boston and
     New York: Houghton, Mifflin Company, 1923.

Ellmann, Richard. James Joyce. New York: Oxford
     University Press, 1982.

"The Ephemeral Sex." The Double Dealer, I (March
     1921), 84-85.

Evans, Bergen, coll. Dictionary of Quotations.
     New York: Delacorte Press, 1968.

Ewen, David. American Popular Songs. New York:
     Random House, 1966.

----------, comp. and ed. Composers Since 1900: A
     Biographical and Cultural Guide. New York:
     The H. W. Wilson Company, 1969.

Fagin, N. Bryllion. "Sherwood Anderson and Our
     Anthropological Age." The Double Dealer, VII
     (January-February 1925), 94-95.

Farnsworth, Marjorie. The Ziegfeld Follies.
     London: Peter Davies, 1956.

FitzGerald, Edward. Letters and Literary Remains
     of Edward FitzGerald. London: Macmillan &
     Co., Ltd., 1903.

Fitzerald, F. Scott. The Great Gatsby. New York:
     Charles Scribner's Sons, 1925.

----------. "The Off-Shore Pirate." Flappers and
     Philosophers. New York: Charles Scribner's
     Sons, 1920.

Flaubert, Gustave. The Temptation of St. Anthony,
     trans. Lafcadio Hearn. New York and Seattle:
     The Alice Harriman Company, 1910.

Frazer, Sir James. The Golden Bough. London:

MacMillan & Co., Ltd., 1919.

Freud, Sigmund. Beyond the Pleasure Principle.
    London: Hogarth Press, Ltd., 1922.

----------. A General Introduction to Psycho-
    analysis, trans. G. Stanley Hall. New York:
    Boni & Liveright, 1920.

----------. The Standard Editions of the Complete
    Works of Sigmund Freud, ed. James Strachey.
    The Hogarth Press and the Institute of
    Psychoanalysis, 1961.

Friend, Julius Weis. Review of A Story Teller's
    Story. The Double Dealer, VII (October 1924),
    72.

----------. "The Philosophy of Sherwood Anderson."
    Story, 19 (September-October 1941), 37-41.

Gautier, Theophile. Mademoiselle De Maupin. New
    York: Boni & Liveright, 1918.

Gibb, H. A. R. and J. H. Kramers, eds. Shorter
    Encyclopedia of Islam. Leiden: E. J. Brill,
    1953.

Gilmore, Samuel Louis, Jr. "Deity." Poetry: A
    Magazine of Verse, II (June 1918), 132-33.

----------. Review of La-Bas. The Double Dealer,
    VII (November-December 1924), 77-79.

Halliwell, Leslie. The Filmgoer's Companion. 4th
    ed. London: Hart-Davis, MacGibbon, 1974.

Hammond, N. G. L. and H. H. Scullard, eds. The
    Oxford Classical Dictionary. 2nd ed. Oxford:
    Clarendon Press, 1970.

Harvey, Sir Paul, ed. The Oxford Companion to
    Classical Literature. Oxford: Clarendon
    Press, 1940.

Hergesheimer, Joseph. The Bright Shawl. New York:
    Alfred A. Knopf, 1922.

----------. Cytherea. New York: Alfred A. Knopf,
      1922.

----------. Linda Condon. New York: Alfred A.
      Knopf, 1919.

Housman, A. E. The Collected Poems of A. E.
      Housman. New York: Holt, Rinehart and
      Winston, 1965.

Huxley, Aldous. Crome Yellow. New York: Harper &
      Brothers, 1922.

----------. Leda. New York: George H. Doran
      Company, 1920.

----------. Those Barren Leaves. London: Chatto
      & Windus, 1925.

Huysman, Joris Karl. La-Bas, trans. Keene Wallis.
      New York: Albert & Charles Boni, 1924.

James, Rev. Thomas. Aesop's Fables: A New
      Version. London: John Murray, 1848.

Jones, Howard Mumford with Walter B. Rideout.
      Letters of Sherwood Anderson. Boston:
      Little, Brown and Company, 1953.

Joyce, James. A Portrait of the Artist as a Young
      Man. New York: B. W. Huebsch, 1916.

----------. Ulysses. New York: The Modern
      Library, 1934.

Keats, John. The Poems of John Keats, ed. Jack
      Stillinger. Cambridge: Belknap Press of
      Harvard, 1978.

Lawrence, Gordon. "An Encounter in Hades." The
      Double Dealer, VII (April 1925), 126.

----------. "Parade." The Double Dealer, VII
      (January-February 1925), 99.

Lewis, Sinclair. Arrowsmith. New York: Harcourt,
      Brace & Company, 1925.

----------. Babbitt. New York: Harcourt, Brace
     and Company, 1922.

Lewisohn, Ludwig. "Literature and Life." A Modern
     Book of Criticism.

----------, ed. A Modern Book of Criticism. New
     York: Boni & Liveright, 1919.

Loos, Anita. Gentlemen Prefer Blondes. New York:
     Boni & Liveright, 1925.

Louisiana: A Guide to the State, comp. Writers'
     Project of the Work Projects Administration.
     New York: Hastings House, 1951.

Lovett, Robert Morse. "Education." Civilization
     in the United States: An Inquiry by Thirty
     Americans, pp. 77-92.

Mann, Thomas. Stories of Three Decades, trans.
     H. T. Lowe-Porter. New York: Alfred A.
     Knopf, 1938.

Marlowe, Christopher. The Works of Christopher
     Marlowe, ed. C. F. Tucker Brooke. Oxford:
     Clarendon Press, 1910.

McClure, John. "Notes on the Theory of Beauty."
     The Double Dealer, VI (July 1924), 139-46.

Milton, John. The Complete Poetical Works of John
     Milton, ed. Douglas Bush. Boston: Houghton,
     Mifflin Company, 1965.

Moore, George. Louis Seymour and Some Women. New
     York: Boni & Liveright, 1922.

Morison, Samuel Eliot. Three Centuries of Harvard
     1636-1936. Cambridge: Harvard University
     Press, 1936.

Munson, Gorham. Letter in The New Republic (1
     November 1922), 252.

----------. "The Single Portent of Carl Sandburg."
     The Double Dealer, VII (October 1924), 17-26.

New Orleans City Directory. N.p., 1924.

New Orleans City Guide. Boston: Houghton Mifflin
    and Company, 1952.

New Orleans Times-Picayune. (1 May 1927), Sec. 3,
    p. 4.

Noyes, Alfred. Collected Poems of Alfred Noyes.
    New York: Frederick A. Stokes Company, 1913.

Opie, Iona and Peter. The Classic Fairy Tales.
    London: Oxford University Press, 1974.

Ovid. Metamorphoses, trans. Frank Justus Miller.
    New York: G. P. Putnam's Sons, 1916.

Partridge, Eric. A Dictionary of Slang and
    Unconventional English. 7th ed. New York:
    The Macmillan Company, 1970.

Parsons, Elsie Clews. "Sex." Civilization in
    the United States: An Inquiry by Thirty
    Americans, pp. 309-18.

Pater, Walter. The Renaissance: Studies in Art
    and Poetry. London: Macmillan and Company,
    1910.

Perrault, Charles. Old-Time Stories told by Master
    Charles Perrault, trans. A. E. Johnson. New
    York: Dodd, Mead & Company, 1921.

Pierson, George Wilson. Yale College: An
    Educational History 1871-1921. New Haven:
    Yale University Press, 1952.

Poe, Edgar Allan. The Works of Edgar Allan Poe,
    collected and edited by Edmund Clarence
    Stedman and George Edward Woodberry. New
    York: Charles Scribner's Sons, 1914.

Pound, Ezra. Personae: The Collected Poems of
    Ezra Pound. New York: New Directions Books,
    1926.

Rigdon, Walter. The Biographical Encyclopedia &
    Who's Who of the American Theatre. New York:

James H. Heineman, Inc., 1966.

Rose, Al. Storyville, New Orleans. University,
    Alabama: University of Alabama Press, 1974.

Rose, H. J. A Handbook of Greek Mythology. New
    York: E. P. Dutton & Co., 1959.

Rossetti, Dante Gabriel. The Poetical Works of
    Dante Gabriel Rossetti. Introduction by
    William M. Rossetti. New York: Thomas Y.
    Crowell & Company, 1886.

Rostand, Edmond. Cyrano de Bergerac, trans. Brian
    Hooker. New York: The Modern Library, 1923.

Sandburg, Carl. Selected Poems of Carl Sandburg,
    ed. Rebecca West. New York: Harcourt, Brace
    and Company, 1926.

Santayana, George. Winds of Doctrine: Studies in
    Contemporary Opinion. New York: Charles
    Scribner's Sons, 1913.

Scott, Sir Walter. The Complete Poetical Works of
    Sir Walter Scott, ed. Horace E. Scudder.
    Boston and New York: Houghton, Mifflin and
    Company, 1900.

Shakespeare, William. The Complete Work of
    Shakespeare, ed. Hardin Craig. New York:
    Scott, Foresman and Company, 1961.

Shipley, Joseph T. "The Esthetic Emotion." The
    Double Dealer, VII (October 1924), 61-64.

Snell, Susan. Phil Stone of Yoknapatawpha. Ann
    Arbor: University Microfilms, 1978.

Spengler, Oswald. The Decline of the West, trans.
    Charles Francis Atkinson. New York: A. A.
    Knopf, 1926-28.

Spingarn, Joel E. "Scholarship and Civilization."
    Civilization in the United States: An Inquiry
    by Thirty Americans, pp. 93-108.

----------. "The Seven Arts and the Seven

Confusions." A Modern Book of Criticism, 1919.

Spratling, William. File on Spratling. Boston:
    Little, Brown & Company, 1967.

Stearns, Harold E. Preface to Civilization in the
    United States: An Inquiry by Thirty
    Americans, iii-viii.

Sutton, William A. The Road to Winesburg: A
    Mosiac of the Imaginative Life of Sherwood
    Anderson. Metuchen, N. J.: The Scarecrow
    Press, Inc., 1972.

Swinburne, Algernon Charles. The Complete Works of
    Algernon Charles Swinburne, ed. Sir Edmund
    Bosse and Thomas James Wise. London: William
    Heinemann Ltd.; New York: Gabriel Wells,
    1925.

Symons, Arthur. "An Appreciation of Havelock
    Ellis." The Double Dealer, III (February
    1922), 78-83.

Thompson, Stith. Motif-Index of Folk-Literature.
    Bloomington: Indiana University Press, 1957.

Treharne, R. F. and Harold Fullard, eds. Muir's
    Historical Atlas. New York: Barnes & Noble
    Inc., 1964.

Townsend, Kim. Sherwood Anderson. Boston:
    Houghton Mifflin Company, 1987.

Tugwell, Rexford Guy. "An Economist Reads Dark
    Laughter." The New Republic, 45 (9 December
    1925), 87-88.

Wilde, Oscar. The Complete Works of Oscar Wilde.
    Garden City, N.Y.: Doubleday, Page & Company,
    1923.

----------. Salome, trans. Lord Alfred Douglas,
    illus. Aubrey Beardsley. New York: Three
    Sirens Press, 1906.

Who's Who in America 1928-29, ed. Albert Nelson
    Marquis. Chicago: The A. N. Marquis Company,

1928.

Yeats, William Butler. The Collected Poems of
    W. B. Yeats. New York: Macmillan Publishing
    Co., Inc., 1956.

Young, William C. Famous Actors and Actresses on
    the American Stage. New York: R. R. Bowker
    Company, 1975.